# Table of Contents

# Preface to the second edition

We are delighted with the way in which the first edition of this book, published in 2002, has been received. Not only is the book now almost out of print, but we have received many positive comments that show that the heritage of European universities is a living reality, not least as the European Higher Education Area is about to come into place in 2010. The importance of clarifying the values of higher education was further underscored by the conference on "The Cultural Heritage and Academic Values of the European University and the Attractiveness of the European Higher Education Area" organised by the Holy See from 30 March to 1 April 2006 in association with the Council of Europe and UNESCO/CEPES as a part of the Bologna Process.

The strong interest in the heritage of European universities also led to Recommendation Rec(2005)13 of the Committee of Ministers to member states on the governance and management of university heritage. This recommendation grew out of the same project that gave rise to the first edition of this book, namely the project on the heritage of European universities that was first launched as a part of the Council of Europe's "Europe: a common heritage" campaign. The work that led to the recommendation constituted the second phase of this project, and it focused on a topic that had been identified in the first phase as one on which there was a strong need for guidelines adopted by an international organisation.

The second edition of the book has allowed us to include this recommendation with its explanatory report. In addition, a few minor corrections have been made.

The second edition also allowed us to include this book on university heritage in the Council of Europe's Higher Education Series, which was launched in late 2004. This is entirely fitting as – particularly at a time of extensive reforms – it is important to have a clear view of the developments that have led European higher education to where it is today as well as of the values embodied by higher education.

We hope the second edition of the book will be as appreciated as the first, and that it will continue to stimulate discussion and awareness both among higher education specialists and policy makers, multilateral organisations and the international community at large as well as among those whose main interest is cultural heritage.

*Sjur Bergan*                                             *Nuria Sanz*

# Foreword

In October 1997, the (then) forty-one heads of state and government of the Council of Europe member countries held their Second Summit in Strasbourg. Among other things, they decided to launch a campaign in 1999 on the theme "Europe, a common heritage", respecting cultural diversity. Thereby the heads of state and government reaffirmed the commitment undertaken at their First Summit in Vienna in 1991 to pluralist and parliamentary democracy, the indivisibility and universality of human rights, the rule of law and a common cultural heritage enriched by its diversity.

This publication thus stems from one of the main efforts the Council of Europe has undertaken in any area of education and culture over the past decade: the Europe, a Common Heritage Campaign. This campaign ran from September 1999 to December 2000 and encompassed some 1 000 national events as well as fifteen transnational projects. Five of the transnational projects were co-financed by the European Commission, under a Covenant between the two Institutions.

The project on the heritage of European universities was one of these five projects. It also deserves mention for another reason: it was a joint project between two different departments and committees of the Council of Europe, namely those responsible for cultural heritage and those responsible for higher education. This co-operation was natural if one looks at the topic chosen and on the origin of the project. When the campaign was launched, the Higher Education and Research Committee asked itself – as well as the Cultural Heritage Committee – whether the universities did not constitute an important part of the common heritage of Europe. The answer could only be a resounding affirmation, and the project was set on its course. Both committees undertook the project as a joint commitment, and this book is the outcome of a fruitful co-operation.

However, anyone with experience of large institutions will also know that while co-operation may seem both necessary and logical, this alone does not ensure that co-operation will actually take place. It is our pleasure, as those responsible for the sectors of cultural heritage and education, to present to the readers today a publication that shows a will to rethink aspects of two sectors which certainly have things in common, but which under normal circumstances happily live their separate lives.

We believe the project on university heritage managed to take this fresh approach and to explore a transversal theme that deserved the effort. The success of the project owes much to a wide range of people. The contributors to this volume provided background essays and presentation to the four meetings of the project and thus laid the basis for a stimulating discussion. In this context, we would also like to thank the CRE – Association of European Universities (since then merged with the Confederation of EU Rectors' Conferences to form the European University Association (EUA)) for helping us draw on the expertise of Professors Walter Rüegg and Hilde de Ridder-Symoens, respectively general editor and editor of its four volume *History of the University in Europe*, as well as of Professor Paolo Blasi, then CRE Vice President, and Ms Mary O'Mahony, then CRE Deputy Secretary General.

The CRE and the Confederation were, and the EUA continues to be, an invaluable co-operation partner for the Council of Europe in the higher education field.

The project has also afforded us an opportunity to become acquainted with other activities in the framework of the Forum Unesco – University and Heritage as well as Icom's (International Council of Museums) International Committee for University Museums and Collections (UMAC).

Then there were the representatives of the participating universities who greatly contributed to the debate and whose contributions are reflected in parts of this publication. A particular thanks goes to those who completed three different questionnaires that helped orient the discussion and that are a basis for one of the articles in this volume. For one of the questionnaires, the circle of respondents even went beyond those of the direct participants in the project. We would also like to thank those who helped organise the four meetings in Alcalá, Montpellier, Bologna and Kraków, without whom the project would not have been possible.

The generous financial support of the European Commission was also instrumental to the project, as was the support and participation of the (then) Chairs of the CC-PAT and CC-HER, Juris Dambys and Krzysztof Ostrowski, both of whom hail from countries that joined the Council of Europe over the past ten years. Our thanks also go to Professor Robin Sibson, former Vice Chancellor of the University of Kent at Canterbury and a member of the CC-HER Bureau, who launched the idea of including the university heritage in the campaign in the first place. We would also like to thank all the members of both Committees who wholeheartedly supported this joint venture.

We would, however, like to end by thanking our two colleagues Nuria Sanz and Sjur Bergan who ran the project.

*José María Ballester*
*Director of Culture and*
*Cultural and Natural Heritage*

*Gabriele Mazza*
*Director of Education*

# Introduction: a word from the editors

*Nuria Sanz and Sjur Bergan*

That the universities are an important part of the cultural heritage of Europe is hardly a controversial assertion, and it is one that met with the immediate approval of the two Council of Europe committees involved with the project that gave rise to this publication: the Cultural Heritage Committee (CC-PAT) and the Higher Education and Research Committee (CC-HER). The present publication sets out to prove the point, but even more to explore what this assertion actually means.

To do so, it is necessary to stop and think about what heritage is and what universities are. By definition, the university continues to function as a transmitter of messages through time, in a world that is accelerating day by day. In a society where the mechanisms of communication abound and those of transmission become fewer and further between, the university can function as the Transmission Institution par excellence. As a guarantor of knowledge and traditions, it enters into a logic of filiation between generations but also of the ruptures that are necessary if the formulas of thought are to advance. The university also appears as a kind of tradition of disruption, as a continuity of fractures without for this reason ceasing to participate in the successive accumulation of advances. This institution has transformed transmission into a necessary value across time and in everyday life.

This is not a work on the history of universities. Our explicit purpose is to address the heritage of universities, and not their history. The heritage of universities and the university as heritage will not be treated in terms of history. In terms of cultural heritage, the university presents itself as an actor of collective responsibility guaranteeing the sense of certain moral, intellectual and technical values. Freedom of belief, freedom of teaching and the preservation of memory – physical or intellectual – teach values for life and for respect between generations.

The project embarked from an attempt at defining a conceptual and contextual framework for the concept of university heritage as well as for the considerations deriving from the role of universities as heritage in Europe. In addition, the university appeared as a space for reflection on the delimitation or enlargement of the term "heritage". This programme was inserted into a discussion already underway concerning a heritage that was constantly widening its definition and its basis for social, cultural, economic and symbolic action. In the construction of the transmission and the definition of the university heritage there is as much of the technical as of the affective, recognition – even of oneself – in the practice and the evidence of this transmission.

By itself, the university can be considered as a special built historical environment in which collections, monuments, traces and also perceptions of what has been inherited is labelled to make an inhabitable and transferable heritage possible. Libraries and archives, collections and museums, built spaces, philosophies, scientific laws and achievements have warped around how the university heritage in its own way builds a special model of transmission through teaching and learning.

11

We are talking about enormous forgotten or disregarded heritage waiting not only for a preservation policy but also for recognition from the academic community and from the wider society as well as recognition in everyday life, in the daily functioning of the institution. This was the challenge: to situate institutional memory and projects for the institutional future within the same framework for planning.

At a time of daily crisis of transmission and in a context defined by moving roots, the values conveyed by the university heritage can function as a response to the segmentation of policies and of knowledge, and they can also be transformed into an antidote to cultural distances. We clearly discern the need to define the university heritage as a passage to the future that contributes to preventing the knowledge society from turning into the society of ignorance.

In several cases, we have found that there is total assimilation between producing a university history and heritage related activities. When universities are asked about their concern for the heritage of the institution, the immediate response points to the elaboration of an institutional history, which normally consecrates the celebration of its jubilees and specifically focuses on commemorating the most glorious moments the institution has seen in the course of time. This assimilation may arise from two specific reasons: the first the absence of the concept of heritage in the day to day life of the institution as an independent part of its concerns, and the second an identification that is frequently found even among professionals of either disciplines, who know how difficult it is to separately identify the concerns and practices of the two concepts.

Heritage and history can co-operate and compete on the same ground. Heritage needs history in order to narrate and to join, while history needs heritage to convince.[1] To some authors close to this line of thought,[2] the attempt of the successive present times to recount and explain aspects related to the past is the concern of historical disciplines, while the collection, preservation and documentation of the registers and the physical testimony of the past is the task of archivists and antiquarians. These authors end up maintaining that if these concerns are presented from the perspective of the current use of the past or to use this evidence of the past to make certain predictions for the future, the new are talking about heritage.

Of course, this definition could be seen as operational. When it comes to practice, it is far from satisfactory if we try to see the implications for heritage and history in the most profound way. The authors quoted take as their point of departure the difference in the use of the past without being very explicit about it and take a present based approach to heritage. Nevertheless, there has been much discussion about the practice of writing history that, in the face of positivist attitudes, is defined as the interpretation of the past from the viewpoint of the present, implying that all

---

1. Lowenthal, David: *The Heritage Crusade and the Spoils of History* (Cambridge 1998: Cambridge University Press).
2. Graham, B., Ashworth, G. J., Tunbridge, J. E.: *A Geography of Heritage. Power, Culture and Economy* (London and New York 2000: Arnold/ Oxford University Press).

history is contemporary. Therefore, "presentism" – the predominance of the present – is common to both disciplines.

History, for what and for whom? For the historians, as passive readers of a message with the audacity to present itself as the correct version of events past, an intrinsically correct version, a bearer of innate values that endows it with qualitative meaning. The recipients read a "scientific" interpretation.

Heritage, for what and for whom? Not only for the professionals, but also for the people creating their own heritage, to the benefit or at the expense of many or of few, according to many objectives. The interpretation process is one of production and exchange of meanings, which functions in a way akin to language: heritage is a fertile field for social interaction that uses the past to create identities or to convert them into a market. It is a significant social practice, and all publics are recipients – producers – buyers.

On what are the different ways of reading the past based? History and heritage "own" the past in very different ways.

The foundations of history are confounded with those of heritage, in spite of the fact that the traditions of the disciplines have brought historians closer to written sources, while archaeologists, antiquarians and anthropologists have served themselves well from the remaining material. A documentary source[3] such as a historical archive may be used for researching its contents or for conserving it as an object, from which arises the difference between a historian and a professional in heritage conservation. Therefore, the difference is less in the foundations than in the objectives of each kind of practice: to the former the document is a tool, whereas to the latter, the document as monument is an end in itself.

The past is also explored through the memory that makes us conscious of our continuity as individuals through time; accepting this as heritage also implies responsibility.

Heritage is conceived of as inheritance, as a cultural product and as a political resource. This practice includes more possible kinds of usage, not only those aiming at improving our knowledge of the past, as in the case of history. Rather, heritage conveys contemporary economic, cultural, political or social use.

History is guided by intrinsic merits and heritage by contemporary values shaped by distinct demands and depending on different cultural values. Whereas the discourse of history is created by the profession, the nature of heritage knowledge is always negotiated through social or intellectual circumstances, as with the case we are considering here, the heritage of European universities.

A key element in heritage policies is the idea of continuity, of connecting the object of the past to the present through uninterrupted trajectories. History places us in a

---

3. From the Renaissance onwards the reliability of written sources is beginning to be discussed and ruins are beginning to be researched, in order to put an end to false morals.

reality different from that of our own, more or less remote, but terminated, interrupted at some stage between the present and the past. Heritage situates us within a sequence that is not interrupted and makes us participate in the continuity. History reads through what remains, while heritage is a social practice. Current society produces the meaning and creates and negotiates the message. Heritage permits an individual representation of the values of the past, a deep social implication in the construction of the message. It is particularly interesting to appreciate the discordance of this message in multicultural environments like that of the university.

Heritage presupposes transmission from one generation to another. What is not transmitted, and that with which nobody longer identifies, is no longer heritage. Andrić, Cervantes, Chekhov, Dante, Goethe, Homer, Ibsen, Kafka, Molière and Shakespeare are not only great writers. They are a part of the cultural heritage of their language areas through their contribution to their language, imagery, consciousness and self-understanding. They are a part of our common European heritage because, even in translation, they have contributed lasting concepts with which we identify: the fight against imaginary windmills, vivid visions of the hereafter, the fight of the lonely upright individual against corrupt authorities or the existentialist doubt of to be or not to be. Even a work with as resolutely a national title as *Ma vlast* – My Fatherland – is a part of the European musical heritage, and not all listeners give thought to the Czech origins of Bedrich Šmetaná. Moreover, these works and concepts are part of our intellectual and non-material heritage, which is a less easy part of the heritage to grasp than monuments and buildings. Fernando Pessoa said that *a minha língua é a minha pátria* – "my language is my country". We would make the point that our language is an important part of our heritage. Nonetheless, monuments are also a part of our heritage only to the extent that someone identifies with them and the ideas, events or symbols they represent. The material of heritage may have its roots in the past, but its effect and its interest are to be found in the present. In the words of a historian, *avoir été, c'est une condition pour être* – "having been is a condition for being".[4]

The choice of the term "universities" also needs a word of explanation. Today, higher education in Europe presents a diverse picture of different systems and institutions, many of which are so called "non-university higher education institutions", bearing a variety of names such as polytechnics,[5] *Fachhochschulen*, *főiskola*, *hogescholen* or *statlige høyskoler*. This publication is aimed also at these institutions, which are of more recent origin, but which in many cases build on a common European academic heritage. However, this heritage was developed at universities, which were the original academic institutions. European higher education is currently engaged in a period of profound reform, starting with the massification of higher education in the 1960s and continuing today at European level with the Bologna Process of higher education reform.[6]

---

4. Fernand Braudel : *La Méditerranée, l'Espace et l'Histoire* (Paris 1985: Flammarion), p. 8.
5. Still used as a generic term even though the United Kingdom has reverted to a unitary higher education system under which almost all former polytechnics have become universities.
6. The Bologna Process gets it name from the Declaration signed in Bologna in June 1999 by the Ministers responsible for higher education of 29 European countries. The Declaration is reproduced in Appendix II and will be referred to extensively throughout this publication.

Precisely because of the profound changes higher education is undergoing today, a look at what has been carried over from its past is of particular interest. The call for a higher education more closely adapted to what are perceived as the needs of society is by no means new, nor has higher education generally been as far removed from society as its critics have wanted that society to believe. The fact that theology and law graduates were numerous in the early years of higher education does not mean that the university was out of step with society. It means, rather, that society has since changed, and that new needs have arisen which universities have also sought to meet, hence their departments of, say, geology, economics, computer science and Chinese. Change takes time – not only in the academic world – but change also builds on the traditions of the past. There may have been considerably fewer Chinese study programmes fifty years go, but today's programmes build on the traditions of linguistics and literature studies developed over generations. Computer science is a relatively recent field, but the principles of mathematics on which it builds are not. Yet, the readiness to change has not been uniform – it has varied from institution to institution and from one age to another, as shown particularly well in Professor Hilde de Ridder-Symoens' contribution to the present volume.

Even more important than the traditions and innovations of specific disciplines, however, are the common fundaments on which the European heritage of the university builds, such as the principles of academic autonomy, intellectual curiosity, the freedom to teach, pursue research and publish its results and the rigorous standards of peer review. The same is true of fundamental societal values such as participation, community and equal opportunity. Traditionally, the university is a community of scholars and students, where participation is open to all qualified candidates. A couple of caveats are, of course, in order: the possibilities to earn entrance qualifications were not equal to all regardless of their social and financial background or their gender. Institutionalised higher education was indeed closed to women throughout most of its existence. In this area also, universities did, alas, conform to the societies of which they were a part.

A word about Europe may also be in order. At a time when reality was mostly local, higher education was truly European. The university may have been an élite world, but it was a European elite. The European and international dimensions have been a feature of higher education throughout its existence, but the strength of this dimension has varied considerably. Today's emphasis on European and international mobility is in a sense a return to the sources of higher education, before the age of passports and immigration departments, but also before the age of easy and comfortable travel. While today's goals for student mobility may not surpass the actual mobility of the Middle Ages if expressed in terms of percentage, the actual numbers are of course of a totally different order. Nonetheless, it is worth underlining that the European dimension of higher education was one of its defining features from the outset. In organised form, this was evident at least as early as the twelfth century, when the king of Portugal, Dom Sancho I, established scholarships for Portuguese students abroad.[7] An early example of what we would today call a "free mover", ie someone who studies abroad without the assistance of an organised exchange programme, is found in the Icelandic tale of Sæmundur the Learned, who studied in Paris but was unable to secure a passage back to Iceland after graduation. He hitched a ride with the devil, disguised as a seal, by gambling his soul. It is a part of the story that Sæmundur, presumably thanks to his higher education, managed to trick the devil, and that his portrait – with the seal and a book – is now the emblem of the University of Iceland.[8]

Therefore, it was clear that universities could not be absent from a campaign focusing on "Europe, a common heritage". At any rate, insisting on heritage as something local or national is a dubious undertaking in an age of global communication, and Europe has no shortage of examples of what can happen if the attempt is made. The Council of Europe grew out of the aftermath of one of the most massive attempts ever made to deny the value of the Other – the Nazi regime that caused the second world war – gained new impetus with the arrival of new member states after the fall of another set of regimes that tried to practice the art of self delusion – the communist regimes of central and eastern Europe – and has tried to cope with the abuse and selective use of heritage in South-eastern Europe, an area that, to paraphrase a popular saying, has produced too much heritage for its own consumption.[9]

Therefore, the European dimension of the university heritage was an important aspect of the project, and it was one of the main factors that dictated the choice of participating institutions. Another was, inevitably, tradition. The bias in the selection of the universities participating in the project has been towards the older, traditional universities, and thus towards what unites rather than the various forms that have developed from the common university idea. While the choice may be open to criticism, it is a conscious one in that in an age when we take the diversification of higher education for granted, we believe it is worth reflecting on the road that took us to where we are now. However, the choice of participating universities was not limited to the earliest period. The inclusion of some institutions founded at a later date is due to two considerations. First of all, we wanted to include at least some examples of the development of the original university model. Secondly, we thought it important to show the geographical expansion of this model. In this case, success would be another term for expansion. From its origins in south and central Europe, the university model spread towards the east and the north. This expansion – a European dimension – is reflected in the project, where even within the very strict limits of a project working within clear restrictions of budget, human resources and time, we aimed to show the blend of common features and diversity which we believe is a salient feature of the common heritage of Europe. This led to a project

---

7. José Hermano Saraiva: *História concisa de Portugal* (Lisboa 1980: Publicações Europa-América), p. 109.
8. The tale was told by former President Vigdís Finnbogadóttir in her keynote address at the Conference on Regional Co-operation in Higher Education organised jointly by the Council of Europe and the Nordic Council of Ministers in Reykjavík in September 1997, cf. p. 9 of the conference report, issued as TemaNord 1998:553.
9. This is admittedly a simplistic view. For a thorough analysis of the background for the disintegration of Yugoslavia, see John B. Allcock: *Explaining Yugoslavia* (London 2000: Hurst).

with the active participation of the universities of Alcalá, Bologna, Cluj-Napoca (Babes Bolyai), Coimbra, İstanbul, Kraków, Leuven/Louvain, Montpellier III – Paul Valéry, Santiago de Compostela, Tartu, Vilnius and Zagreb.

The second choice was the kind of heritage to be included. While material remains are perhaps the feature most commonly associated with cultural heritage, and while many universities certainly have treasures in the form of buildings, museums, libraries and collections, the non-material aspects of the heritage are also important, not least in a project focusing on the university heritage. Both aspects had to be treated with equal emphasis to give an adequate coverage of the subject, and this, added to the emphasis on the European dimension that we have already addressed, structured the project as follows:

– an introductory meeting in Alcalá de Henares from 9 to 11 December 1999;
– a second meeting on the intellectual heritage of European universities in Montpellier from 13 to 14 March 2000;
– a third meeting on the heritage of European universities as represented by built heritage – town planning, university collections, museums, libraries and archives in Bologna from 28 to 29 July 2000;
– a final meeting on the European dimension of the university heritage in Kraków from 23 to 24 October 2000.

The present volume is based on the main presentations and background documents for the project. The order of the contributions in this book does not, however, follow the order in which they were presented in the project. Rather, with the benefit of hindsight, we have sought to order the articles around five main themes.

The project was originally conceived as the Ancient Universities Route. However, the participants quite rapidly moved away from this title in favour of an emphasis on the heritage of European universities, for at least two reasons. Firstly, while the origin of European universities may well be termed ancient, not all the institutions that identify with and continue to live this tradition are marked by old age. Secondly, while the European university tradition provides a link in space and time between a variety of institutions in Europe and beyond, the concept of a route is too simplistic a way of conceiving this relation. Therefore, we shall refer to the project as one addressing the heritage of European universities or sometimes, for the sake of simplicity and legibility, simply as "university heritage".

The first part of the publication sets the scene and provides the background for the discussion. While heritage is not history, Claudia A. Zonta's overview of the development of European higher education in its earliest stages will help situate the discussion of the university heritage within its historical context. She shows the different stages of the early developments of European universities and the different models that coexisted and competed. Through a university curriculum that essentially consisted of law, theology, medicine and the liberal arts (*artes liberales*), the medieval state covered its limited needs for a literate and highly trained labour force. Zonta underlines the importance of international recognition of university qualifications, including the doctorate, which gave the holder a right to teach at any university (*licentia ubique docendi*). This recognition remained even if, with time, universities diversified and were coloured by their national or local circumstances, and it was, of course, fundamental to the mobility of students. Zonta also outlines the effect of the Reformation and Counter-Reformation and the expansion of the university model into central and eastern Europe.

Professor Walter Rüegg – the general editor of the CRE[10] *History of the university in Europe* – quotes Rousseau, who regretted that in his age, there were no longer any Frenchmen, Germans, Spaniards or even Englishmen, but only Europeans, since they had all been educated in the same way. He goes on to show how the university developed into what he calls a "European bridge" and the role that the humanities played in this development. A key part of this function as a bridge was the principle of dialogue, which recognised the "other" – who could be a foreigner – as a partner in intellectual conversation. The *Corpus christianum* of the earliest universities was replayed by the role of the university in a "republic of letters", meant in both an intellectual and a literal term. Knowledge and learning literally spread through the mail. However, the humanist tradition also implied a certain superficiality, even sterility, of both form and knowledge, satirised by Molière, that engendered a decline of the university, which recovered only through the reforms inspired by von Humboldt and an emphasis not so much on erudition as on intellectual curiosity and problem solving. At the end of the past century, specialised higher education institutions started emerging outside of the universities, but as a complement to, rather than a replacement of, the traditional higher education institutions.

In the third background article, we aim to discuss the specific heritage function of the university. The article in large part builds on questionnaires sent out in the course of the project and addressing the main topics covered by it. It reveals the ambiguity of the university's relationship to its heritage, and the lack of conception of an integrated heritage. At "home", the lack of a definition prevents consistent heritage management, while in relation to the outside world, this ambiguity is translated by punctual contacts that are unable to define a general framework for European co-operation in terms of heritage on a professional and not only voluntary basis. For example, the replies to the questionnaires show that there is little or no European co-operation in heritage training and heritage research.

There also seems to be a lack of specific heritage concerns in management and decision-making. That management models will vary from one university to another is hardly surprising, nor is it a matter of great concern. What is of concern, however, is that heritage issues do not seem to play much of a role in the decision making, even at universities that manage a substantial heritage. Only four universities tried to estimate the proportion of their budgets used for heritage purposes, mostly for their historical buildings. The answers to the questionnaire also seem to indicate that the conservation of heritage, teaching and research and awareness raising are managed separately, even within each faculty. In other words, in addition to transdisciplinary research and teaching with a specific heritage approach, institutions also need to develop a policy for their heritage. With our article, we also attempt to provide a

---

10. CRE – Association of European Universities, an NGO gathering some 700 European Universities. On 31 March 2000, the CRE and the Confederation of EU Rectors' Conferences merged to form the European University Association (EUA).

bridge between the background articles and the contributions addressing the specific heritage themes of the project.

In the second part of the publication, we start this exploration with the theme that most commonly comes to mind in a discussion of heritage, namely its material traces.

Professor Patrick J. Boylan outlines the role of museums and collections in relation to the university heritage. He traces their evolution from the early "curiosity chambers" and underlines that museums and collections do not lead their separate lives as university "extras". Rather, from an early stage, museums and collections have been an integral part of university teaching and research, even though this link may now be loosened, at least in certain disciplines. For example, in biology, geology and anthropology, research is no longer as dependent on museums and collections as previously, and the leading researchers in these fields have less experience with collections and museums than their predecessors. This could, at least in the medium term, endanger the position of museums and collections within universities. On the other hand, there are some encouraging signs. The role of museums and collections seem to be increasingly important in popularising the university to a larger public. The increase in cultural tourism is one example of this, particularly where – like in Oxford and New Haven – a renowned university is the main attraction in town. Professor Boylan also refers to examples from the United Kingdom to show that many "new" British universities have sought to emulate the traditions and customs of ancient universities, and that some of them even seek to acquire historical buildings or build up collections of their own. Whether at older or newer institutions, however, museums and collections have to be an integral part of the university, also in terms of management, decision-making and staffing, and every university needs to consider possibilities for co-operation between their various museums and collections.

The third part of this book addresses the more elusive but equally important concept of intellectual heritage. Professor Hilde de Ridder-Symoens – editor of the CRE *History of the university in Europe* – explores university historiography, universities and national identity, the tension between theory and practice, academic freedom and the Humboldt university and European and North American concepts of the liberal arts. Her article ends with a summary of the discussions on the intellectual heritage at the second meeting of the project, for which she was rapporteur. Professor de Ridder-Symoens maintains that universities in their development have been through cycles of vitality and decay, but that these cycles have not been uniform for all universities nor indeed for all academic disciplines within the same university. Few of these fluctuations may, however, be surmised from official university histories, the jubilee publications, which tend to concentrate on achievements and neglect problems. One of the less successful chapters of university development concerns precisely their failure to adapt their curricula to new developments in the early modern age, when the traditional emphasis on theoretical training in theology, law, medicine and liberal arts threatened to marginalise the universities with regard to new and more practically oriented knowledge. However, university response to the new challenges was not universally lacking, and anatomical theatres, botanical gardens and laboratories were a part of the response by the more progressive institutions from the sixteenth century onwards. Institutional freedom was exemplified by the medieval university as an independent institution with specific rights and privileges which is well illustrated by the Spanish concept of *fuero*, and by the individual academic freedom that is central to the Humboldtian university concept.

Professor Gian Paolo Brizzi, the Director of the Student Museum of the University of Bologna, directly addresses the question of whether universities constitute a part of the cultural heritage and identity of Europe. The Middle Ages were a period of change and innovation, and Professor Brizzi maintains that the university was one of the major innovations of its day. Moreover, their origin was closely linked to the cultural environment of the Europe at the time, and this was a European rather than a local or national phenomenon.

The term university itself implies universality, both in terms of the fields of knowledge covered – although this has not been entirely true at any period of its development – and in terms of geography and culture. The European aspect was also evident in the high mobility of scholars – the *peregrinatio*. At the same time, the members of the university constituted a body that may well have been international, but that was also quite distinct from the society that surrounded the university. And there was diversity amid the unity, both in university models, the origin of professors and students, the different characteristics of small and large universities and – somewhat later – in outlook. Universities and their members took opposing views as to the questioning of religious doctrines and the development of empirical science.

Professor Brizzi's article already points to the fourth main part of this publication, which focuses on the European dimension of the university heritage. Professor Paolo Blasi – then Vice President of the CRE – Association of European Universities[11] – underlines the importance of the European dimension throughout the development of the universities, from the international community of scholars and students through social and economic processes like urbanisation to the European dimension of the values on which the universities were based. As they have evolved over time, these values are not only the basis for the university but also for European citizenship. The origin of the university in a certain area of Europe and the subsequent expansion of the university model to other areas of Europe has also contributed to a common European dimension of the university. The picture might have been quite different had university-like institutions arisen in various parts of Europe at approximately the same time without much contact between the various institutions. It is also a part of the European dimension of the university heritage that its fortunes have ebbed and flowed with the major political, social, intellectual and cultural movements of Europe. The development of mass higher education, which seems a natural fact to today's students and younger university teachers, but which is a recent phenomenon in a historical perspective, presents some particular challenges if the European dimension of the university is to be maintained: the organised mobility programmes like Erasmus and Socrates answer a part of this challenge, but improved recognition of periods of teaching and research abroad in

---

11. Now the European University Association (EUA), see previous footnote.

career advancement for staff as well as a Europeanisation of social security and pension rights would be important measures. Not least, however, higher education policies, on the part of both institutions and governments, must seek back to the European roots of the university heritage and be based on common fundamental values, transparency and the concept of the academic world as a shared community.

The role of the university as the basis for a common European culture is the topic of Professor José Luis Peset's article. Taking the establishment of the University of Alcalá in 1499 as his point of departure, Professor Peset shows that the university was deeply influenced by a culturally rich world dominated by European humanism and international contacts and exchanges. The emphasis on languages – mostly classical – was also an emphasis on access both to information that was not available in Spanish or Latin – such as the Arabic mathematicians and physicians – and to an important part of the European cultural heritage: the classical authors that were being rediscovered in this age. Professor Peset insists on the importance of books as the principal instrument of communication in universities. Books allow communication in space because they can easily be sent all over the world. Equally important, however, they allow communication in time, because they are a source of information, views, values and culture that can easily be transmitted from one generation to the next. Therefore, they are an important part and source of the cultural heritage of universities.

In an article originally written for another Council of Europe project and published in this context,[12] Professor Alain Renaut explores the role of higher education in developing a European democratic culture. This culture rests on a European dimension and a European identity that have been part and parcel of higher education from its inception in the Middle Ages. One could even make the point that the etymology of the term university is that of universal and universality, but then it should be kept in mind that Europeans of the time did not easily recognise the value or relevance of things non-European. However, Professor Renaut sees the end of the eighteenth century and the beginning of the nineteenth as a crucial time for the adaptation, development and dissemination of the university model, with roots on the one hand in the changes in French higher education in the wake of the French Revolution and on the other hand in the Humboldtian university model. By the end of the nineteenth century, the Humboldtian model was largely accepted, not necessarily in the sense that all institutions strictly conformed to it, but at least in the sense that the underlying notion of the university was that of institutions sharing a conscience and common values and ideals. The emphasis on intellectual conscience and reflection in addition to specialised knowledge has been a characteristic of the European university ever since, and it has been preserved through a period of rapid expansion of student numbers and improved access to higher education. The mission of the university is not only to train, but also to educate. The university of today is in a period of transformation, under the impact not only of student numbers but also of the rapid increase of the mass of knowledge and changing requirements from the

---

12. The project European Studies for Democratic Citizenship was run by the Higher Education and Research Committee (CC-HER). Professor Renaut's article was originally published in *Concepts de la citoyenneté démocratique*, Editions du Conseil de l'Europe, ISBN 92-871-4451-6, December 2000 (French version) and *Concepts of democratic citizenship*, Council of Europe Publishing, ISBN 92-871-4452-4, Council of Europe, December 2000 (English version).

surrounding society, and Professor Renaut does not believe that the Humboldt model will survive intact. Nevertheless, he is optimistic that in what he calls a transformation towards "multiversities", higher education will still be able to play a role as the conscience of Europe, as a place of reflection and values.

In the final section, the general and theoretical issues addressed in the first part are illustrated through case studies of some of the universities that participated in the project. Professor Gian Paolo Brizzi gives a brief overview of the rich material heritage of the oldest university of Europe and illustrates it in some detail through the Bologna Student Museum and the university's historical archives. The Student Museum is dedicated to an important part of the academic community, but at the same time a group that has not always been well considered by the senior members of that community. The museum looks at both the life of the student as an individual, the phenomenon of studenthood as a phase of life or a rite of passage and the position of students as a group, where Professor Brizzi discerns a line leading from the autonomous student corporations of the Middle Ages to the student activities in 1968, although this line is certainly not a straight one. The Historic Archives of the University of Bologna are typical in that they are faced with the problems of split collections – in the case of Bologna those parts dating from before the Italian unity were transferred to the National Archives in 1892 – and a lack of specialised staff, and also by being faced with the challenge of preserving its heritage by using modern information technology as well as to adapting to serving a university which has grown dramatically over the past generation. This implies not only being at the service of a larger number of students and teachers, but also having to absorb a far higher number of documents and acts that will in their turn become part of the university heritage.

In her article on the heritage of the University of Coimbra, Professor Maria da Fátima Silva in particular explores the role of university traditions and rituals, which are at a crossroads between the material and immaterial university heritage. Whether we talk about the inauguration and graduation ceremonies, the promotion of *doctores honoris causa* or student traditions such as the *queima das fitas*, they all contribute to giving the university community a distinct identity. This identity is two fold: as a part of the larger, universal or European academic community and as a part of the local academic community of Coimbra. The academic dress worn by both professors and students on ceremonial occasions also contributes to building identity, as do student associations and the rich musical traditions of the Coimbra *fado*. Indeed, Professor Silva's article shows that university life is itself a part of the university heritage.

Professor Béatrice Bakhouche illustrates the intellectual heritage of universities through the example of Montpellier. The origins of the university are closely linked to three academic areas: liberal arts, medicine and law. In law, Montpellier was home to a large number of *légistes* who played an important role in elaborating the theoretical and practical foundation of the France of Philippe le Bel. Professor Bakhouche also points out that in Montpellier, as at other medieval universities, the fundamental organisational structure of faculties and degrees had already been laid. While the forms of these have changed over time, and the medieval university hardly thought of in terms of learning paths, the original organisational structure is very much a part of the heritage of modern higher education. However, much learning and research also took place outside of the universities, particularly in the convents of Montpellier. The most famous example is perhaps the Catalan Franciscan Ramón Llull, who worked in Montpellier in several periods, but probably not at the university. The medieval intellectual heritage is the topic of a new interdisciplinary research programme established at the University of Montpellier called *Mémoire et Patrimoine*, a heritage which includes a rich exchange between Montpellier and other early universities on the northern shores of the Mediterranean.

This external aspect of the university is the topic of Professor Antonio López Díaz's article on the European dimension of the heritage of the University of Santiago de Compostela. Santiago is in fact an early example of a European city, in that the pilgrimage brought people from all over the continent to the city in spite of its peripheral geographical location. Professor López sees Europe as a dialogue between cultures, and he underlines that the university has not contented itself with a passive, receiving role, but that it has on the contrary been an active disseminator of culture, and through it of a European dimension. Today, the new information technologies can be of great use to the universities in carrying out this mission. The European dimension of the university is linked to the general political context, as is illustrated by the Spanish case, where attention was so focused on the Spanish colonies in Latin America and the Philippines that the loss of the last colonies in 1898 implied not only a national trauma, but also a period of relative isolation which was reinforced by the long years of the Franco regime. It was only with the democratic change of 1975 that Spanish universities could again fully develop the European dimension of their heritage. Building on the traditions of the pilgrimage of Santiago de Compostela, which was declared the first European Cultural Route by the Council of Europe and the European Commission, the Compostela Group of universities was established in 1993 to reinforce the means of communication between the participating universities, to organise joint activities, to participate in the European debate on higher education and, not least, to promote exchanges and foreign study as a basis for improving knowledge of European languages and cultures. Today, some eighty universities from more than twenty European countries participate in the Compostela Group. The University of Santiago de Compostela combines this European commitment with an active co-operation with other parts of the world, in particular Latin America.

In the final article of this volume, we explore some possibilities for continuing work on the European heritage of universities beyond the confines of the present project. If we are to give this heritage the attention it deserves, the efforts of many actors is required, including international organisations and national, regional and local authorities. While these can help create a framework that will make it easier to preserve and raise awareness of the university heritage, the main tasks will fall on the universities themselves. Only they can fully promote their heritage, make it an element of their institutional plans and policies and develop research and study programmes that will ensure that the heritage remains heritage by transmitting it to future generations. Only they can convince the rest of society that the traditions on which universities build are an important part of our common European heritage, and that the relevance of the university heritage does not dissipate where the gown ends and the town begins. Only the universities can ensure that their past be not only a history for specialists, of which the general public will catch a glance through jubilee publications, but a heritage that is lived in the present by most members of the academic community as well as by the wider society, whether the local community, schoolchildren, policy makers or European civil society. Only the universities can ensure that the ongoing higher education debate and reform be lived not as a threat and a break with the past, but as a process that builds on and adds to the heritage of European universities as institutions that had a measure of distance to the surrounding society through their autonomy and their basic research, but which also contributed actively to the development of this society through their study programmes, their graduates, much of their research and not least through their role in defining ethics and values.

Universities have an important role in constructing our common future, and in this they must balance a concern for immediate results with respect for and acceptance of a mission that also includes long term priorities in developing the fundaments of research and learning without which the immediate results cannot be obtained. An understanding of and respect for the university heritage as a current responsibility for the long term past is essential to this goal.

In the age of the sound bite, it is no easy task to build one's work on a heritage of centuries. It is, however, a task that European universities must undertake, without distinction to their age and location. In fact, some of the newer universities, as well as institutions in countries and areas where higher education has to be rebuilt, are more acutely aware of the European university heritage than many established universities and look to their heritage for guidance and inspiration, but also to shape new policies for integrated conservation. We hope that this book may in a modest way contribute to keeping the heritage of European universities well and alive in the new millennium so that the European university may continue to contribute to an ethics and values based European civil society with a high level of competence in a wide range of fields.

# Part I

# Background

# The history of European universities: overview and background

*Claudia A. Zonta*[1]

## Introduction

At first glance, the university, as a place of learning and research, today appears to be a thoroughly modern institution and phenomenon. However, as we shall see by studying their history, universities have developed over hundreds of years and can look back on centuries of tradition. The earliest universities were established in the Middle Ages, and the fact that universities were founded right up to the present decade, and are still being founded today, is proof that the model is not outdated. If we consider the university system from our own national standpoint we lose sight of the common roots of this pan-European phenomenon. Our aim here is to show that, despite their individual differences, all universities have many things in common.

In the universities of Europe people read, lectured and debated in Latin, not in the local language(s). The subjects studied and their content were the same everywhere: law, theology, medicine and the *artes liberales*, the liberal arts. The degrees awarded were also recognised by all European universities. This made it possible for students from any country to study in any university, whether in France, the Netherlands, Britain, Germany, Italy, Spain or Portugal.

This European education was primarily based on constant interaction between academic staff and students. The very fact that students and lecturers travelled from one university to another and between the countries of Europe guaranteed a certain degree of universality of university studies. This does not mean, however, that the universities adhered to a rigid, immutable structure over the centuries. The individual seats of learning definitely specialised, and there were differences in the teaching which they dispensed. Academic staff also came from a variety of educational backgrounds. In the final analysis, it was worth studying at the university which had the best qualified lecturers.

The political and social transformation of the feudal state of the Middle Ages into the early modern state brought about corresponding changes in society and in contemporary culture, for example in the army, in administrative circles, in finance and in diplomatic relations. It was of prime importance to these new states that they train a civil service, a new social class which became responsible for the state's territorial administration. Members of the civil service needed a sound education in specific branches of the law, moving away from a religious interpretation of legal concepts towards a civil one. The result was a civil service which was both ideologically and physically dependent on the state itself, not on an institution such as the Church, whose members were clerics and therefore first and foremost

---

1. This article was commissioned from Claudia A. Zonta as a background document for the first meeting of the project on the heritage of European universities. It has been slightly reviewed by the editors.

proponents of the Christian ideology. It was in the universities of Europe that this new caste was trained.

## The origins

Researchers do not dispute the fact that the modern universities can trace their origins back to the twelfth century. The three oldest universities are Bologna, Paris and Oxford, which were founded between the end of the eleventh century and the late twelve hundreds. We have no definite date for the establishment of these three universities, just as there is no founding text. In principle, it must be assumed that their creation and consolidation was a fairly lengthy process. The process was completed, and the university came into being, only when the institution qualified as a *studium generale* or a *universitas magistrorum et scholarium*.

The initial building blocks for these completely new educational establishments were the ancient school of law in Bologna, various schools of philosophy in Paris and the monastic schools in Oxford.

There are a number of theories on how the universities came into being:

– The tradition theory, whose proponents argue that there is a direct structural link between the educational institutions of the Arab-Oriental world, of Byzantine civilisation and of the monasteries of the High Middle Ages, on one hand, and the twelfth-century universities, on the other.
– The intellect theory, whereby interest in knowledge is believed to have prompted the establishment of a forum for free intellectual development.
– The social theory, which regards the universities as a new form of community where people lived, worked and studied together.

A combination of all three theories comes nearest to the truth.

It must be borne in mind that the medieval universities were marked by the "new scientific concept of scholasticism" and by the "social revolution" of the twelfth century. The forms of teaching and learning – and the founding principles – which shaped the modern university system only became possible, firstly, with the scholastic approach to teaching and academic life and, secondly, with the emergence of new corporate bodies within society (the guilds and the holy orders).

*The meaning of* universitas

Having begun by holding lectures and debates in the street, in the homes of academic staff or in churches, the universities went on to rent premises, publish curricula, discover a need to endow themselves with statutes, collect fees, keep their own matriculation registers and adopt their own symbols of authority (seals, sceptres, etc.). In these educational establishments paid teaching staff imparted knowledge to students according to a fixed curriculum, using set textbooks. At the same time, the institution's corporate and democratic nature was preserved, and the masters, who evolved into a professional teaching corps, acquired enormous influence.

28

A *studium generale* was a university attended by scholars from outside its own region which had been granted privileges by one of the two world powers of the time (the Pope or the Holy Roman Emperor) and which also had faculties in the four classic branches of knowledge: philosophy, theology, law and medicine.

The privileges made the institution's reputation and, above all, guaranteed international recognition of the degrees which it awarded. Holders of a doctorate, or of the *licentia ubique docendi*, were entitled to teach at any university. The privileges also secured the university's independence *vis-à-vis* state and local authorities.

The universities were both a result of and a driving force behind the rationalisation and urbanisation process that went hand in hand with the opening-up of society. This process began in Europe in the eleventh and twelfth centuries and in the end encompassed the entire world and broad sections of the population. The expansion of the university system is intimately linked to this development. By the Middle Ages the law as habitually practised no longer enabled people to master the complexity of social and political problems. In the texts of Roman Law, which, as the unifying legal tradition of the empire and the papacy was partly handed down from Roman times and partly rediscovered, it was possible to find generally applicable rules for the solution of new legal problems, which when put into practice, constituted new legal precedents.

People also sought the beginnings of solutions to the complex philosophical and theological questions, rife with inconsistencies, which were posed at the time. What was at stake here was the very substance of traditional dogma and knowledge. Power struggles between pro- and anti-papal factions, between the empire and the papacy, and contradictions between the holiness of religious office and the venality of Church officials, between piety and worldliness, between the monetary economy and the prohibition of usury, between the recognition and the condemnation of reform movements, destabilised the intellectual élite.

The opening-up to the East through the crusades and through trade revealed the superiority of Arab-Islamic ways of life and patterns of thought. Europe rediscovered the body of Greek philosophical and scientific thinking in Arab translations and commentaries. Science was faced with a huge challenge: the quest for truth. Bologna and Paris came to typify the two fundamental roles which universities were required to play in the course of their history: on one hand, establishing the theoretical foundations of the knowledge imparted, subjecting that knowledge to critical analysis and expanding it and, on the other, providing theoretical training in the practical solution of problems of importance to society.

*The universality of the university*

It is not possible to talk about Europe's universities without discussing the importance of universality to the development of the university system seen from a social historian's point of view. In the thirteenth century universality meant that a university, Paris for example, was not in the strict sense an educational institution that belonged to a given city or diocese, and therefore all the intellectual activity that went on there could not have been geared to satisfying specific local needs.

In terms of legitimacy, the universities' claims to universality were linked to the legends concerning their foundation (Bologna was alleged to have been established by Theodosius, and Paris by Charlemagne).

For about 600 years the external involvement of one of the two universal powers – the papacy or the empire – was an inescapable condition of existence for Europe's universities.

The universities' universality rapidly took on further dimensions. An essential aspect was the universality of university studies, in the sense that all branches of knowledge were covered. The fact that, in principle, everyone had access to university teaching was yet another facet of this universality. The criterion of a public education open to all could also be a substitute for coverage of all branches of knowledge (the four faculties).

It was precisely because of their structural openness that the universities were able to give a universally recognised framework to the discovery and transmission of fundamental scientific knowledge.

Lastly, the universities' universality also had a topographical connotation – all universities were established in towns or cities. Unity of place was a prerequisite if the bringing together of all the publicly taught branches of knowledge was to be effective.

The turning point in the development of the modern state and church was the foundation of sovereign states independent of the empire and of denominations other than Catholicism. The transition from universal sovereignty to territorially limited sovereignty marked the birth of the modern state. The Catholic Church also lost its claim to universality since there were too many other denominations which it could not rank among the "infidels". In both spheres – state and church – pretensions to universality therefore had to be curtailed.

The advent of the self-governing state and of a multi-denominational religious environment had an important influence on the development of the early modern university. Limitations on the universality of the other two universal powers also decided the history of the universities, but did not result in limitations on the universities themselves. The groundbreaking early modern universities, such as Padova, Göttingen and Leiden, also partly managed to escape the restrictions inherent in these new trends or even succeeded in giving those constraints a new universalist definition.

*Types of university*

The first generation

### The Bologna model: *universitas magistrorum et scholarium*

A university formed by the students, who chose the lecturers. This model favoured the students (who selected the Rector, an office which was held by a student, and exercised control over the academic staff in matters of teaching and pay).

"Nations": The students divided up into groups or "nations". Students who, although Italian, did not originate from the city of Bologna formed the *citramontana natio*. Students from the other side of the Alps grouped together in the *ultramontana natio*. However, this model soon gave way to the Parisian one.

### The Paris model: *universitas magistrorum*

A university of teachers (not of scholars), which was divided into faculties. Students were merely members of the university. This has remained the pattern on which European universities have been formed up to the modern day.

The universities of Oxford and Cambridge were also organised along these lines. Both came into existence through a process of gradual development, with the result that they too cannot be given an exact date.

Migration universities: Universities established through the secession of students or lecturers from another university. Examples are Padova and Siena, both of which were formed by students who seceded from Bologna.

The second generation

### *Universitas ex privilegio*

A university granted privileges at the time of its foundation. Certain universities were founded by royal decree, by decision of a city authority or under some other form of government act. Their history began with a founding instrument, a document establishing in clear terms the sources of their funding and the related control possibilities. Examples are the universities of Salamanca, Naples, Toulouse, Prague, Vienna, Heidelberg and Cologne.

The specificity of the universities of Spain and Portugal lay in the fact that they were founded by virtue of the royal prerogative, were linked to a cathedral or other religious authority and were at the same time supported by the city in which they were situated. The universities of Huesca, Zaragoza, Alcala, Coimbra and Lisbon were all founded by the ruling monarch, as was the university of Salamanca – the "mother of the liberal arts and all the virtues".

*The significance of the Church*

The medieval university's evolution into an independent corps of teachers and scholars principally took place within the Church, but was at the same time an emancipation from the Church.

The college system

Religious orders had a major influence on academic life. The *collèges* of the French universities, the colleges of Oxford and Cambridge and the Spanish *colegios mayores* were communities of teachers and scholars, learning and living together, which took various forms modelled on the monasteries of the mendicant orders. This was above all apparent in the architectural features of university buildings, the daily academic routine – with fixed mealtimes and study and lecture periods – and the wearing of a uniform.

The *Modus Parisiensis*, where students boarded at their place of study, as was customary in France and England, was influenced by the monastic way of life. It contrasted with the *Modus Bononiensis*, prevalent in Italy and Germany, where scholars in the advanced faculties were free to study as they wished. The college system is a striking illustration of the close links that existed between the Church and the universities in the Middle Ages.

*University structure and* studium

During the fifteenth century the faculty structure, first attempted in Paris, began to gain ground everywhere. As a result, the encyclopaedic knowledge previously imparted gave way to specialisation. The four specialist schools of learning which emerged from this process – medicine, theology, law and philosophy – known as the *facultates* were entirely separate from each other. These faculties were basically oligarchies governed by the teachers. To qualify as a *studium generale*, a university did not need to include all four of these faculties. In principle it was enough if one of these four specialist schools existed alongside the compulsory faculty of arts. The faculty of arts was the school of the seven liberal arts, which were sub-divided into the *trivium* and the *quadrivium*, that is to say into philological-philosophical and scientific subjects.

*The* nationes

A specific feature of the medieval and early modern universities was the scholars' division, or rather grouping together, in corporations, known as "nations". The *nationes* were co-operative associations of fellow countrymen, in which students banded together according to their geographical origin in order to defend their common interests.

However, the *natio* of the medieval and early modern university did not have a national basis in the current sense of the term, but included scholars from a number of countries. In Paris there were four nations, the French, the Normans, the Picards and the English. The French nation included Spaniards and Italians, and the English nation not only scholars from the British Isles but also north Europeans and Germans.

In Bologna there were seventeen nations, of which fourteen were *ultramontanae*. The German nation played a major role in Bologna up to the eighteenth century. It not only provided its members with board and lodging, but was also their legal representative in dealings with the city authorities and safeguarded their interests within the university.

The *natio Bononiensis* spread to become the dominant model in Italy, Spain and southern France, although the number of nations decreased considerably. At Oxford and Cambridge only two such groups existed.

*Openness and (religious) discrimination*

To satisfy the demands of an increasingly open society and a more mobile population the universities were obliged to practice the principle of open access to the different branches of knowledge. This applied to both enrolment of students and selection of teaching staff. The knowledge imparted was perceived as a gift of God, something which was common property. Open access to the universities only concerned men; women were not admitted until the nineteenth century. Until the fifteenth century it also applied solely to Christian men; only then were men from other religious backgrounds – such as Jews – allowed to study at the universities.

After the Reformation religion became a factor of discrimination in the majority of universities. Open admission was of fundamental importance to local religious toleration and to academic quality. Jews were allowed to study in Montpellier, Padova, Leiden and Basel even before the Enlightenment. Prussia did not ban its nationals from studying in foreign universities until the early eighteenth century.

*Mobility*

Student mobility at European level was a contributory factor in the foundation and spread of the universities and the emergence of an academic culture. Scholars undertook the *peregrinatio academica*, establishing the custom of a "pilgrimage" from one seat of learning to another. They studied for a certain time at each university. Many students earned a degree from one of these universities before returning to their homeland. However, graduation was not an essential component of their studies, nor was it a prerogative granted solely to successful students. Students frequently availed themselves of this possibility of studying at a number of universities. They could rely on the fact that both first degrees and doctorates, for those who went on to sit the necessary examinations, would be recognised in their homeland. In an age where a large part of the overall student mobility takes place within organised mobility schemes, such as Erasmus, Nordplus or Ceepus, it is interesting to note that there was a genuine migratory student movement on a pan-European scale, in which tens of thousands of young men participated. The *peregrinatio academica* reached its apogee in the sixteenth century.

In the early seventeenth century this academic migration underwent a transformation. The students' goals changed, as did the nature of their peregrinations. This launched the tradition of the educational journey – or Grand Tour – which no longer entailed lengthy studies at any individual university. In the early modern universities mobility concerned some 10% of students. At least 20 000 Germans studied in Italy between 1500 and 1700. Young men making the Grand Tour visited the universities and academies of Germany, France, Italy, Spain, England and the Netherlands.

*Property and funding*

The funding of the universities posed extremely complex problems. The principal difficulty arose not with their ownership of assets, such as buildings, lighting, furniture, libraries and means of heating, but with payment of the teaching staff. Since there was no state budget *per se*, lecturers were allocated stipends or other church livings. Professors and lecturers were often simultaneously choir masters or canons. They held a prebend, and allowed someone to replace them in their ecclesiastical duties. This necessitated special permission from the Pope, who thus came to play an important role in the financial history of the universities.

This form of indirect funding was also frequently supplemented by transferring estates or other properties yielding interest or taxes to the academic corporations, which then had to administer these themselves. Colleges might moreover be endowed with their own property, and the collegiate bodies often paid the keep of masters of the arts.

With the advent of the early modern period the structure of university financing changed, in detail if not in principle. Protestant rulers transferred buildings and assets to the universities following the dissolution of the monasteries; Catholic ones earmarked donations to church foundations for the universities' purposes. The universities were no longer financially independent, as they had been in the Middle Ages. The principalities of the seventeenth and eighteenth centuries had to fund the universities out of their own budgets and took advantage of this to interfere extensively in academic matters.

**The modern age**

The changes in the university system in the early modern age can be summed up in three words: expansion, differentiation and professionalisation. In concrete terms, expansion meant extending the university network to the whole of Christian Europe. Differentiation came with the emergence of a system of many different educational establishments, of which the universities were only a part. Lastly, the professionalisation of the universities began in the early modern period and was completed in the nineteenth century as, under government pressure, the universities and the graduate professions grew closer together and geared themselves to serving the state's needs.

Until the sixteenth century European universities were to a large extent all organised on the same lines. They showed no national particularities or local focuses. They were international in spirit and in principle and open to all. They constituted self-governing legal entities, autonomous in their comprehension of knowledge. The picture changed with the decline in the authority of the papacy and the empire, the two "guarantor powers", and the emergence of the European nation state. This led countries to adopt their own national ways of doing things and to develop particularities, including in the academic field. The early modern universities were no longer solely committed to knowledge; they became a factor in the local ruler's calculations and were transformed into places of training for State and Church officials.

Under the influence of humanism, the social role of the universities changed between the fifteenth and the eighteenth centuries. They began to turn their backs on theory, in favour of practice. Their former secondary function of training people in the professions – above all as civil servants, members of the clergy, teachers, judges, notaries, lawyers and court and urban physicians – became their principal task. The fact that academic research was closely identified with its practical benefits to society led university teaching staff to gain in self-esteem.

However, a further consequence of this change in the universities' role was a decrease in the number of major scientific discoveries made within the universities themselves. Although such activity did not completely cease in the universities, in early modern Europe the most important research was done by academies, botanical gardens, royal observatories or other non-university institutions. This development points to our own day, when a substantial part of the research effort takes place outside of the university. A marked feature of the higher education system of central and eastern Europe over the past fifty years is the proportion of research carried out in the Academies of Science whereas universities played the predominant role in academic teaching.[2]

## Reformation and Counter-Reformation

As we have already seen, the territorialisation of politics (a continuous process) and the emergence of many religious denominations (the Reformation, a discontinuous process) were the key developments in the early modern age. These two trends also transformed education and the university system. The Reformation began in universities such as Tübingen, Wittenberg, Strasbourg and Geneva.

The combination of humanism and the Reformation first spelt the end of the universal university concept which had prevailed in the Middle Ages and second led to the universities' lasting integration into the territorially independent state and hence their harnessing to the needs of the emerging early modern state's machinery of government. Wittenberg university became the model for the new Protestant universities and for the reform of some other universities already in existence. The Wittenberg model was adopted in the universities of Basel, Frankfurt an der Oder, Leipzig, Heidelberg, Tübingen, Königsberg and Strasbourg.

---

2. See Recommendation No. R (2000) 8 of the Committee of Ministers to member states on the research mission of universities.

The Catholic universities, which the Reformation had plunged into a state of crisis, found a solution to their problems in the *Societas Jesu* or Society of Jesus. This religious order, which was founded by St Ignatius Loyola and recognised by the Pope in 1540, set itself the main objective of spreading the Catholic faith. It was in the *gymnasia* and the universities that the order principally performed its mission of preaching the faith. In Europe and overseas (America) the Jesuits established a system of colleges, which were both religious institutions and higher education establishments. These were patterned on the college system as practised in Oxford and Paris but included humanist elements, following the examples of Leuven and the Spanish state universities. On account of its strict management, organisation and discipline this system was a huge success. The Jesuits provided qualified teaching staff, and there were no financial or other obstacles to the management of the colleges.

During the period of the Reformation and the Counter-Reformation, ie the late sixteenth century, the universities also underwent an architectural renewal. Until then they had pursued their academic activities in purchased or rented houses or secularised monastery buildings. Now new university buildings – whole building schemes – sprang up almost everywhere. As with all building projects certain conditions had to be met: a comprehensive, consistent development scheme and sufficient financial resources and energy to implement the project. These requirements were mainly fulfilled in the smaller independent states, the Papal states and the German principalities. La Sapienza was built in Rome (1575 to 1660), and in Germany the universities of Tübingen (1588 to 1592), Helmstedt, Würzburg and Altdorf (late sixteenth century). At the beginning of the seventeenth century Lemercier rebuilt the Sorbonne.

## Universities in central and eastern Europe

Humanism, Renaissance, Reformation and Counter-Reformation: these are the key concepts, which characterise the period of the fifteenth, sixteenth and seventeenth centuries. All of these currents were already perceived as distinctive features of the age by people living at the time. The question is to what extent the spiritual unrest and great variety of movements embodied in these key concepts encompassed eastern Europe, or even whether they reached that part of the world at all. The answer must clearly be yes. The whole of eastern Europe was indeed caught up in the general European spiritual unrest of the time. The frontiers of Latinity moreover moved further east in the process.

The social and political effects of the above-mentioned movements were also felt to the full in eastern Europe. In this connection, it is important not to overestimate the gulf between the scholars and the illiterate common people. Many members of the urban bourgeoisie and the nobility had been educated to various levels. In educational terms they formed a literate middle class between the scholars and the populace. The members of this class functioned as intermediaries between the academics and the ordinary people, popularising the ideas of the time. Laypersons were primarily concerned with questions of theology and religion. This new form of popular participation in the debate on reform of the Church had specific consequences in central and eastern Europe, which led to the nationality problems of the nineteenth century.

The specifically west-European university concept reached central and eastern Europe in the fourteenth century (Prague in 1348; Krakow in 1364; Vienna in 1365; Pécs in 1367; Kulm in 1386; and Buda in 1389, although the last three universities mentioned did not develop on a lasting basis). The foundation of these universities marked a new epoch in eastern and central Europe and a new stage in Latin/European expansion. The *universitas*, as conceived in Paris and Bologna, was a typically western phenomenon on the educational scene. In contrast with other schools of higher education – that is to say scribal education – which already existed in the Byzantine-Russian world, the universities enjoyed relatively unrestricted intellectual freedom and were largely self-governing.

From the twelfth to the fourteenth century growing numbers of north and east European scholars travelled to the universities of northern Italy, and sometimes also to Paris, where they devoted themselves to their studies and were also awarded degrees. It was only with the foundation of Prague university that eastern European scholars wishing to study were offered any real alternative in their own geographical catchment area. However, the universities' eastward expansion was limited. Kraków remained the university, which reached furthest to the east, particularly with regard to Lithuania, the Ruthenian border territories (Ukraine) and Hungary.

The new universities of central Europe were all founded by local rulers or city authorities and were at their service. However, it would not be correct to say that their role was reduced to that of a mere local place of training. They were granted papal privileges at the time of their foundation and were therefore also part of the sole general higher education institution of the time, the Church.

From the sixteenth century various academies were founded in eastern Europe:

– the Catholic academy in Vilnius in 1578;
– the Catholic academy in Zamość in 1594;
– an Orthodox academy in Kyiv in 1632, including an arts faculty and schools of languages and theology;
– a Slav-Greek-Latin academy in Moscow in 1687, also including an arts faculty and schools of languages and theology;
– a science academy in St Petersburg in 1724. This institution was organised along very complex lines and was multifarious in nature. It included a western style science academy, a university with faculties in the advanced branches of learning, and a college which prepared students for university entrance. In 1755 the university became an independent part of this educational institute, which continued to go by the name of academy.
– a university in Moscow in 1755. This university had three faculties and housed two colleges, one for the nobility and the other for the bourgeoisie.

The universities of Moscow and St Petersburg were founded as part of the Russian rulers' westward-looking modernisation policy. These two Russian universities were modelled on Leiden in the Netherlands. It is of importance to note that they were founded by the secular power, the Tsar, not by the Church.

In the seventeenth century neither St Petersburg nor Moscow had a faculty of theology. The teaching of theology remained in the hands of the Russian-Orthodox church. Nor was either university divided into the four main faculties: law, theology, philosophy and medicine.

## Concluding remarks

As we have seen, the university is the most important academic institution of our time. Modern civilisation and contemporary culture are unquestionably built on the foundations laid by the medieval universities and by the "republic of learning". As part and parcel of Middle Ages Christianity, education and knowledge, institutionalised in the universities, took on fundamental importance in Europe. In our European tradition the universities and science have always been closely related, and contemporary science is undoubtedly one of the cornerstones of the modern world. The same university tradition also gave rise to a pan-European awareness, based on common principles. The university system constituted a network of individuals and knowledge transcending geographical and political frontiers, which was underpinned by the constant migration of teachers and scholars. Only with the self-contained, self-centred nation state did that system come to a standstill. It is only by overcoming the competition-based thinking and conduct typical of the nation state and by looking back to our common roots, traditions and ideals that we can found a new European awareness. In an increasingly united Europe this is also, and in particular, a task for the universities.

## Bibliography

Boehm, Letitia and Raimondi, Ezio: *Universitá, accademie e societá in Italia e Germania dal Cinquecento al Settecento*, Bologna, 1981

Brizzi, Gian Paolo and Verger, Jacques (editors): *Universitá dell'Europa. Gli uomini e i luoghi nei secoli XII e XVIII*, Milano, 1993

Brizzi, Gian Paolo and Verger, Jacques (editors): *Universitá dell'Europa. Dal Rinascimento alle riforme religiose*, Milano, 1991

Conrads, Norbert: *Ritterakademien der frühen Neuzeit. Bildung als Standesprivileg des 16. und 17. Jahrhunderts*, Göttingen, 1982

Julia, Dominique; Revel, Jacques; and Chartier, R. (editors): *Les universités européennes du XVIe au XVIIe siècle*, two volumes, Paris, 1986-89

Müller, Rainer A.: *Geschichte der Universität. Von der mittelalterlichen universitas zur deutschen Hochschule*, München, 1990

Rüegg, Walter: *Was lehrt die Geschichte der Universität?* Sitzungsberichte der wissenschaftlichen Gesellschaft an der Johann-Wolfgang-Goethe-Universität, Frankfurt am Main, Volume 32, No. 6, Stuttgart, 1994

Rüegg, Walter (editor): *Geschichte der Universität in Europa*, Volume I (Mittelalter), München, 1993

Rüegg, Walter (editor): *Geschichte der Universität in Europa*, Volume II (Von der Reformation zur Revolution, 1500-1800), München, 1993

Rüegg, Walter and de Ridder-Symoens, Hilde (editors): *A History of the university in Europe*, Volume II (Universities in Early Modern Europe (1500-1800)), Cambridge University Press, 1996

Stichweh, Rudolf: *Der frühmoderne Staat und die europäische Universität. Zur Interaktion von Politik und Erziehungssystem im Prozess ihrer Differenzierung (16.-18. Jahrhundert)*, Frankfurt am Main, 1991

# The Europe of universities: their tradition, function of bridging across Europe, liberal modernisation[1]

*Walter Rüegg*

In 1987 the European Communities embarked upon the Erasmus programme to increase student mobility in Europe from 1% to 10%. If efforts under that programme and the successor programme, Socrates, achieved that aim, they only brought the figure back up to the previous proportion of students who, until the eighteenth century, travelled between the ancient universities of Europe. The *peregrinatio academica* enabled the intellectual élite of the *Ancien régime* to acquire a common European culture based on the same studies and developed through direct interaction with the academics and university environments of other countries, to such an extent that Rousseau complained in 1772 that there were no longer any Frenchmen, Germans, Spaniards or even Englishmen, but only Europeans, since they had all been educated in the same way.[2]

This common culture of the European élite was the product of the university as the European institution par excellence. Researchers of the Carnegie Commission on Higher Education found sixty-six European institutions which had survived without interruption from the Reformation until the present day: the Catholic church, the Protestant church, the parliaments of Iceland and the Isle of Man, and sixty-two universities.[3] I will not dwell on this result in detail but I would go even further by suggesting that the university is the sole European institution whose fundamental structures, together with the universal nature of its social role, have been maintained and even reinforced in the course of its history. Of the three powers of the Middle Ages – the *regnum*, the *sacerdotium* and the *studium* – political power underwent sweeping changes and the *sacerdotium* of the Catholic church, despite retaining its structure and spreading throughout the world, lost the universal monopoly of spiritual power that it had possessed, while the *studium*, the university, conquered the globe, asserting itself everywhere as the supreme institution of higher education.

This was not achieved without overcoming crises threatening the nature of the university and even its very existence. My contribution will seek to explain, therefore, how the university managed to adapt its heritage to the changing cultural, social and political contexts through the regions and the centuries. I begin by outlining the medieval tradition which opened up the old universities route, then analyse how the universities succeeded in fulfilling their bridging function despite the religious and political schisms from the sixteenth century onwards, and end by demonstrating that the process of modernisation in the nineteenth century enabled

---

1. Article presented at the first meeting of the project (Alcalá de Henares, December 1999).
2. Jean-Jacques Rousseau, *Considérations sur le gouvernement de Pologne et sur sa réformation projetée*, ed. Jean Fabre, Oeuvres complètes, ed. Bernard Gagnebin and Marcel Raymond, vol. III, Paris 1964, 960. The erroneous attribution to Voltaire (eg in *Nationalism in the Age of the French Revolution*, ed. Otto Dann and John Dinwiddy, London/Ronceverte 1988, 14) was rectified thanks to the perspicacity of Charles Wirz, curator of the Voltaire Institute and Museum in Geneva.
3. Wolfgang Frühwald, Hans Robert Jauss, Reinhart Koselleck, Jügen Mittelstrass, Burkhart Steinwachs, *Geisteswissenschaften heute. Eine Denkschrift*, Frankfurt am Main 1991, 88).

the university to recapture and broaden its traditional role as the European institution par excellence.

## Medieval tradition[4]

The university as a corporation, enjoying special privileges and broad legal and administrative autonomy, setting its own programme of studies and awarding academic qualifications recognised by the public authorities, is a European invention of the twelfth and thirteenth centuries. It has to be said that the methods and knowledge that they taught went back for the most part to antiquity. The Bible and the seven liberal arts had always been studied in medieval cloisters and schools. At the end of the eleventh century law scholars began to teach Roman law privately, a fact which has prompted the University of Bologna to celebrate 1088 as its founding date. Galenic and pseudo-Hippocratic medicine as well as the philosophy of Aristotle and Platonism had been studied by Arab scholars and were taken up and taught in the Western world in the twelfth century.

It was this flowering of intellectual study that sparked a great trend towards mobility among academics and students, resulting in the organisation and typically European role of the university by about 1200. But laymen – and very often even clerics – did not benefit from any protection outside their home town, were exploited by the local population, had to pay for the debts and crimes of their compatriots or academic colleagues and were even executed without trial. At the request of law scholars teaching in Bologna, the emperor Frederick Barbarossa promulgated a law in 1155, the famous *Authentica Habita*, promising imperial protection from abuses by local authorities to *omnibus qui studiorum causa peregrinantibus* (all those travelling as a result of studies) and authorising them to choose their own judges where necessary. This law was incorporated into the *Corpus iuris* and today takes the form of the "fundamental charter of the medieval university".[5] However, it did not have an immediate impact, which prompted the foreign students in Bologna in around 1200 to defend their own interests by organising themselves into two corporations: the Italians who were not citizens of Bologna formed the *universitas citramontanorum* and the others formed the *universitas transmontanorum*, each *universitas* having its elected director, the rector. At the beginning of the thirteenth century, the teachers and students of Paris established a *universitas magistrorum et scholarium* to defend academic freedom from the control of the bishopric and encroachment by the urban provost. The example set by Paris was soon followed at Oxford. These universities were the fruit of long struggles, during which the teachers and students elected to move to and fro between other towns, which resulted in other universities, such as Orleans, Cambridge, Padua and Vercelli, being founded. So the first universities, these university corporations, were the result of efforts to make the *peregrinatio academica* to these meccas of learning less perilous and form the starting point for the transnational project on the heritage of European universities.

4. Cf. Walter Rüegg (ed.), *Geschichte der Universität in Europa*, vol I: Mittelalter, Munich 1993, in particular: chap. 1: "Themen, Probleme, Erkenntnisse" (by the editor); chap. 3 "Die Hochschulträger" (by Paolo Nardi).
5. W. Stelzer, "Zum Scholarenprivileg Friedrich Barbarossas (Authentica 'Habita')", in: *Deutsches Archiv für Erforschung des Mittelalters 34* (1978), 123-165, "Grundgesetz der mittelalterlichen Universität" (p. 132).

The university corporations were backed in their struggles against the local authorities by the central authorities. The pope and the emperor had both understood that these corporations could, more so than individual academics, secure them the ideological support and intellectual frameworks that were vital to their bid to maintain the unity of the *Corpus christianum* and the Holy Empire. They reserved for themselves the sovereign authority necessary to create higher education institutions bearing the name of *studium generale*, which conferred upon individuals the right to teach in all of papal Christendom, the *licentia ubique docendi*, while in the *studia particularia* run by the cathedrals, towns and individual academics the right to teach was granted and restricted by the bishopric. In their official documents, the universal authorities hailed the university as a place capable of enlightening the world through the love of science.

At the same time, the central authorities looked to the universities and academics to meet a growing need of their expanding administration, namely intellectual and practical support in in-fighting between papal and anti-papal forces and between pope and emperor but above all against centrifugal forces, heresies and regional and local political powers. Through centralised administration and distribution of ecclesiastical benefits to graduates, the popes strongly accentuated the European role of the universities, and this universal aspect constituted the second medieval tradition opening the way between the old universities.

The third tradition important for the subject of this project is the open structure of the university corporations. Other medieval corporations were defined by their regional scope, such as the *universitas vallis de Schwyz* within the original Swiss Confederation covenant, or by a *numerus clausus* in technical professions, such as architecture or navigation, whose public importance was at least equal to university studies. But these studies were accessible to any Christian capable of pursuing them in the universal language of the period, Latin. The knowledge thus acquired was considered as a gift of God, a public asset, whereas other knowledge was taught and exercised on worksites and within professions where access and financial return were monopolised by the corporations concerned.

While architects applied their highly intricate theoretical knowledge to build magnificent cathedrals, university academics constructed great theoretical edifices, the theological *summae*, the *corpus* of civil law and *corpus* of ecclesiastical law, the philosophical mirrors of the *specula*, astronomical models, maps and tables, all with a view to better understanding and applying the divine and human laws governing the spiritual and physical unity of the world. Verticality did not only reign supreme in the gothic cathedrals and ecclesiastical and secular hierarchies. The identifying point of all the theoretical edifices were their highest point, with God at the summit of the universe and his spiritual and political representatives on Earth, and transcendental ideas becoming reality down here. Researchers compared themselves to dwarfs sitting on the shoulders of the ancients to be able to see further. The study syllabus was illustrated with an ascending chart going up from the ground floor via the intermediate floors of liberal arts and philosophy to theology, which formed the crenellation of the tower of sciences.

Ultimately, then, it was thanks to this hierarchical unity stemming from medieval tradition that the students moving between the ancient universities found the same methods and study disciplines everywhere and gained identical qualifications entitling them to teach in the universities themselves. It goes without saying that most of the young men who undertook perilous and costly journeys to study law in Bologna or Orleans or medicine in Montpellier, Paris or Padua did not wish to become teachers.

The latent function of the university was to pass on to them knowledge and methods enabling them to exercise intellectual professions in societies undergoing sweeping change. It has been said that no period in European history has undergone economic, political, intellectual and spiritual crises comparable to those of 1200 to 1600. Europe was opening up to the outside world. Monetary economy and bureaucratic administration were developing in the towns, giving rise to political and social conflicts. The spiritual and secular powers were tearing each other apart and these conflicts, together with famine and plague, threatened the physical safety of individuals. Their psychical and spiritual security was shaken by the contradictions between the message of the Church and their actual experiences. The university offered intellectual security by playing off the contradictions and conflicts of opinion and experience as thesis and antithesis in a dialectical process culminating in a logical synthesis. The *disputatio* where this dialectical process was exercised was a mandatory supplement to classes and the crowning point of study in every faculty.

This scholastic method corresponded to the Aristotelian and monastic ideal of contemplative life. From the fourteenth century onwards it was criticised for disregarding man and his tangible problems. The emphasis had swung too far towards the theoretical side and caused a reaction which overturned the university's role, transforming its latent function of training doctors, lawyers, judges, notaries, registrars, secretaries and other public officials into a manifest one. The universities were subordinated to the needs of regional authorities and found themselves competing with new types of higher education, the navigation colleges in Spain and Portugal, military academies, theological colleges for Protestant clergymen and academics, seminaries for priests, *gymnasia academica*, colleges and *colegios mayores* for public office-holders. But there was also the trade in printed books and the foundation of learned societies and scientific academies, which from the fifteenth century onwards toppled the universities' medieval monopoly in developing and disseminating scientific knowledge.

One might deduce that this dispersal of higher education, reinforced by the decline of the universal powers in favour of national and regional states, together with the religious and political schism in Europe caused by the Reform, brought movement between the universities to an end. Only a few years ago, people were still talking of the decadence, atrophy or even coma into which the universities had plunged in the seventeenth and eighteenth centuries. The second volume of our *History of the university in Europe* shows that this was not the case and, on the contrary, the universities made a substantial contribution to European culture that reached beyond the splits between Catholic, Protestant and Reformed states. Although this division favoured international movement between universities of the same confession, movement across confessional boundaries was not prevented. A great many universities which facilitated the matriculation of foreign students for financial reasons found ways of dispensing them from declaring their faith, and teachers whose doctrines did not correspond to those accepted by a given university were welcomed elsewhere for precisely that reason. However, it was no longer the universal nature of global powers and the unity of the intellectual world that determined the route of the universities.

## Their function of bridging across Europe[6]

The initial bulwark for this European bridge was formed by the *studia humanitatis*, the humanities, studies whose curricula differed from the liberal arts only through the addition of history and the importance attached to rhetoric and moral philosophy. But their orientation was quite different. In the same way that the vertically oriented gothic style of cathedral gave way to the Renaissance and baroque styles with their horizontal perspective, the university education ideal was now the *honnête homme,* the gentleman, the enlightened citizen cultivated through conversation "with the finest men of the past centuries, conversation that would offer up the best of their thinking" as Descartes maintained,[7] reiterating the principle of dialogue which the Italian humanists of the fourteenth century had introduced in their study reform.

This dialogue with the lessons of the past incremented the medieval tradition of *Aetas aristotelica*, oriented towards the nature of things, with the interest of *Aetas ciceroniana* for human relations, if I may borrow the comparison made by the great medievalist Etienne Gilson. Dialogue was becoming a preferred form for scientific and philosophical treatises. It enabled the author to present the different viewpoints in their theoretical and practical context and, instead of resolving the divergences through dialectical processes, to leave it to the reader to draw the conclusions. It was not so much logic, therefore, as rhetoric, the art of directing words at others, that characterised the intellectual discourse in the universities and the civilisation of the age.

The principle of dialogue whereby the foreigner was recognised as a partner in intellectual conversation determined the university's bridging function. In place of the unity of the *Corpus christianum*, the Europe of the universities constituted itself as a republic of letters, whose members exchanged thousands of letters across confessional and political boundaries. Guillaume Budé, the founding father of what became the Collège de France, heralded this mentality in a letter he sent in 1518 to the former rector of the University of Vienna, the Swiss humanist, Vadian: "could there be such a person who, through his humanities studies, has built friendships with colleagues abroad and would be capable of renouncing those friendships were their governments to tire of peace and gain a taste for war?"[8] Among the most

---

6. Cf. Rüegg, *Geschichte der Universität* (note. 3) vol. II, *Von der Reformation zur Französischen Revolution* (1500-1800), in particular 21-52.
7. Gustave Lanson, *Histoire de la littérature française*, 12th ed., Paris 1912, viii.
8. *Vadianische Briefsammlung VII, Ergänzungsband*, St Gallen 1913, 9. Text corrected in line with the original by Walter Rüegg, Humanistische Elitenbildung in der Eidgenossenschaft zur Zeit der Renaissance, in: *Die Renaissance im Blick der Nationen Europas*, ed. by Georg Kauffmann, Wolfenbütteler Abhandlungen zur Renaissanceforschung 9, Wiesbaden 1991, 133.

famous teachers loyalty to the European republic of letters often surpassed the loyalty they owed to their fatherland or their church.

The function of the universities as a bridge across Europe is also reflected in the development of the idea of Europe. In the thirteenth century, that time when the universal powers were backing the founding of the universities to develop the unity of the *Corpus christianum* and the Holy Empire, Alexander von Roes was seeking to give the geographical notion of Europe political significance by attributing distinct functions to the three great European nations: the *sacerdotium* to the Italians, the *regnum* to the Germans, the *studium* to the French. While this medieval vision of the university was endowed with a piecemeal European function, Pope Pius II gave it its function of European bridge. In 1463, as sovereign pontiff, he justified the proclamation of a crusade against the Turks by claiming that what they were attacking was not the *Corpus christianum* but Europe, our "fatherland, our own home, our house". Versed in humanist wisdom, he justified the unity of Europe in his cosmography by turning to the thinkers of Greek and Latin antiquity.[9] So it was not union through Christian faith but historical origin that gave Europe its political and cultural significance, and the university had the dual function of a bridge, on the one hand linking the Christian present with pagan antiquity through humanist and Cartesian conversation with the *honnêtes hommes* of the past and on the other hand via the route linking the universities, each one of them a different chamber within the common European home.

Although that universities route enabled students to form their minds in some excellent old universities such as Salamanca, Padua, Edinburgh, Vienna and Kraków or in newly founded establishments such as Leiden, Halle and Göttingen, the humanist leaning towards the *vita activa* and the civility of the *honnête homme* degenerated in most universities into sterile knowledge and superficial culture captivatingly caricatured in the comedies of Molière.

This resulted in the disappearance of a great many universities following the French Revolution and the Napoleonic conquests, which devastated the university scene in Europe. In 1789 there had been 143 universities but by 1815 only 83 remained. In Germany and Spain nearly half of them had disappeared. The twenty-two French universities had been abolished and replaced in twelve cities by special colleges and isolated faculties. This policy reflected the dominant trend during the Enlightenment, which steered higher education towards practical knowledge and careers that would serve the public good. From Spain to Russia, the governments set up their own colleges for military officers and public officials. The universities seemed doomed to extinction like the other medieval institutions. So how is the expansion of the universities in the nineteenth and twentieth centuries to be explained? This is my third and final point.

---

9. Manfred Fuhrmann: *Alexander von Roes: ein Wegbereiter des Europagedankens? Sitzungsberichte der Heidelberger Akademie der Wissenschaften, Philosophisch-historische Klasse*, Jahrgang 1994, Bericht 4, Heidelberg 1994.

## The liberal modernisation of the traditional role of the university

The document prepared by Professor Alain Renaut quite rightly explains an unexpected expansion by a policy of modernising refoundation, symbolised by the opening in 1810 of the University of Berlin. The great scholar and statesman Wilhelm von Humboldt had introduced this policy by persuading the King of Prussia, who favoured the French model of vocational colleges, to found a university in Berlin based on the ideas of the theologian and philosopher Friedrich Schleiermacher. In Schleiermacher's view the function of the university was not to teach accepted knowledge that could be directly used as the colleges did, but to demonstrate how that knowledge was discovered, awaken the idea of science in students' minds and encourage them to think back to the fundamental laws of science in their every act.[10]

Freedom applied equally to the manner of studying, subject matter and the university's relations with the public authorities. In Humboldt's eyes, the state had only two tasks to perform as far as the universities were concerned, namely protecting their freedom and appointing academics. Obviously, this idealist model was not as easy to put into practice as the French state-controlled model of special colleges, subject to a calculated, often military discipline, organised and closely controlled by an enlightened despotism which regulated, down to the last detail, the study courses, the conferment of grades, compliance of the opinions professed with official doctrines and even personal habits through, for example, the prohibition of beards in 1852.

Humboldt's scheme of giving the new university a large area of land to ensure its material independence was abandoned by his successor; academic freedom was restricted in 1819 by control and censorship measures following student demonstrations, and was not restored until after 1848. Similarly, introducing students to scientific research through seminars and laboratories was slow to progress. But liberal modernisation bore its fruit. Whereas, at the beginning of the century, Paris had been the Mecca for scholars the world over, from the 1830s onwards the French government sent representatives to Germany to investigate advances in higher education. And young Frenchmen, later followed by English and American students, went there to train in the new scientific methods. From the end of the nineteenth century, the German model embodied the modern university in Europe and also the United States and Japan.

An extraordinary expansion in the number and attendance levels of universities resulted. By 1939 there were some 200 establishments, as opposed to barely a hundred in 1840. The number of teachers had quadrupled and student numbers were seven times higher.[11] Even greater still was the expansion in the number of specialised colleges (some 300) in the military, technical, commercial, medical, veterinary, agricultural economic, teacher training, political and music sectors. But

10. Walter Rüegg, "Der Mythos der Humboldtschen Universität", in: *Universitas in theologia – theologia in universitate, Festschrift für Hans Heinrich Schmid zum 60. Geburtstag*, publ. by Matthias Krieg and Martin Rose, Zürich 1997, 155-174, in particular 162-166.
11. Christophe Charle, chap. 1, Matti Klinge, chap. 5, Walter Rüegg, appendix in *Geschichte der Universität* (note 3), vol. III: *Vom 19. Jahrhundert zum Zweiten Weltkrieg* (1800-1945), in preparation.

they had not replaced the universities and were attended by only a relatively small minority of students.

In France, the universities had been reconstituted in 1895, and one of the first acts of the new nation states of eastern Europe was to set up universities, allowing the notion of "university as the European institution par excellence" to take on its full meaning. With the exception of France, where the rigorous selection and training systems of the *grandes écoles* placed them at the summit of higher education, special colleges had to strive for the rights and titles of universities – which they achieved in Germany and Austria towards the end of the century – or integration into universities, which was the case in Great Britain and Italy. Most special colleges today form part of the membership of the European University Association.[12] But beyond Europe too, universities have become the global institutions of higher education, whereas at the beginning of the nineteenth century, other than in Latin America, there were only colleges, academies, seminaries, madrases or other schools for training the intellectual, political or spiritual élite.

In this expansion process, one of the flagships of the French model, the *Ecole polytechnique*, was highly influential in terms of theory in the sector of the special colleges, founded in the eighteenth century to provide technical training for state officials. In the nineteenth century they became polytechnical colleges by introducing advanced training in the mathematical and physical sciences. But they did not adopt the other aspect of the French model, namely a college for officials structured along the lines of military discipline and subject to meticulous state control. On the contrary, they aspired to the fundamental rights of universities, gaining first corporate autonomy for their internal organisation, then the right to accredit lecturers and, at the end of the century, the entitlement to confer the title of doctor, which put them on a par with universities and established the model for transforming colleges of commerce, veterinary medicine, agricultural studies, etc. into university institutions.

When we take a closer look at the impact of the German model on the French-style universities and especially on the British universities, which retained their medieval and humanist structures, we can see that it was above all the scientific spirit of the German university that led to the modernisation of traditional university structures in Europe. That modernisation was boosted by models that geared the corporate autonomy of the traditional university to the freedom of its members in the sphere of teaching, study and research. The great merit of Humboldt and his adviser Schleiermacher had been their refusal of the state model of vocational colleges and their liberal modernisation of the university's medieval structures, which made it possible in the long term to overcome state constraints on academic freedom. The example of the great Anglo-American universities demonstrates the fundamental importance of freedom and corporate autonomy. The striving of universities for corporate autonomy and freedom of their members is all the more impressive and explained only by extrinsic reasons. The real cause of this success has to be sought in the scientific mind itself.

---

12. Editors' note: on 31 March 2001, the CRE – Association of European Universities and the Confederation of EU Rectors' Conferences merged to form the European University Association (EUA).

The spiritual fathers of Berlin University distanced themselves from the scientific spirit of the humanist university, which they regarded as merely exploring the outward aspects of things and not penetrating their essence. The theologian and philosopher Schleiermacher wrote in his plan for Berlin University that he expected "scientific thought, awakened by philosophical teaching, to move from the centre and penetrate more deeply into individual detail, to seek, compile and create its own judgement confirming, through its accuracy, natural science and the coherency of universal knowledge".[13]

Savigny, the great law historian, gave an example of this "scientific thought" in the prologue to his masterpiece *The History of Roman Law in the Middle Ages*. He rejected the superficial separation of the history of law and the history of legal literature. If his work was to go beyond the description of previous studies and engage in new research, he would need to take "a specific point to explain how the most recent law resulted from the pure and simple development and constant transformation of the Roman law determined by the circumstances of the Western Empire".[14]

Niebuhr, in the prologue to his famous *Roman History*, also spoke of the "decisive point" which emerged in discussion with Savigny[15] and enabled him to describe history from a critical viewpoint. Previous works had dealt with Roman history like "geographical maps or painted landscapes and had not even attempted to bring forth from these rudimentary media the image of the subjects they were considering".[16]

Wilhelm von Humboldt sought, as a philosopher of language, the specific point in the "faculty of the mind whose depth and abundance influenced the course of world events and which was the founding principle in the hidden and somewhat mysterious development of humankind".[17]

There are many other examples illustrating this turning of scientific thought to the "centre", the "specific point", the "decisive point", and the "founding principle". In particular, it prompted philosophical speculation in the natural sciences, which only slowly gave way to empirical research. But no one defined this scientific mind better than the fifth and most influential of the spiritual fathers of the new University of Berlin, the philologist and historian of Greek antiquity, August Böckh. In his view the only method suited to the scientific mind was the concentric method "which entailed linking all phenomena to their centre and from there moving step by step to all the outer sides". This centre of scientific research and education constituting the essence of the university was located, in Böckh's opinion, "in the innermost core of

13. Friedrich Schleiermacher, *Gelegentliche Gedanken über Universitäten im deutschen Sinn. Nebst einem Anhang über eine neu zu errichtende*, Berlin 1808, 39.
14. Friedrich Carl von Savigny, *Geschichte des römischen Rechts im Mittelalter, vol. I*, Foreword to first edition, Nachdruck Darmstadt 1956, vii.
15. Barthold G. Niebuhr, *Römische Geschichte, Berichtigte Ausgabe in einem Bande*, Teil I, Berlin 5 1853, xvf.
16. Ibid., xv.
17. Wilhelm von Humboldt, "Über die Verschiedenheiten des menschlichen Sprachbaus" (1827-1829) in *Werke in fünf Bänden*, publ. by Andreas Flitner and Klaus Giel, vol. III, Schriften zur Sprachphilosophie, Darmstadt 1965, 155f.

its coherent whole" (*im innersten Kern seines Gesamtzusammenhanges*).[18] I believe that this new method would be better termed "nuclear", since it goes to the core, the philosophical essence and historical or physical origin of natural and spiritual phenomena. This new scientific thinking, which Niebuhr saw as animating the early years of Berlin University with its "enthusiasm and bliss" (*die Begeisterung und Seligkeit*)[19], this nuclear method of pushing research to the innermost core of all things, blazed the trail on which the modern university picked up speed and which today forms the itinerary of modern universities of either ancient or recent origin.

---

18. A. Boeckh, *Encyclopädie und Methodologie der philologischen Wissenschaft*, ed. by Ernst Bratuschek, Leipzig 1877, 47.
19. Niebuhr, *Römische Geschichte* (note 13), xvi.

# The cultural heritage of European universities

*Nuria Sanz and Sjur Bergan*

## Introduction

The purpose of the project on the heritage of European universities was to raise awareness of the key role of universities to the cultural heritage of Europe as well as to encourage universities to co-operate at European level to define a common approach to their common problems with regard to their heritage. It thus had a double aim: the heritage of European universities and the European university as heritage. The project comprised some twelve traditional European universities and was built around four thematic meetings. The launching meeting was held in Alcalá de Henares in December 1999. Subsequent meetings focused on the intellectual heritage of universities (Montpellier, March 2000), the material heritage of universities (Bologna, July 2000) and the European dimension of the university heritage (Kraków, October 2000).

While the number of universities participating in this project had to be limited for structural reasons, an effort was made to obtain a reasonable geographical diversity as well as a diversity of traditions. Thus, the project included some of the earliest European universities as well as some more recent. While south central Europe, the region where the European university originated, was strongly represented, the participating institutions also illustrated the spread of the university idea to other parts of Europe.

## Heritage and history

There is a general consciousness that the universities have a long history, and that they have survived a number of crises. Universities are in fact among the few institutions that have survived in more or less continuous form since the Middle Ages; other candidates include the Icelandic Parliament – as well as that of the Isle of Man – and the Catholic and Orthodox churches.[1]

There is far less consciousness of the heritage of universities: how the accumulated experience of universities as well as their material culture have been transmitted from one generation to the next, and the role this heritage plays today. This is particularly important because higher education institutions are in a period of great change. The change is exemplified by the emergence of mass higher education, of a large non-university higher education sector and of a continuing discussion about the mission of higher education. The Bologna Process has launched a major movement of higher education reform throughout Europe, while higher education in many new member states also needs to address the problems arising from a long period of totalitarian rule.

---

1. See Professor Walter Rüegg's article in the present volume.

In this context, a project addressing the heritage of universities as quintessentially European institutions seemed particularly pertinent. Heritage looks at the past with a view to the future. Even if the conscience of the heritage of universities is not as strong as one would have liked, the university heritage is nevertheless very much a living heritage.

## Intellectual heritage

Policies for the immaterial heritage of universities were an important aspect of the project. In this sense, the university constitutes an important point of reference in beginning to define and valorise the intellectual heritage of Europe. The uniqueness of the intellectual heritage is shown through the integrative power and freedom of learning and scientific research with regard to language, esthetical, mythical, religious and historical endeavour.

Universities are places of organised discussion (*disputatio*). The creativity resulting from discussion and friction is an integral part of the intellectual heritage of the European university. Heritage is a process in which conscious transmission of values to future generations is a key element.

In preparation for the meeting in Montpellier, the participating universities were invited to complete a questionnaire helping to define the concept of intellectual heritage. The overall approach of the answers was historiographical rather than heritage oriented. All replies saw the university heritage as an instrument, and there was little focus on heritage on heritage terms. The main components of the intellectual heritage were considered to be the values of the university, the material traces of its work (collections, museums, buildings, etc.), the scientific and educational achievements, the ideas developed and the prominent individuals who had contributed to these achievements. The role of the university in the process of nation building was also emphasised, as was the importance of the multi-cultural university. Interestingly, none of the replies referred to transmission as a key element of the intellectual heritage.

Some universities felt that the notion of "two cultures", ie a cultural distinction between the "hard" sciences on the one hand and the humanities and the social sciences on the other, was accurate, whereas others rejected this division of what they perceived as one common academic culture.

A question about the social commitment of the intellectual heritage gave rise to very different interpretations of the term "social": society, social class, and equal opportunities. Perhaps interesting statements on the traditions of both the university and the society concerned could be discerned from these different interpretations.

The contribution of the intellectual heritage to the European construction was strongly emphasised by all respondents. This emphasis was universal, but it was particularly strong in the case of central and eastern European universities. Two universities in addition emphasised their role in contacts with other parts of the world. In both cases, this reflected a long-standing orientation of their respective societies: Coimbra with respect to Latin America and Africa, and İstanbul as a bridge between East and West.

Since the first Council of Europe campaign on cultural heritage, in 1975, the heritage concept has developed towards a wider and more inclusive view. The latest text adopted so far, Recommendation No. R (98) 5 of the Committee of Ministers to member states concerning heritage education, defines cultural heritage as including any material or non-material vestige of human endeavour and any trace of human activities in the natural environment. This gives rise to a number of questions:

– How does the heritage belong to all of us as Europeans?
– How is fragility defined? Is our heritage fragile?
– How can we distinguish between memory, legacy and heritage in relation to transmission, responsibility and values?
– What does heritage mean for the university community today?
– How can a sustainable curiosity about the university heritage be established?

Some of the participating universities had given particular consideration to their heritage under different circumstances. For example, at the partition of Louvain/Leuven in the 1960s, the *Université catholique de Louvain* defined each of the components of its name. "University" implied academic freedom and institutional autonomy, even under economic constraint. "Catholic" implied universal, hence open. There were no ideological or religious requirements with regard to staff and students, except that they were expected to show respect for the beliefs of others. "Louvain" implied a commitment to this city, which had originally been chosen as the location of the university because the city was in a deep recession at the time a university needed to be established. At the same time, the university saw it as part of its mission that it should be open to both Europe and the wider world, in particular the Third World.

The representative of Coimbra underlined that this town distinguished itself from other Portuguese cities because of its university, which was also an important element in the old town, which had been declared a heritage monument. Nonetheless, the university has often had to question its role in the city, where many inhabitants know very little about the institution. On the other hand, Cluj-Napoca is now engaged in recovering its history, which was necessary for it to play a conscious role as a multi-cultural university in a region with a rich and diverse heritage.

The host institution, Montpellier, has traditions dating back to the fifteenth century, yet it is also very much a modern university. Its heritage is reflected in its historical buildings and its Botanical Garden, but also in its traditions and current policies.

We thus see that a heritage project is a project of and for society. Its object is traces of human existence and activities, whether material or immaterial, in their capacity to be rediscovered, reinterpreted and reread. Heritage is not a static phenomenon, but a process and an exercise of selection. Heritage is a memory that is formed on a daily basis, and the project aims at discovering how the heritage of universities can become a common project. Heritage can also be thought of as a shared frame of reference and comparison. While many parts of the European heritage were generally shared, there are also interesting differences, for example in the importance given to the classical European heritage in school curricula – and hence in its transmission to future generations.

Values are important in the development and transmission of heritage, but values also change, and hence the interpretation of heritage. For example, whereas national greatness, military prowess and glory were important values in the interpretation of the national heritage at the beginning of the twentieth century, tolerance and justice are now generally seen as core values and indeed as measures of a country's greatness. Also in this respect, it is therefore important to think of heritage as a process.

A definition of the intellectual heritage of universities should aim at being operational. Universities have to define the elements of their own frame of reference through heritage, what they can share with others, and how. Among other things, an operational definition of the intellectual heritage of universities could provide a platform for:

– defining what a university is, and what distinguishes it from other higher education institutions;
– assisting those who want to establish new institutions within the tradition of European universities, or who want to reform existing institutions to comply with that tradition;
– providing guidance to the (re)construction of higher education in zones of recent conflict or civil strife, such as Kosovo or the universities recently liberated from the constraints of the authoritarian 1998 Serbian Law on Universities, in which conforming to European standards and traditions are an important factor in the reconstruction effort.

A common identity should be a part of the definition of intellectual heritage. Heritage should contribute to the definition and construction of the past, as relevant to the present and the future. In this sense, heritage should be operational and not nostalgic – we should study the past to construct the future. In political terms, a part of the task is finding how, in the age of the sound bite, one could create understanding for an institution that, by definition, takes the longer view and is concerned with complex issues.

**The traces of cultural heritage**

In preparation of the Bologna meeting, we invited the participating universities as well as a number of other traditional universities to complete a questionnaire on their material heritage. This part of the article builds on returned questionnaires and supplementary material from universities participating in the projects as well as some additional institutions, in all some twenty-five institutions. Northern, southern, eastern, central and western Europe are all represented. Some of the universities play – or have played – a role as the central higher education institution of their country (eg Coimbra, Tartu, Vilnius, Zagreb, Oslo). Others are important universities in countries where no single institution can claim historical or current pre-eminence

54

(eg Bologna, İstanbul, Padova, Salamanca). At least two universities (Santiago de Compostela and Åbo Akademi) play a pivotal role in a region with a distinct language and culture, which does not prevent them from also playing an important role at national level.

Initially, universities were asked to state what they consider as traces of their cultural heritage. Predictably, all mentioned material traces. Just about every questionnaire mentioned built heritage as a first reference, and most also mentioned collections, archives and libraries. It was, however, interesting to see that even in a context that favoured the material heritage, other associations were made. For example, the University of Bologna considered that the whole work of its teachers and students constitutes traces of its heritage. Bologna also specifically mentioned the normative aspect that is an important part of its heritage. Related to the points made by Bologna is the one mentioned by the University of Coimbra: university life as heritage. The point was further illustrated during the meeting through a presentation by Professor Maria de Fátima Silva on university ceremonies and festivals,[2] ranging from solemn commencement and doctoral ceremonies to the *queima das fitas* and *tunas* of student life.

The reply from St Andrews went an interesting step further and included the historical environment among the traces of its heritage. Vilnius specifically mentioned intellectual freedom and religious tolerance. While these are universal academic values,[3] the fact that they were mentioned specifically by Vilnius is interesting in view of its history.

In the case of Zagreb, the university saw values as traces of its heritage and considered educating and developing attitudes toward the heritage values of the university an important task. Zagreb also gave a very extensive interpretation of the traces of its heritage, encompassing language, artistic and aesthetic appreciation and creation, mythical elements, scientific and technological achievements, religious involvement and expressions, as well as modes of social organisation and structure. Whereas Zagreb refers to language as manifestations of human thoughts and a means of human – and therefore also scholarly – communication, Åbo Akademi invokes its commitment to a specific language and culture: that of the Swedish speaking minority in Finland.

It is worth noting that while all answers referred to material traces, none considered the symbolic value of the space dedicated to teaching and learning.

We also asked about the legal basis for the protection of all or parts of the university heritage. Here, replies were disappointingly general, with reference to national heritage laws without specific provision for university heritage. For example, under Norwegian heritage legislation, the Archaeological Museum of the University of Oslo is one of five regional authorities for the implementation of the heritage

---

2. The presentation is reproduced in the present volume.
3. Cf. the 1988 *Magna Charta Universitatum*.

legislation.[4] This legislation, however, says nothing about the heritage of the university.

There was also little or no reference to laws or rules establishing university ownership of its heritage, even though most respondents stated that they own their built and movable heritage. What does ownership mean in the case of a state institution? Is each state institution the legal owner of its buildings and artefacts, or is the state – admittedly a nebulous concept – the owner, exercising its ownership through a specialised institution? It was also interesting to note that only two replies referred to internal university rules that specifically address management issues.

## Research on the university heritage

Here we asked specifically about research and development (R & D) programmes linked to the university heritage, laboratories conducting research on heritage conservation and restoration (focusing on techniques, not on individual items or collections) and scientific publications devoted to the heritage of the university.

The answers revealed that the most developed R & D programmes concern technical aspects of restoration and conservation. Archaeology departments in particular are pioneers with regard to R & D programmes. Universities also offer professional services that public authorities need for the management of heritage. As in many other fields, they are centres of competence. However, these services seem to be offered mostly on a case-by-case basis, without any overall planning or management.

There is an imbalance in that some universities have well-developed heritage policies but no specialised laboratories, whereas some universities that have well-developed study programmes do not let students participate in and contribute to the cataloguing of the universities' own heritage.

The list of publications concerning heritage is impressive and probably far from complete. Publications range from books through regular specialised journals to occasional articles. Topics range from the history of Åbo Akademi[5] through a collection on the history of Portuguese art (Coimbra), urban policies around the university (Louvain) and bibliographies and academic registers (Vilnius) to publications on university museums and collections (Bologna) and the historical heritage of the university (Santiago de Compostela). However, the European or comparative perspective is absent from these publications. Each institution seems to work on its own without any attempt to co-operate at European level.

---

4. Two linguistic points may be worth making: the Archeological Museum is known as *Oldsaksamlingen* – literally "the collection of ancient objects" or, less charitably, "old things". In Norwegian, the name itself gives a connotation of antiquity. The heritage law is known for short as *Kulturminnevernloven*, literally "the law on the protection of the cultural memory".
5. Which properly speaking is a history rather than a heritage publication.

## Teaching and training

The most remarkable feature of the replies to this part of the questionnaire was that none made any connection between research and teaching programmes. Since one of the characteristics of universities is the intimate connection between teaching and research, this lack of connection is surprising, to say the least. The most obvious explanation would be that unlike other university programmes, heritage-oriented study programmes are divorced from research. This, however, is an unlikely explanation in view of what we know about universities. We should therefore ask why the respondents did not make what would seem to be an obvious connection. It would be interesting to see whether this is because heritage study programmes are differently structured from heritage research. However, the question transcends the scope of this article.

Cultural heritage is a transdisciplinary field. Almost without exception, however, the examples of study programmes provided were not of heritage courses *per se*, but of traditional academic disciplines related to heritage. Archaeology and art history were the programmes most frequently mentioned. Conservation and museology were also mentioned by more than one university, as were courses related to the history of the university. Courses mentioned only by a single university covered a very broad range of fields and specialisations, from library science (Zagreb) through a Master level programme on historical cities and town planning (Bologna) to maritime studies (St Andrews).

Two comments seem pertinent with regard to this list. The first is that most of the courses mentioned are disciplinary rather than transdisciplinary. The structure of the study programmes therefore does not seem to explain why no connection was made between teaching and research. The staff teaching archaeology and art history most likely carry out research in the same disciplines.

The second comment is both more substantial and more worrying. It concerns the lack of specific heritage training courses. Heritage is neither the historiography of collections – the study of things past without regard to how one identifies with the traces – nor the consideration of the discourse of the past with the same disregard as to identification. History and material objects are both important to heritage but what makes them heritage is that someone identifies with them. Heritage is kept alive because it means something to individuals or groups of individuals. The main aim of the project is how to define the relevance of the heritage for the academic community and for its social context.

What are labelled as heritage programmes are therefore mostly heritage related studies. Among the respondents, only three universities (Bologna, Santiago de Compostela and Vilnius) listed heritage courses as such, and of these, only Santiago offers a substantial course at advanced level. Our overriding conclusion is that there is a great need for heritage study programmes, because heritage forges a community of interest. Such courses should by definition be a transdisciplinary and co-operative effort, and they should be linked to heritage research.

A logical extension of this conclusion is that heritage programmes should have a comparative approach and be built on European co-operation. There is no evidence of either in the replies. On the contrary, programmes often build on very specific concerns arising from local circumstances with no participation of other universities or institutions. The lack of a European perspective is also shown by the fact that there is no information on the number of European (or non-national) participants in these programmes.

## Conservation and restoration

The first part of the questionnaire concerned the tasks of the university with regard to all kinds of material heritage, with special emphasis on the university's two main tasks: research and teaching. The second part of the questionnaire focused on the university's own material heritage.

We first asked about the conservation and restoration of the heritage of the university. The replies indicated a difference between built and movable heritage in that policies for the built heritage show a larger degree of co-operation with external bodies, whereas movable heritage policies tend to be specific to the institution or even faculty or museum concerned. It could therefore lend itself to co-operation with other institutions both for restoration and conservation – it could for example be sent to another institution with a particularly well-developed conservation laboratory – and for events such as travelling exhibitions. However, the built heritage is the more massive one, often the one representing the largest financial value and perhaps in many cases the one representing the greatest challenges for conservation and restoration.

Where the replies are specific, they indicate little propensity to turn heritage into "museum objects" after the Linné system of classification, in other words to keep heritage objects – including buildings – for display but not for use. Nevertheless, the use made of facilities and objects that are considered a part of the university's heritage is quite restricted. Their use is often reserved for special occasions such as academic ceremonies, regulated institutional use, museums, exhibitions or research centres. The *aula magna* is a special case in that it is often located in the historical part of the university buildings and used for academic ceremonies and other solemn occasions. The *aula magna* of the University of Bologna is a reconverted church, Santa Lucia, and has acquired a special meaning in European higher education policies because it was here that two important policy documents were adopted: the *Magna Charta Universitatum*, adopted by university rectors in 1988 on the occasion of the 900th anniversary of the University of Bologna, and the Bologna Declaration signed by the Ministers of Education of twenty-nine European countries in June 1999. The *aula magna* of the University of Oslo is a part not only of that university's heritage but of the heritage of Norway for two reasons: its walls were decorated by Edvard Munch, and, until 1990, it was here that the Nobel Peace Prize ceremony was held each year on 10 December.

The information available on the built heritage of the university is highly uneven. Some universities have a complete documentation, whereas this is largely lacking in others. Related to the information available is the issue of what is done with the university's material heritage. The replies indicate that only Salamanca has a master plan for its built heritage. This is absent in the other universities, many of which nonetheless have a very valuable built heritage. Overall, there is in fact little evidence of sustained planning, whether for the built or for the movable heritage.

A particularly interesting issue is the relationship of the university heritage to the overall development of the city in which the university is located. This is perhaps a more salient issue in small towns hosting a historical university – university towns – than in large cities that include a historical university as one among many of their distinctive features. The replies indicate that urban development is highly uneven, as is the university's role in it. In many cases, the impression is that while the university may have played an important role in town planning in the past, this is no longer quite the case. It would also seem that the university's informal role is stronger than the formal one. Nevertheless, universities like Santiago de Compostela, Bologna and Vilnius constitute significant features of the urban landscape and do have a role in urban planning. Coimbra is the exception that confirms the rule: there are many difficulties in the relationship between the university and the city and they go back a long time. The situation has been described as a conflict between two potential centres of local power: academe and the civil authorities. An example of a sharp conflict arose with the building of the new university city in the part of Coimbra known as Alta in the 1930s. It is interesting to note that this part of the conflict was played out under an authoritarian regime, many of whose leading figures, including Salazar himself, had strong ties to the University of Coimbra.[6]

**Management**

We then asked how the heritage of the university is managed and how heritage policies are made. The answers showed that only one university – Salamanca – has a clearly centralised model. From other contexts, we know that this is also the model of the Universidad Central Autónoma de México. In Salamanca, one physical and legal person is responsible for the heritage of the university. The other universities that answered this question all have different types of decentralised models, ranging from Santiago de Compostela, which has a Vice Rector with a specific responsibility, to Zagreb. At the latter university, a high degree of decentralisation and the correspondingly high degree of autonomy of individual faculties is linked to the general structure of university management in which the faculties are legal entities. Within a decentralised model, the relationship between the central and lower levels may vary considerably, but at several universities, Faculty or Department officials are responsible for specific buildings, collections, etc. These include Bologna (where responsibility lies with specialised centres rather than faculties), Coimbra, Zagreb, Tartu and St Andrews.

The point to be made is not that centralisation is a goal in itself, or that a centralised model is necessarily preferable to a decentralised one. The issue is rather whether heritage concerns are present in the decision making process. Heritage concerns will

6. Cf. Luis Reis Torgal: *A Universidade e o Estado Novo* (Coimbra 1999: Livreria Minerva Editora).

have to be weighed against other considerations, but at a historical university, the administrative system should ensure that heritage concerns enter the equation.

One area in which the various concerns of the university are brought together is the budget discussions, which at most institutions are an annual occurrence. The answers we received show no clear evidence of a clear budget policy for the heritage of the university, with an estimate of annual foreseen expenditures, nor was there any evidence of systematic fund raising or efforts at obtaining funds through specific projects. Only four universities (Padova, Tartu, Vilnius and Zagreb) gave an estimate of the share of the university budget spent on protecting and preserving its material heritage. These estimates ranged from slightly less than one per cent to six per cent of the overall university budget. Padova remarked that the overwhelming part of this budget is spent on the built heritage.

Statistics imply making a choice as to which parameters are considered most relevant, and the statistical base is designed with a view to identifying these factors for analysis. Other information, considered less relevant, is not specifically identified. Financial statistics – budgets and accounts – are no exception to this rule. Providing information on the share of the budget spent on heritage implies a conscious choice as to the relevance of this information over other parameters. An added difficulty, particularly for the built heritage, is that it may not be straightforward to distinguish buildings of heritage value from other buildings. On the other hand, Bologna underlined that while the maintenance costs of historical buildings were high, spending on maintenance contributed to sustainable use of the facilities, in that it is cheaper to maintain old buildings than to build new ones. Nonetheless, we believe the fact that only four historical universities gave even a rough estimate of expenditures on their material heritage gives reason for concern. Certainly, to improve heritage policies, it would be useful to know what means are at the disposal of the university and what is already spent.

When funds are scarce, one response is to look for alternative sources of funding. While it is reasonable to assume that such solutions are being sought, the answers gave little indication as to how and to what extent. The relationship between the university and external bodies (such as foundations, patronage boards of other museums, valorisation committees) remains unclear from a heritage perspective. However, Alcalá, Kraków and Santiago de Compostela provide interesting examples of the use of external funds for maintaining the university heritage.

**Raising awareness**

Raising the awareness of the heritage of European universities has been a key concern of our project. The replies give us reason to believe that much remains to be done in this area. There seems to be a separation of the conservation of heritage, teaching and research and awareness raising. In several universities, awareness raising is mainly left to the press or external relations department, but we know little of the specific heritage competence of these departments, nor do we have information on the composition of the teams carrying out these tasks and their co-operation with the relevant parts of the university. It is clear that heritage is not an essential part of the communication strategies of universities.

Everything seems to indicate that to be successful, awareness raising must be adapted to various target groups. In this context, it is interesting to note that while several universities emphasise their role as tourist attractions, only Coimbra showed a clear concern for communication with the local community. Coimbra was also the only institution that mentioned efforts directed at schoolchildren. The example of Coimbra seems to show that a greater effort aimed at schools is important in raising awareness of cultural heritage.

## The European dimensions of the university heritage

For the final meeting of the project, we asked the participating institutions to answer a questionnaire focusing on the European dimension of their heritage. The first question concerned the definition of the European dimension of the heritage of the responding university. Four common traits emerged from the answers:

– interaction with other European universities through teachers and students from many countries;
– the impact of the university institution and its ideas beyond the restrictions of political frontiers;
– the European origin of the university;
– the concept of Europe as a synthesis of cultures in which universities play an important role.

In other words, the university is clearly seen as a transnational phenomenon closely linked to society but not restricted by the institutions of that society. In addition, the University of Santiago de Compostela underlined the impact of the pilgrimage as an additional European element in its identity,[7] and it referred to the importance of university networks, such as the Compostela Group, as a modern and more institutionalised version of the cultural exchanges of other areas. In both their modern and older versions, these exchanges are centred on the mobility of people.

The respondents generally asserted that the European heritage is a recurrent theme in the development of their university, but they were economical in providing details to justify and support this assertion. Nevertheless, Santiago de Compostela underlined the historical dimension as a characteristic element of its institutional identity, and this dimension was very much a European one. Today, it is reflected in the strategic plan of the university. Vilnius found that the heritage was very much present in the concept of the university as a classical one, but was more reluctant as to whether this underlying heritage was consciously reflected when the university adapted its research and teaching to face the challenges of the present.

A closer look at the factors that constitute the European dimension of the heritage of the responding university revealed that student and staff exchanges, European research programmes and other European Union programmes as well as the

---

7. See also the article by Professor Antonio López Díaz in the present volume.

consciousness of a European origin and dimension of the university idea were considered the most important factors. There is an element of contradiction if one compares these answers to those given to the questionnaire on the intellectual heritage of the university. While staff and student exchanges and European programmes are seen as important parts of the European dimension of the university heritage, they are, as we have noted earlier, curiously absent from research and teaching in heritage related disciplines. While most universities actively participate in both European and regional exchange programmes, they do not seem to take advantage of these programmes to help students and staff engaged in heritage related studies gain a European and comparative perspective on their work. One of the aims of any further work on the university heritage should certainly be to eliminate this discrepancy between what is felt to constitute the European dimension of the university heritage and the lack of a similar dimension to the universities' heritage work.

European influence on teaching programmes, European standards in teaching and research and joint publications were ranked as "somewhat important" factors in the European dimension. While joint publications are seen as less important than exchanges and research programmes, there is again a discrepancy between general university policies and their ramifications in the heritage field, where joint publications seem to be a rare phenomenon.

Foreign language teaching, the material heritage, including traditions and festivals, and academic language were seen as the least important of the factors we listed in the questionnaire as potential elements of the European dimension. This is somewhat surprising. Knowledge of foreign languages is essential to communicate with other Europeans. No explanation was given, or solicited, for the respondents' ranking, so we can only guess at the reasons. One potential reason is that languages are seen as tools rather than as carriers of culture. Another is that much communication across borders takes place in a language that is foreign to both communicants, which would seem to underline the function of language as a tool. While the widespread use of English as an international *lingua franca* may further communication, it may also take away from that communication the link between expression and heritage. If this were the case, it would be a serious warning that an important part of the European cultural heritage is in danger.

We had also assumed that academic traditions and festivals would serve to underline the common heritage of universities. Again, we can only guess at the reasons why this does not seem to be the case, but the answers may indicate that while such traditions are very much alive at some universities, they are absent or at least in decline in many others. Another possibility is that they may serve more to distinguish the university from its immediate surroundings – distinguish gown from town – than to unite the academic community across political boundaries. Again, this is a potential warning sign.

The answers to the questionnaires unanimously agreed that students and staff identify with the European dimension of the university heritage. While the replies were somewhat short on specifics, the University of Santiago de Compostela underlined that a university is not an island confined to its geographical environment, but that, on the contrary, it must occupy a space in the global scenario. Coimbra underlined the importance of strong research co-operation in this respect, whereas the heritage dimension remains to be developed. All but one of the respondents also felt that the awareness of the European dimension of the university heritage is stronger today than it was twenty years ago, largely due to the European exchange programmes, a general "opening up" of Europe and a general trend towards internationalisation.

The question on how the European heritage of universities can contribute to creating a more cohesive Europe based on democratic pluralism, human rights and the rule of law elicited fewer responses than the other parts of the questionnaire. Nevertheless, some helpful suggestions were received. Notably, it was pointed out that the basic principles of the construction of Europe – pluralism, freedom in its different manifestations and autonomy – are also integral parts of the university heritage. Santiago was confident that the expansion of higher education would increase awareness of the European dimension, but with an important caveat: higher education must include education for values.

## Conclusion

By 1600, Europe had some 130 universities.[8] Although the date is randomly chosen, the number illustrates the fact that traditional universities represent an important part of our cultural heritage, whether at local, national or European level. These levels are in fact complementary rather than contradictory, and the university is a European institution par excellence. Albeit in an age of low student numbers, the medieval university was a cosmopolitan institution. The importance accorded to higher learning was also expressed through university buildings. Later, collections, museums, archives and libraries formed an integral part of the university because they were not only showpieces or curiosity chambers, but played an important role in teaching and research. The answers to our questionnaires show that this heritage is very much a living heritage. However, the answers also show that much remains to be done. This is true of almost all the areas we have outlined in this article. Yet the most striking feature of the role and practice of heritage at European universities is that in spite of their intellectual and analytical traditions and international orientation, heritage is not treated in a transdisciplinary way, and a comparative perspective and European co-operation are largely absent. We believe that these are the main challenges to academic heritage specialists as well as to higher education policy makers concerned with the heritage of their institutions. In the final article of this volume, we will try to address some of the issues arising from the project and offer some suggestions as to how the challenges can be met.

---

8. H. De Ridder-Symoens (editor), W. Rüegg (general editor): *A History of the Universities of Europe*, vol. II, (Cambridge 1996: Cambridge University Press), pp. 90 ff.

# Part II

# The material heritage of European universities

# Museums and collections in relation to the heritage of the university[1]

*Patrick J. Boylan*

Having chaired the City University's centenary year celebrations in 1994-95, I am very conscious of the fact that I come from a relatively young University in comparison with most of those taking part in this Council of Europe project on the heritage of European universities, carried out jointly by the Cultural Heritage Department and the Higher Education and Research Section. However, much of my doctoral and postdoctoral research in vertebrate palaeontology and the history of geology has focused on historic collections and institutions across Europe (and beyond), but particularly those of the 800-year-old University of Oxford: the oldest university in the British Isles, which also has in the 300-year-old Ashmolean the country's oldest museum.

It is most appropriate that this meeting should be held in Bologna, which taught the world what a university should be, and which has one of the widest and richest ranges of university museums, historic buildings and collections anywhere in the world. The University of Bologna and its academics also has a many centuries-long tradition of taking its scientific and other programmes to the city: bridging the more usual separation of "town and gown", to use the traditional English expression. Obvious examples here in Bologna include the seventeenth century solar image projection onto the floor of the Duomo, created by the University's Professor of Astronomy, G. D. Cassini, who in effect turned the nave of San Petronio into a gigantic *camera lucida*, (and hence almost certainly the world's largest pre-twentieth century scientific instrument). Almost as remarkable is the public statue of 1879 by Cencetti of Professor Luigi Galvani (1739-98) illustrating his famous experiment demonstrating the reflex reaction in the muscles of a dead frog when stimulated by electricity. It was good to hear in the opening address from the Rector Magnificus, Professor Fabio Roversi-Monaco, that the University remains so strongly committed to the conservation of its cultural heritage while remaining at the leading edge of contemporary university practice and life. It is of course also good to see our host city recognised by the European Union as one of Europe's Cultural Capitals for Millennium Year.

Any consideration of the present state and future prospects of university museums and collections, as with their historic buildings, monuments and sites, has to recognise the changing nature of the museum sector in many parts of Europe, and more widely around the world. The United Kingdom situation is not untypical. For centuries universities were essentially private foundations constrained only by the terms of their Royal Charters and with only the rarest of interventions by either the Privy Council or Parliament. However, during the years following the second world war, successive national reforms in education and its funding quite quickly brought even the most ancient universities much closer to the public sector, and – critically –

---

1. Article presented at the third meeting of the project (Bologna, July 2000).

increasingly dependent on public funds for all three key aspects of their budgets: teaching, research and capital development. During the same post-war period numerous new university-level educational institutions were created (or elevated) within the national and local government sectors.

Then, between 1988 and 1992, most of these newer public sector institutions such as the Polytechnics, were separated from their mainly local government origins and are now governed and managed as educational corporations subject primarily to a system of company law devised over the years for the regulation of industrial and commercial enterprises rather than public bodies, and are funded by central government. In the course of these reforms the polytechnics, and some of the other higher education institutions, were re-titled as universities, though without the traditional system of university governance through a Royal Charter within which academic standards and academic freedom are primarily the responsibility of the university's academic community through an elected Senate. In parallel with this merging of the two higher education systems, the arrangements for close regulation, scrutiny and "accountability" to government, already long established in the polytechnic sector, was extended to the "old" universities. The United Kingdom's Committee of Vice-Chancellors and Principals has recently estimated that the various systems of inspection, regulation, "measurement" and general "accountability" covering in particular the universities' quality systems, teaching quality and research output quality, now cost the institutions and the government agencies around €0.5 billion a year – out of a total higher education budget that is in marked decline in real terms, particularly the annual funding per student.

There are other serious economic pressures facing universities in many parts of Europe, which will be very familiar to many here today. Particularly significant are the future prospects in terms of student recruitment. With perhaps just two or three exceptions, most European countries have both established many new universities and other higher education institutions over the past twenty or thirty years and in addition increased student capacity in many of the longer established universities, while the increased freedom of movement in relation to advanced study within the European Union (and the wider European Economic Area) also adds a new dimension to student access to higher education. On the other hand, major demographic changes already here, or at least in prospect in the near future, are bringing about a marked decline in the numbers of people of traditional university age, reversing a fifty year (or longer) trend in which the young greatly outnumbered the "third age" of still-active retired people. Also, while non-European students remain an important, valued, indeed prized, part of our student population, the rapid development of the higher education sector in other parts of the world means that advanced overseas study in Europe or North America is no longer the academic imperative that it was even fifteen or twenty years ago, let alone in colonial times.[2] As a consequence of these various factors, universities across the continent are facing very considerable competition in recruiting students, at the very time that in many if not all European countries they are having to become at least more market

---

2. Editors' note: one of the main aims of the Bologna Declaration, signed in 1999 by the ministers responsible for higher education of twenty-nine European countries, is indeed the competitiveness and attractiveness of European higher education.

orientated in terms of student recruitment, even if not totally market-driven, as some commentators would argue.

In such an atmosphere universities and other higher education institutions are inevitably focusing their priorities onto core areas of activity in teaching and research, and questioning the future of those activities, which are not seen to be paying their way within circumstances that are increasingly market-driven. Thus, when whole subject areas and individual courses that do not cover their way in terms of student numbers, external research grants or other funding are called into question, or even closed down completely, a university's expenditure on its heritage buildings and – particularly its, perhaps ancient, museums – is similarly thrown into sharp relief, and comes under threat. I believe that such a narrow view of the university's inherited past, whether in physical form, such as historic buildings or university museums, or intangible, such as traditional colourful institutional and student traditions, is misguided. Instead, an ancient university's heritage should be recognised, protected, promoted, indeed positively exploited as a very valuable advantage in the increasingly competitive and market-led world in which higher education has to operate these days.

It is, I believe, very significant that many of the British "new" universities immediately and very actively sought to adopt or emulate the traditions and customs of ancient universities in relation to their ceremonial practices, academic dress, etc. It is also significant, in my view, that at a time when many long-established universities are questioning the financial burden of their historic heritage in terms of the cost of historic building maintenance, running museums, etc., some of the newest institutions are actively creating galleries, cultural centres and theatres, or are positively seeking out such prestigious historic buildings. For example, in England, only Oxford and Cambridge had important buildings by the country's greatest seventeenth century architect, Sir Christopher Wren. However, the post-1992 University of Greenwich in southeast London has very recently joined them in this with its expansion into Wren's Royal Hospital/Royal Naval College of 1694 – a World Heritage List complex, and arguably the grandest building occupied by any British university today.

In addition to the contribution that a historic university's proud and visible heritage can make to student recruitment, there can be similar benefits in relation to the recruitment and retention of high quality academic staff and of researchers, as well as in terms of maintaining and developing relations with the university's own alumni. A high profile in this area also helps greatly in the university's relations with its wider community, not least with potential private and business benefactors and sponsors, and indeed with government. Both the university itself and a wide range of commercial and other interests can also benefit greatly from a historic university's heritage, particularly in terms of what is now termed cultural tourism – which is widely recognised as one of the two or three most important factors in terms of tourism development potential. Mass tourism as a phenomenon, and the average European population, are now both rapidly maturing, and there is a declining demand for the typical 1960s to 1980s beach resort holiday – often characterised as an annual search for the four "S"s – sun, sand, sangria and sex! Instead, a more sophisticated, and on average older, tourist market is looking for new and more cultural experiences, and for more and often shorter holiday experiences such as weekend breaks in historic cities, rather than the traditional one holiday a year consisting of two or three weeks in the sun. Again, when they are well promoted, the values, traditions and historic features of an ancient university can be one of the main, or indeed the most important, attraction for visitors, as for example at Oxford in England, or New Haven (Yale University) in the USA.

Within universities, especially longer-established ones, the university museums are often amongst the most important publicly recognised expressions of the institution's heritage. After all, universities were amongst the earliest public institutions to develop museums in a form that would be easily recognised today, with the oldest dating from the seventeenth century or even earlier. However, increasingly many universities are seeing their museum inheritance as a problem rather than an opportunity.

As part of this contribution it is necessary to explore, if only very briefly, the origins and main types of university museums which today's generation of scholars, curators and university administrations have inherited from the past.[3] Though only very limited information is available about them, it does seem clear that teaching and display collections existed in university-like academic institutions in ancient times, including that of the second millennium BC at Lasa and of around 530 BC at Ur, both within ancient Mesopotamia. The fourth century BC Greek "Lyceum" is presumed to have had demonstrations of original dissections and reference specimens of the over 500 species described and classified by its founder, Aristotle, and to have set a trend which would have been carried on in support of much of the teaching of Aristotelian science over the following 800 or 1 000 years or more. Similarly, we know little about the details of the original museum within the great library and academy of Alexandria, founded by Ptolemy Sotor in about 290 BC, and which survived for many centuries, though this almost certainly had a large and growing collection of works of art, antiquities and natural history.[4]

After this there is a major gap in our knowledge, though it seems clear that in Europe at least the scholastic tradition placed the main emphasis in academic studies on written sources, predominantly Greek and Roman texts of the Classical period, rather than on physical objects and collections, or even original observation and experimentation. Even well into the seventeenth century, essentially practical or observation-based sciences, including zoology, anatomy and geography were taught in academies and the emerging universities largely if not wholly from the writings of the Classical authors of up to 2 000 years earlier such as Aristotle, Galen, Pliny or Ptolemy. However, from the late medieval period onwards some academic institutions began to gather and use original objects. What is probably the earliest

---

3. The evolution and role of university museums, and their interaction with their universities, has recently been explored in much more detail by the present author, see: P. J. Boylan, 1999. Universities and Museums: Past, Present and Future. *Museum Management and Curatorship* vol. 18, No. 1, pp. 43-56, which was developed from an address of the same title in the University Museum Inaugural Lecture Series: *I y II Journadas de Museos*, (Universidad de Alicante, 1999). The following notes are a very brief summary of the main findings and conclusions of this study.
4. See for example M. El-Abbadi, 1990. *The Life and Fate of the Ancient Library of Alexandria* (UNESCO/UNDP, Paris).

university art collection is at Christ Church College, Oxford, where the Picture Gallery was founded in 1546, while soon afterwards the college also became England's first university centre for the revival of practical anatomy – involving both human and comparative zoology, following the pioneering work of the Flemish anatomist, Vesalius, at Padua. A further major influence on both the ancient English universities (and beyond) was the Cambridge educated scholar and politician Francis Bacon. He sought to replace or at least greatly update the traditional 1 500 to 2 000-year-old scholastic texts by systems of direct and practical observations from nature, a position that was to greatly influence first the conduct of contemporary exploration of the Americas, and of the African and Asian coastal regions, and then the emerging national academies of science, particularly London's Royal Society, established in 1666, some forty years after Bacon's death, but imbued from the beginning with the Baconian agenda. In 1630 and 1631 two different continental scholars visiting Oxford reported seeing the collection of "natural curiosities" in the Anatomy School. This was in turn visited by King Charles II in 1681, while the earliest surviving catalogue of the collection, prepared between 1705 and 1709, listed 386 specimens.[5]

The Oxford Anatomy School in Christ Church was just one example of what rapidly became a Europe-wide phenomenon by the early seventeenth century, which saw the creation of anatomical dissection demonstration theatres and supporting collections in dozens of universities and other academies from the south of Europe, including Padua, Bologna, Ferrara and other Italian cities, and Montpellier in France, through to Uppsala in Sweden in the north, and Valencia, Spain in the west. Other sciences soon followed, with the collecting of mineral, ore, rock and mining technology specimens at the Saxony Mining Academy at Freiberg, to marine zoology and botany at Naples.

What was almost certainly the first purpose-designed museum (as opposed to picture gallery) in the world was the original Ashmolean Museum in Oxford, built in 1683 to house the rich collections or geology, natural history, antiquities and ethnography brought together by Elias Ashmole, and donated to the University on condition that the university provided a suitable building for it and took responsibility for the Museum's future care and maintenance.[6] In the original Ashmolean Museum building (which happily survives to this day, now serving as the Oxford University Museum of the History of Science) was developed a role and an organisational structure that became a typical model for very many traditional university museums even to the present day. The building was designed not just for the display and storage of the original museum collection and subsequent additions to these. For over two centuries it also accommodated the teaching staff of the academic subjects covered by the museum and lecture rooms and demonstration rooms or laboratories for the teaching and studying of these subjects, and when the natural history and geology collections were removed to the new Oxford University Museum in 1860 all of this was duplicated on a much larger scale in the new building. The museum

5. K. C. Davies & J. Hull, 1976. *The Zoological Collections of the Oxford University Museum: A Historical Review and General Account* (University Museum, Oxford).
6. A. MacGregor (editor), 1983. *Tradescant's Rarities. Essays on the Foundation of the Ashmolean Museum, 1683, with a Catalogue of the Surviving Early Collections.* (Clarendon Press, Oxford).

consequently formed an integrated small academy of the natural sciences in its own right. Further, the Keepers and other staff of the Museum usually held other university or college positions as professors, lecturers or tutors in their respective specialisations, while traditionally the most senior professor in each subject was the *de facto* director or curator of that part of the museum and of the relevant collections. Again, this is a pattern that was, and very often still is, found in university museums around the world.

The eighteenth and nineteenth centuries saw a series of revolutions in knowledge relating to many areas traditionally covered by university museums. This began with the world of Linnaeus from 1735 onwards in developing standardised systems of first botanical and then zoological classification and nomenclature, and was quickly followed by the development of geology and scientific palaeontology and the establishment of historic and archaeological chronologies for the Egyptian, Biblical and Classical periods around the turn of the century, and was followed by the proposed threefold classification of the Prehistoric period (Stone Age, Bronze Age and Iron Age) by the Danish archaeologist Thomsen in 1836, and finally Darwin's launching of his theory of evolution in 1858-59.

Each of these developments, especially the application of Linneus principles in botany, zoology and palaeontology, relied heavily on identification and classification by direct comparison of the new or unknown object with established standards, represented above all by the designated "type" or other "voucher" specimens used by the original author in establishing the scientific name of a species or other established category within accepted classifications, principles which the emerging science of archaeology to a considerable extent adopted and adapted to its own purposes. Such approaches placed both reference and teaching collections at the very heart of both research and teaching, and universities across the world quickly established or developed the necessary facilities for all of this in the form of teaching and research collections and museums. In the case of those universities which already had such museums by the early to mid-nineteenth century these were being rapidly given a new lease of life. What had all to often become moribund and neglected "cabinets of curiosities" were totally reformed and given a new direction and position at the centre of the newly emerging sciences.

To take Oxford as an example again, by the early 1820s the geological collections of the Ashmolean had been totally transformed in accordance with modern principles, and greatly augmented, by William Buckland, appointed Reader in Geology and Mineralogy in 1818. By the end of the decade the zoology collections of the Ashmolean had similarly been massively improved by John Shute Duncan (significantly a close friend of Buckland), appointed Keeper of the Ashmolean Museum in 1823, who was in turn succeeded by his brother, Philip Bury Duncan in 1829, while Henry Acland had carried out a parallel revolution with the collections of the Christ Church anatomy school.[7] All three collections were finally brought together in the new University Museum opened in 1860, already referred to above, while the art and antiquities collections of the Ashmolean Museum were eventually rehoused in the "new" Ashmolean Museum, still in use.

Similar stories can be told about the emergence and development of natural history, archaeology and anthropology museums in ancient universities during the eighteenth and early to mid-nineteenth centuries in many other places. Just a few examples include Cambridge, Glasgow and then Manchester in Britain, Tübingen, Bonn and Münster in Germany, Harvard in the United States and Melbourne in Australia.

Many universities, both ancient and modern, also have important art museums. For example, the Fitzwilliam Museum in Cambridge, opened in 1816, was endowed by an alumnus, while a century and a half later Yale alumnus Paul Mellon donated both a major collection and funds for a new building for what was named the Paul Mellon Centre for British Art in his honour.

The present generation of university managements and university museum curators across the world have inherited from past generations many hundreds of university museums of many different types and sizes, and very many of these continue to offer an extraordinary range of both academic and wider cultural services and roles, including traditional audiences of university students, staff and researchers, but also increasingly they are serving the general public at all levels. The traditional concern with assisting in the teaching of undergraduate and postgraduate students has been broadened to cover all levels of education – from very young children through formal and informal adult education to support for elderly and disabled community groups. Taking Oxford again as an example, the six university museums[8] between them attract more than 530 000 visits a year, the great majority of which must be by people who are not members of the university.

The very scale of use of so many university museums by the general public rather than the university's students and staff raises serious longer-term questions about the role and especially the funding of such museums, especially in those countries seeking major reductions in levels of subsidy from taxation for almost all public services, and actively promoting a "consumerist" economic model, in which government looks for a closer linkage between services provided and consumers of all kinds including, in the case of higher education, university students. In such a financial climate it is hardly surprising that universities may be questioning their traditional role in providing for the cultural needs of the wider population of their city or region, not just fee-paying students of the university itself.

---

7. For Buckland, see N. Rupke, 1984. *The Great Chain of History: William Buckland and the English School of Geology, 1814-1849*. (OUP, Oxford) and P. J. Boylan, 1984. *William Buckland (1784-1856): Scientific Institutions, Vertebrate Palaeontology and Quaternary Geology*. (PhD, University of Leicester, Leicester, 2 vols.); for the Duncans see A. MacGregor & A. Headon, 2000. Re-inventing the Ashmolean. Natural history and natural theology at Oxford in the 1820s to 1850s. *Archives of Natural History* vol. 27, pt. 3, pp. 369-406; for Acland, see Davies & Hull, 1976 (*op. cit.* – note 3 above).

8. Ashmolean, University Museum, History of Science, Pitt-Rivers Museum, Christ Church Picture Gallery and the Bate Collection of Musical Instruments.

A further widespread threat to university museums is the effect of changes in university curricula and in many sciences that have traditionally been supported by museums and collections for the previous 150 years or more. Taking natural science museums as an example, it has to be recognised that both biological and geological sciences have been utterly transformed since the late 1960s or early 1970s as a result of revolutionary changes that have been at least as great as those brought about by the introduction of Linnaean classification in the eighteenth century and then the theory of evolution in the mid-nineteenth century. As a consequence nowadays very little biological teaching or research takes place at the level of the whole animal (except for behavioural and ecological studies, neither of which is museum specimen-based), and parallels can be drawn in relation to geology and anthropology teaching in relation to traditional museums and collections. Further, and perhaps most significantly of all, many of the present-day academic leaders in subjects which formerly made heavy use of collections-based teaching and research, and in particular the senior professors and heads of department (who are frequently *ex officio* titular directors and curators of university museums) now come from a generation which was itself never schooled in the traditional science of the high point of such university museums and collections.[9] Not surprisingly, many such contemporary academic leaders, especially when faced with ever-increasing financial and other resource problems, can easily come to the conclusion that the cost of such museums and collections, and the valuable, often extensive, space that they occupy, are luxuries that can no longer be afforded.

However, universities need to take a much broader view of their museum inheritance, and should explore their potential in relation to the institution's identity and the now vital promotion of its heritage to gain that competitive advantage in relation to areas such as student recruitment, alumni relations and broader marketing and fundraising previously discussed. For example, the Hunterian Museum of the ancient Scottish University of Glasgow has for a considerable number of years offered a substantial exhibition on the origins and development of the University itself, together with some of its most famous alumni, such as the economist Adam Smith. It is good to hear during this meeting of the plans of the University of Bologna to develop a permanent museum exhibition on student life including the very distinctive tradition of student fraternities found in several of the most ancient universities of continental Europe, and subsequently adopted elsewhere, most notably in American universities.

Beyond this, however, university museums must find new ways of demonstrating their continuing relevance despite the great changes in many academic fields traditionally, but no longer, heavily dependent on museums and collections for teaching and research. Also, the organisation and management problems so

---

9. A national survey for the Australian Vice-Chancellors' Committee of university museums and collections in Australia found that very many, almost certainly the majority, of important university museums and collections are nowadays almost totally detached from their subject area, with little or no specialist staff even at the Honorary Curator level, so that their very survival is in question, see: University Museums Review Committee, 1996. *Cinderella Collections: University Museums and Collections in Australia* (Australian Vice-Chancellors' Committee, Canberra).

frequently found in the university museum sector need to be addressed. All too often even still-active museums are isolated and marginalised within the academic departments and faculties responsible for them, and frequently have very little formal or informal contact with other museums and collections within the same university, let alone more widely.

They, and their staff, need to be properly integrated into the university's overall structure and staffing, and given a clear identity and operational autonomy (within allocated budgets and overall development plans, of course). The university's most senior management, such as the Rectorate, should accept responsibility for the museums of their institution by, at the very least, setting up some sort of museum committee or board which can oversee all of the university's museums, collections and related heritage. Certainly the tradition of imposing the nominal or (even worse) real directorships or curatorships of the museums on a perhaps reluctant or even positively hostile professor or other head of department *ex officio* needs to be changed as a matter of priority, though of course there is no reason why a senior academic with a special interest in the field should not continue to serve in such a capacity if he or she wishes to do so, and can find the necessary time for such duties.

Also, every university needs to examine the possibilities for co-operation between the institution's perhaps several different museums and collections, with a view to sharing expertise and specialised professional and technical staffing, such as conservation, documentation, exhibition and display, and security staff, at the same time offering better career prospects and progression than could ever be achieved within just one small and specialised museum. A good example is the arrangement being developed in University College, London, which has seven or eight different museums and important collections (at least one of which, the Petrie Museum of Egyptology, is of international importance) though these had traditionally been entirely the responsibility of the different academic departments. In 1998, however, the college set up a college-wide Centre for Museum, Collection, Heritage and Conservation Studies, led by the head of the college's highly regarded MA courses in museum and heritage studies, to which all museums and collections were affiliated, while remaining within their traditional departments. Under this, for the first time a salary, career and professional training structure has been developed for all curatorial and support staff, co-operation between the different museums has been actively fostered, and for the first time the college is providing some funds from "central" resources for museum, collections, and related developments agreed through the new structure. Further, the new arrangement has greatly increased the specialised staffing and development resources for previously very isolated small museums and collections within the college.

Historic – and indeed new – museums and collections need to be regarded as an important part of the university's resources offering great opportunities in respect of the competitive advantage that most if not all now need to positively seek in the increasingly international marketplace within which universities are now operating.

# Part III

# The intellectual heritage of European universities

# The intellectual heritage of ancient universities in Europe[1]

*Hilde de Ridder-Symoens*

The organisers of this meeting have asked me to present reflections on the definition and the role of the intellectual heritage of Europe as represented by its universities. I am happy that, as a historian, I can present this introduction. As a matter of fact, I have spent almost my whole university career in the service of the European university and of its significance for society. I want to draw attention here to two fascinating scientific experiences dealing with the history of higher education. The first was my contribution to the ESF (European Science Foundation) project "The origins of the Modern State in Europe" with a chapter on "Training and Professionalization of the Power Elite" published in volume 4: *Power Elites and State Building*.

But certainly the most challenging activity was being a board member, editor and author in the joint university research project on *The History of the University in Europe* sponsored by the CRE.[2] The aim of that still on-going project is to gain some insight into the contemporary identity of the university through the internal and external movements that have influenced it over the years, and to highlight the chronological and geographical differences and similarities of an institution that constitutes an integral part of European culture.

In this paper, I will present the changing views on the intellectual mission of the universities, dealing with only five topics that are in the centre of the discussion:

– University historiography
– Universities and national identity
– The tension between theory and practice
– Academic freedom and the Humboldt University
– European and American concepts of the liberal arts

## University historiography

Until about ten years ago, it was generally thought that universities were in a sclerotic condition in the early modern period without serious teaching and without any scientific activity. Not only did the early modern universities have a bad press until recently, but the medieval universities also had a bad reputation thanks to the humanists.

For the humanists, the universities were controversial institutions as were so many of the other institutions inherited from the Middle Ages. Their judgment contributed to shaping the view of these institutions as it was expressed in historiography up to

---

1. This article constituted the main presentation at the second meeting of the project (Montpellier, March 2000).
2. Editor's note: on 31 March 2001, the CRE – Association of European Universities and the Confederation of EU Rectors' Conferences merged to form the European University Association (EUA).

the 1970s. Since that time, however, we no longer think in categories of good and bad, of growth and decline. Rather, we try to consider these phenomena in their historical context and to understand them in all their complexity.

This was the picture: After a remarkable beginning at the end of the twelfth century, the European universities experienced a period of scientific expansion in an atmosphere of intellectual openness that was both disinterested and "democratic", during the course of the thirteenth century. After two subsequent centuries of decline, the humanists would once again infuse life into the ossified sclerotic temples of science. The humanists settled their accounts with the obsolete tradition of scholastic education: they modernised the methods of instruction and the content of the subjects to be assimilated; the *bonae litterae* received a fixed place in the institutions, which were disposed to modernisation. But in the seventeenth century, this whole process had already come to an end. The universities had fallen to the ranks of (glorified) boarding schools for the sons of the rich who spent their time taking courses on subjects that were completely outmoded – that is medieval – taught by uninspired and uninspiring masters. Furthermore, these students dabbled in learning worldly subjects such as modern languages, horseback riding, fencing and dance, often in a French or Italian university on the occasion of their *Grand Tour*. Real scientific research was done outside the universities in academies or other specialised institutions. We can understand how it was then, that, in their pursuit of rationality and modernity, French revolutionaries eliminated with one stroke of the pen in 1793 the universities from their territory as being institutions devoid of meaning and even useless for society.

The image that emerges from recent research by historians on the history of the universities and the sciences, and most notably the research of the CRE, is of a completely different nature.

European universities underwent, in fact, periods of expansion and of decline, but not in monolithic blocks with a rupture at the end of the Middle Ages and again in the middle of the seventeenth century. Despite a structure and an organisation that were relatively uniform, diverse developments took place in accordance with political and cultural circumstances as well as with the economic climate. In addition the periods of expansion and of decline were not those of a block graph but only waves in a continual process of change, or rather of adaptation to the demands and needs of society, often slow, but all the same (always ongoing). Therefore, it is thanks to this flexibility that the university was to be one of the rare institutions of the Middle Ages to defy the centuries, survive different revolutions and become in the end one of the principal export products of Europe, while the institutions which, for differing reasons were not able to adapt, disappeared from the scene.

The evolution of the university is perceptible in different domains: its social function, the student population, the methodology and subjects taught, professionalisation, relations with lay and ecclesiastical authorities. On the other hand, from the outside and with the exception of some experiments, the university underwent few changes in its structure and its organisation up until the nineteenth century.

Evidently this rigid structure caused problems already beginning at the end of the Middle Ages but especially from the middle of the seventeenth century onwards, for the incorporation of new learning and new scientific disciplines in one of the four faculties. I will deal later on with this problem.

University historiography is not only troubled by the prejudices of former historians and opinion makers but also by the most popular kind of university historiography, namely the jubilee publications. Since the nineteenth century, jubilees have generated a wide variety of publications: pious commemorative illustrated coffee-table books of no real scientific value, overviews of the history of the celebrating university for the educated laymen, and serious scientific histories. More recently jubilees have been welcomed as opportunities to publish massive source editions and to set up a proper series.

The threshold experience of a jubilee ought to be accompanied by a complex process of verifications, a critical self-examination and review of past attainments and failures. But jubilee histories tend to omit the dark chapters of the development of individual institutions; there is a tendency either to present apologetics or to publish only the highlights. They also have a tendency to speak about their own institution only, omitting to put the institution in its social context and to look at it as a part of a European higher education system.

There are no general objectives available to guide anniversary-inspired histories. It is perhaps difficult to see how there could be. Recently, however, a group of researchers has started a project, called FASTI,[3] to investigate, among other topics, the possibility of offering some guidelines. It is part of a Scientific Research Network sponsored by the Flemish Fund for Scientific Research with the aim of elaborating "New Tools for University History". Scientists from several Flemish and international research units have undertaken to consider the nature of publications on university history. At the same time, they intend to reflect on the relationship between university history, intellectual history and scientific history. They believe that new theoretical insights in this area could result in greater interaction. New tools are also required if this renewed university history is to be pursued. It is explicitly intended to introduce modern electronic processing, editing and publishing techniques to the field of university history, by producing automated and accessible bibliographies, archive guides, text editions, prosopographic databases of students and professors, etc.

The final objective is to disseminate the results of the discussions in written form and to publish test cases that can serve as models. Another intended result is to provide a paradigm for universities celebrating anniversaries and their historiographers, by indicating how they can best use the historical output of that moment in such a way as to advance university history as a whole, rather than simply that of their own institution.

---

3. FASTI website: www.flwi.rug.ac.be/fasti.

**Universities and national identity**

No one will deny that the intrinsic role of the university nowadays consists of the transmission of knowledge and the development of research. Other functions are more linked to a particular area and time. At the meeting in Alcalá the function of the university dealt with was social and political.

Universities were also called on for defining the cultural identity of the nation. They sometimes play a major role in movements of national revival. Jubilees and other kinds of celebrations are the most welcome tools to sustain these activities. Very good examples in this way are Finland, Iceland, the Baltic States and Flanders, where scholars in the second half of the nineteenth century played an important role in "inventing" traditions of a national identity. Several answers to the questionnaires also point to this role.

Politicians and academic authorities, nevertheless, did not wait until the nineteenth century to involve scholars and students in inventing, defining and propagating political and cultural identity. It was part of the strategies used in early modern state formation, which started in the fourteenth century. It is one of the reasons that universities became nationalised. But even in periods when universities were more internationally oriented, their members were aware of their "national" identity, whatever that might be.

Student nations were an important element in defining the cultural identity of the students living abroad. From the thirteenth century onwards students in a foreign, sometimes hostile city formed associations whose members spoke the same language or shared the same tastes. As a group they could look after themselves better and cope more easily with the difficulties of a long stay abroad. They hired houses in common, met at church or at an inn to celebrate their national and patron saints' days, and organised postal services between the university city and their homeland so as to keep in touch with their families and receive from them money, letters, and parcels. These *de facto* associations quickly became publicly recognised corporations under the name of "nations". The nation to which students belonged depended primarily on their mother-tongue, and secondarily on their birthplace, cultural community, or shared history. Universities such as those of Bologna and Padua, which took in a steady stream of students from elsewhere, could follow this practice fairly strictly and form more than a dozen ultramontane and cismontane nations covering most European regions or provinces. Paris and its imitators (Prague, Leipzig, Vienna, and Louvain) had only four nations, whose catchment area was somewhat fanciful or highly inconsistent. Everywhere the German nation was one of the most important and well-attended nations. In the course of the seventeenth century nations lost most of their functions, and they died out. Almost all universities in Europe had become national and even regional universities.

## Tension between theory and practice

Since the very inception of the university, there has been an ongoing discussion on the relation between theory and practice in university education. How relevant is university education for society? To what extent can universities capitalise on the needs of society?

As I have already indicated, apparently the university did not change fundamentally in structure and organisation until the beginning of the nineteenth century, excluding a few experiments. A complete *studium generale*, the common name for a university in the Middle Ages, includes four faculties: the lower, propaedeutic faculty of arts, and the three higher professional faculties: theology, law and medicine. Northern Italian universities had a different structure during the Middle Ages, but there also the four cited disciplines were the rule. All newly created institutions starting from about 1550 followed the same pattern, even if their teaching methods and content moved to a more modern style.

It is only in the nineteenth century that the four-faculty structure was altered. The faculty of arts was split into an *alpha* section (letters and philosophy) and a *beta* section (exact sciences). Other faculties were added after the introduction of new disciplines. It is clear that this straightjacket had provoked problems at the time of the introduction of humanism and even more during the scientific revolution. How to incorporate recent knowledge and new sciences into one of the four existing faculties was the perennial problem. A discipline in the field of humanities and partially the social sciences could be integrated into the faculties of arts and law. The natural sciences were a more complex problem. Of course the *beta* section of the arts faculty, the so-called *quadrivium,* could house the developing fields of chemistry and physics, but the medical faculty was also a potential faculty within which to integrate these sciences.

Within the functioning faculties special chairs were established in the recently formulated disciplines and the new subject matter was taught in tutorials or private lectures, often by *Privatdozenten*. Integration was not always easy. Universities are, generally speaking, conservative institutions with strong conflicts of interest. Academic government and more specially professors often tried to obstruct the introduction of "novelties" or new fields.

Completely problematic were those disciplines that did not fit the classification of sciences imposed by classical authors, such as management, veterinary medicine, architecture, and the conduct of war. These disciplines combine theoretical knowledge with intensive professional training including practical skills; they did not fit into an exclusively textual education. We can wonder about the fact that medicine was taught at the university, but the teaching of medicine was purely speculative and theoretical. Practical medicine was in the hands of vocationally trained surgeons and midwives.

From the sixteenth century onwards experiments to overcome this problem led to the creation of anatomical theatres, botanical gardens, and laboratories. The first to introduce these experiments were the Italians in the course of the sixteenth century, followed by the Dutch. The rest of Europe followed rather slowly and often reluctantly. The teaching of anatomy offers perfect insight into the scientific and psychological problems with which humanist scholars were dealing. On the one hand they had a sacrosanct belief in Antiquity; on the other hand they learned from an increasing amount of experimental data that the Classical authors made mistakes. The humanists had to accept this dualism. This resulted in schizophrenic situations in which the professor taught traditional views while lecturing but also presented his new concepts in his publications. Those who did not accept this compromise had the opportunity to do research outside the university. These scholars are mainly to be found in the field of natural sciences and technical disciplines not fitting into the regular university curriculum.

That happened, for example, to the training of military officers. In the Middle Ages, a nobleman was prepared and trained to become an officer as a squire at home, in the castle of a friend or relative or even on the battlefield. His theoretical knowledge was minimal. The modern conduct of war in the fifteenth and sixteenth century, on the contrary, asked for knowledge of strategy, logistics, constructions and ballistics. As military strategy and warfare were not taught at the university, the future officers had to follow courses in private schools or with private teaching given by university teachers but outside the university. Leiden University was the first to present a formula combining theoretical lectures with practical training. Prince Maurits of Nassau charged the Flemish mathematician Simon Stevin (1548-1620) with setting up a school for (military) engineers to train surveyors and structural engineers. He needed these technically trained professionals for his war against Spain. Because the engineering school could not be integrated into an existing faculty, it lived in the shadow of the university. Indeed its students were not registered with the university at all. Other Dutch universities followed the Leiden model. Only at the end of the seventeenth century was higher military education in Europe given at specialised schools for officers or military academies.

In Italy, experimental training was also not limited to medicine. In the late fourteenth and fifteenth centuries a class of *technici*, or inventive and ingenious men, was active and combined experiment and theory in different fields. This practical-science concept was also widely spread in the sixteenth-century Low Countries. One finds there first-class cartographers, navigators, surveyors, instrument makers, gardeners, botanists, etc. with international renown.

Slowly the gap between the liberal arts and the mechanical arts was beginning to narrow in the minds of scientists. Universities as institutions resisted longer, until the nineteenth and even the twentieth century, incorporating practically-oriented disciplines into their curriculum. Even now, in 2000, it is a point under discussion whether some subjects and methods actually belong to the university or to technical schools.

This resistance is linked to general concepts about the aims and functions of a university education: the general education of social and intellectual élites, professional training, and scientific education. Consequently, content as well as instructional techniques and methodology have to be adapted.

At the Alcalá meeting, a great deal was said about the changing function of higher education in the course of the centuries. As a consequence I will be brief.

Universities started in the late twelfth and early thirteenth centuries as teaching centres. But already in the thirteenth and certainly in the fourteenth century academic people were selected for ecclesiastical and public service notwithstanding the purely "scientific" and scholastic nature of teaching. Graduates were selected for their capacities to think in an abstract way, to classify and order a lot of information, to cope with disparate and often contradictory data. With the increasing importance of academic education for public life, the discourse on theory and practice grew. During the Middle Ages no solution was found. Moreover, it was firmly believed that universities were not the appropriate place to educate the social élites. The medium of communication was Latin, and the lectures were too intellectual, too abstract and too theoretical. The knowledge and the skills necessary for a nobleman, or a burgher with noble aspirations, were not taught at the university. From the fifteenth century onwards Italy started with special schools for young noblemen (*Ritterakademien*, academies), a model that spread to the whole of Europe by the seventeenth and eighteenth centuries. These schools were select places to be for the young aristocrats during their *Grand Tour*. Often they functioned as pre-military academies.

These examples show that although universities were no doubt the most important modellers of the intellectual heritage of Europe, certainly if one considers that intellectual heritage to be purely cognitive, other institutions and forms of education also contributed to the formation of the intellectual mind of the Europeans and to the development of knowledge: for example, ecclesiastical institutions such as abbeys and chapters, ecclesiastical and princely courts, printing houses, academies, scientific and cultural societies, and so forth. From the fifteenth century onwards personal networks of men of letters, scientists and artists played a very important role in the diffusion of ideas, knowledge, norms and values. Thanks to the printing press and a better postal system worked out by the family Thurn und Taxis at the command of emperor Charles V who needed it to govern his imperium, communication between intellectuals improved considerably. Letters, books, gifts and samples were sent all over Europe. The *Respublica Litteraria* or Republic of Letters was universal and did not take into account geographical, political or religious barriers. Finally, in the nineteenth century scientific journals and conferences became the scene for professional and academic contacts all over the world.

## Academic freedom and the Humboldt University

As we have seen, from the seventeenth century onwards new institutions of higher education were erected to compensate for the deficient university education. Universities had to accept this variety of higher education. From the nineteenth century onwards academics stressed their significance by claiming that a university is an institute for fundamental research that consists of a variety of disciplines that needs academic freedom and where teaching is closely linked to research. Everybody recognises the so-called Humboldt University in this concept.

Let me first say something about academic freedom and then about the Humboldt university concept.

A medieval university was a corporate body distinguished by its liberties and immunities. The first and most important of these privileges was autonomy, the so-called "academic freedom". It means that the academic community had the right to deal autonomously with the outside world, to supervise the recruitment of its members, whether students or teachers, to make its own regulations and to exercise some degree of internal jurisdiction. In the course of the centuries, more and more personal privileges of students and masters were subject to growing supervision from civic authorities. This was not only due to the greater interference of the state in educational matters but also to misgovernment by the university bodies. In the early modern period universities seemed to care less about their academic freedom, or rather they were no longer in a position to defend themselves.

Academic freedom, and then more specially *Lernfreiheit* and *Lehrfreiheit* or freedom of learning and of teaching, became a real issue in the so-called Humboldt universities; it is considered as the essence of a university, together with the concept of unity of science (*Einheit der Wissenschaften*). During recent years university historians and historians of science have been dealing with the nature of the German university model, the Berlin model and the Humboldt university model. A real debunking is taking place. A recent conference in Bern entitled "Humboldt International. The export of the German university model in the nineteenth and twentieth century" reached the following conclusions:

The German university model is a very vague concept. The University of Berlin is not so much based on the ideas of von Humboldt, as is generally acknowledged, and it was never exported intentionally. The German university model was taken over all over the world in a very eclectic and implicit way; only those elements were taken over that fitted the goals of the particular university. The new views were introduced by individual scholars. Only Japan took over the German model in a more systematic way in the 1880s, to keep pace with the West.

Three elements of the Humboldt conception are still nowadays generally accepted and are considered as its real intellectual heritage:

– the relationship between teaching and research;
– seminars;
– academic freedom for teachers and students (*Lehr- und Lernfreiheit*).

Scholars are concerned about recent developments in higher education. They deplore the fact that universities are more and more considered as business enterprises that have to be managed as such. The institutions have to follow the market, and students are considered their products. Increase in scale, budgeting, efficiency, applied research financed by companies, the concept of direct utility and usefulness, all are threatening the Humboldt University. But even when scholars idealise the Humboldt University concept, it is true that the three basic elements of a modern university are under pressure.

Recently a new element was added to the transformation of this German university model, namely the Bologna Declaration.[4]

## European and American concepts of liberal arts

The export of European university models to other continents falls outside the project on the Ancient University Route. It is nevertheless very important to reckon with the origin and evolution of American higher education in the discussion on the introduction of the Anglo-Saxon or American bachelors/masters models in continental Europe as it was decided in Bologna in 1999.

Until the seventeenth century the *septem artes liberales* constituted the corner stone of general education for young boys. For various reasons linked to the infrastructure and the character of higher education, the universities had an almost complete monopoly on the transmission of non-manual learning from the thirteenth century onwards. Starting in the Renaissance, the universities slowly began to lose this monopoly in favour of other institutions of higher learning (academies, special schools, and so forth). A thorough knowledge of the liberal arts was considered to be both the necessary and the ideal basis for being able to take courses at the higher faculties of theology, law and medicine. But the liberal arts were also a goal in themselves. They provided the intellectual training and the general cultural knowledge – that is, the non-specialised introduction to the principal branches of knowledge – of the "intellectual" in the Middle Ages and in modern times. Almost three quarters of the students left the university after a few years of study at the arts faculty alone, with or without a final diploma (Master of Arts).

The intellectual preparation required for admission to the arts faculty in the Middle Ages was limited to a knowledge of Latin sufficient to allow the student to take university courses. The future arts students could learn Latin grammar in chapter schools, urban Latin schools, or by private instruction. During the fourteenth and particularly during the fifteenth century, several arts faculties began to organise this preparatory education, on the one hand to make up for the manifest deficiencies of the freshmen, and on the other hand to attract future students at a very young age (8 or 9 years old). By the end of the Middle Ages this system was the most developed within the University of Paris. The students there were lodged in private boarding houses or university colleges. In the latter, independent communities of scholar-boarders were set up from the end of the fourteenth century onwards. These were called *collèges d'exercice*. Once the required level of knowledge had been reached, the students began their studies in the faculty of arts proper and thus became true university students. Around 1500 the *collèges d'exercice* introduced the separation of students into homogeneous groups, gradually organised according to level of knowledge. At this time it happened as well that the future arts students were often so well prepared that they could easily follow the university arts curriculum and even skip certain courses. At the end of the Middle Ages, under the influence of pedagogues and humanist professors, "secondary" schools took up part of the task of the arts faculty and, thereby, began to develop, however slowly, into

---

4. Signed in June 1999 by the ministers responsible for higher education of twenty-nine European countries.

an homogeneous scholarly network, which prepared young students for higher education. In Catholic countries, the system was perfected by the Jesuits. In Protestant countries Latin schools – *gymnasia* – were founded on humanist principles; they hardly differed, however, from their Catholic counterparts. This division in scholarly levels – primary, secondary, higher or university – had important consequences for instruction in the arts faculties. As the level of preparation of the new enrolees became higher and higher, the professors of arts could devote themselves to other subjects in the domain of philology and letters, philosophy, and the natural sciences. These changes in the content of university instruction came about slowly, first in Italy and then in other countries. These changes were also reflected in the titles that faculties used to designate themselves. During the sixteenth century arts faculties often changed their names to the faculty of philosophy or the faculty of letters.

The question regarding the place of the liberal arts in instruction, be it secondary and/or university, remains alive today. It is at the heart of the debates on education in the United States. The content of learning – the subjects – that the Americans call liberal arts are almost never taught in the senior high school (students of 16 to 18 years old) but rather during the first two years of college or university at the undergraduate level. After this "general education", followed by two years of specialisation in a major, leading to a Bachelor of Arts (BA) or a Bachelor of Science (BS) degree, the students continue their studies in professional schools (law, medicine, civil engineering etc.) or in graduate schools (letters, history, natural sciences, etc.). A majority of students, nevertheless, leave college or university after having received their Bachelor degree. One of the reasons why the liberal arts are taught in the United States at the university level, and not at the secondary level as in Europe today, is that higher education was organised there before secondary education and the last two grades of secondary school have never been developed to the European level of the last two years of the *collège*, *lyceum*, *atheneum*, or *gymnasium*, etc. This, in fact, corresponds to a certain degree to the situation existing in Europe before the changes, which were brought about largely, but not exclusively, under the influence of humanism at the very end of the fifteenth century and especially in the sixteenth century.

We really have to reflect on the consequences of introducing an educational, or better, an institutional system in Europe that has another background and other traditions.

**Conclusions**

Scientific research and teaching were from the sixteenth century onwards no longer confined to the universities. This is especially true for experiment-related sciences and for disciplines that did not belong to the classical canon of the liberal arts, theology, law and medicine.

As a consequence, a binary system of higher education emerged in Europe in the course of the seventeenth and eighteenth centuries, and it has lasted until the present, although the dividing line between the university and other institutions of higher education is becoming increasingly blurred and Europe is moving towards a more integrated system of higher education as in the USA.

The unlinking of teaching and research resulted for the universities during the early modern period in a double speed evolution. At some universities professors rather quickly introduced experimental research, as in northern Italy and in the northern Netherlands in the sixteenth and seventeenth centuries and some German (Halle and Göttingen) or Scottish universities (Glasgow and Edinburgh) in the eighteenth century. Other European universities expressed more reserve and adjusted only reluctantly to the "novelties". Among those figure most universities in countries dominated by Spain, and the French and English universities, and in several German and eastern European universities. This analysis might indicate a geographical caesura in Europe between "progressive" and "conservative" institutions. Analysis of the individual universities, however, indicates that the global picture is not accurate. Every single institution had from its start ups and downs, trying to conciliate the most opposite goals and interests.

All universities have tried since their foundation to transfer knowledge within the boundaries they were given by the academic and public powers; it could be slow or rapid depending on the times and the political situation. But transfer went on whatever the conditions, universities considering their most important task the training of young adults in scientific thinking. It could be along the lines of the medieval scholastic method or the humanistic experimental-inductive method, or a combination of both; the goal was the same. This means continuity in learning and research.

In spite of criticism that the methods and content of teaching were too conservative and not adapted to the needs of society, there was a constant increase of graduates in all institutions and professions from the thirteenth century onwards despite the many complaints about an overproduction of academics. The discourse on a surplus of university students was very strong in the late seventeenth and eighteenth centuries. It was said that there were not enough interesting and well-paid jobs for all graduates whereas there was a shortage of skilled artisans and technicians. According to several historians these alienated or frustrated intellectuals became revolutionaries and were to a large extent responsible for the many revolutions in Europe.

A real alternative to the university does not seem to be available. Although the French revolutionaries abolished these institutions, deeming them to be useless, the next generation reintroduced them again. And the universities always have been the most successful cultural export products of Europe to the world.

But without any doubt the main contribution of the university in Europe is that it introduced rational and critical thinking, which became the intellectual essence of the western world.

# The intellectual heritage of universities: conclusions of the discussion

*Hilde de Ridder-Symoens*

The organisers asked me to formulate some conclusions, or better, some thoughts, at the end of two days of discussions and confrontations of ideas on the intellectual heritage of the European universities.

I will not formulate a definition of "the cultural heritage of the universities in Europe" – that will be done later on. I will only put the results of the discussion into words as I have interpreted them. During these two days I realised that I was participating with two identities: firstly as a historian of universities, secondly as a concerned academic.

## Reflections of a historian

As a historian, I devote my research to the history of the European university in general. I scarcely deal with a particular university.

It is the task of a historian to reconstruct as accurately as possible what happened in the past, on the basis of the facts and data, and to put these facts and data in their social context, trying to understand and to explain them.

More than once, the results of these investigations do not correspond with our visions and aspirations as professors, as members of the academic community. Working on the CRE project, A history of the university in Europe, and on other occasions, university historians are confronted with explicit or implicit falsifications of historical reality, mostly consisting of myths. These myths are often a result of jubilee historiography or public relations publications. Every university – and certainly the older ones – has a collection of them, starting almost in the beginning of their existence.

University historians can roughly be divided in two categories: those who work almost exclusively on the history of their own university and those dealing in a more global and comparative way with European universities or universities of the Western world.

The first group of historians has a tendency to consider their university as a *cas unique*, as an institution with a unique history in a kind of no man's land, an institution that had many more ups than downs.

Traditionally, an important aim of the second group is to define the place of the university in the whole education system, in the development or the transmission of knowledge and in the improvement of science. From the 1960s onwards much more emphasis has been put on the social role of universities, on the role academics played in the modernisation or professionalisation of universities, and more recently on the transmission of norms and values. In fact, without using the terms, general university historians are trying to define the cultural heritage of the university.

As a consequence, I see the contribution of university historians to the project of the Council of Europe as follows: university historians are equipped with tools to reconstruct the past of individual universities in a relatively accurate way, to retrieve similarities and differences and to interpret facts and events. They do not consider it their task to predict the future on the basis of the past.

University historians are well organised; there are many opportunities to confront the results of individual research at conferences and workshops organised by individual universities or individual departments or by the International Commission of the History of Universities or national committees. As I said in my introduction, the newly created FASTI project intends to create new tools, concrete technical tools, on the level of bibliographies, source editions, the use of electronics etc. But the international network also wants to provide some guidance in the commemoration of universities in writing. As far as I can see, FASTI can provide this expertise to the Council of Europe project.

**Universities, part of the cultural heritage of Europe?**

After four days of intensive discussion, two in Alcalá and two in Montpellier, it is time to formulate to what extent the university is part of the common heritage of Europe. Although from the discussions there emerged a variety of ideas and visions, it is clear that academics have the feeling that there is a common heritage that ought to be protected and to be continued in the future.

As an academic, I agree with this vision but as a historian, I have to warn of the pitfalls of a nostalgic reference to the past, and of an idealisation of the universities as centres of disinterested learning and research and of ethical values. European universities are challenged by the enterprise-university and the market-dominated conceptions of higher education and by the possible consequences of the Bologna Declaration. Since the sixties, there has been a loss of community feeling, of corporate identity. Students and teachers are less committed to their university, considering it as a school from which to get a diploma or as an employer.

The question is: how to keep and protect everything academics consider as valuable against external forces? An answer has to be found quickly. Time is pressing. In several countries, academic and political decision makers are working out new models that do not always take into account the European university traditions and heritage. If we find these traditions valuable, we really need to work fast and to propose to the European rectors and presidents via the European University Association (EUA) and other European organisations an integrated overview of the aims and values of the European academic community that have to be kept alive.

Political and even academic decision makers are often not aware of the values of the common heritage. It is our responsibility to acquaint them of this. But the weakness of universities, or better, academics, was in the past and still is their conservatism, their incapacity or willingness to face problems and to reorganise themselves. Most of the *reformationes,* as they were called in the Middle Ages and Early Modern Period, were done by external authorities, often after having lectured the universities about abuses and bad functioning. A more radical solution was and still is the creation of new institutions responding better to the new demands of society. After a certain time, these new institutions become part of the cultural heritage.

# Universities: a shared heritage in terms of European cultural identity[1]

*Gian Paolo Brizzi*

Do universities present a shared heritage in terms of European cultural and institutional identity?

I want to introduce the theme of my lecture in the form of a query because I think that beyond a standard response, our work should be guided by questioning. I do not wish to challenge the probability of finding elements of shared identity in the history of European universities, but tackling this analysis through questioning will doubtless help us not to be content with ready-made or obvious answers, which would be of very little use to us in this joint work which has already spanned half a century of history.

In the post second world war period, a new development began to take shape within European universities, from which emerged the convergent purpose of redefining the nature of relationships between universities of different countries, while at the same time respecting the constraints of political barriers, a legacy from the second world war. It was in the immediate post-war period that the need was felt to find and follow completely new directions, and from this there arose links between the structures underpinning the intellectual independence of different nations.

After the second world war, there were profound changes in the relationships between the different universities in Europe. The new intellectual situation created by the war in our continent demanded on the one hand a rethinking of the notion of universities themselves, these, on the other hand, appearing to a large extent to be the only institutions in a position to understand the deep meaning of this new mentality and to give it shape for the future.

In the 1950s, Hans-Albert Steger from the University of Münster wrote: "at that time, universities experienced a renewed awareness of their European origins: they began to go beyond the narrow national confines which had surrounded them to embrace a broader debate encompassing the whole continent. However, having been separated for centuries, the institutions they rediscovered appeared very different in many respects. They no longer spoke the same language, in the broad sense of the term: the 'nations' had exerted too much influence on them. In each case, national factors had mingled with historical data of a completely different nature to create vastly different entities".

The Europe which was then in the process of rebuilding itself, by virtue of the commitment of the best men of the time, sought and often found its roots in the Middle Ages, namely in the period of history which gave rise to the definitive institutions, individuals and value systems which form the bases of present-day

---

1. Article presented at the first project meeting (Alcalá de Henares, December 1999).

European society. In the words of Jacques Le Goff: "In terms of politics, economics and culture, Europe was born in the Middle Ages, and, today more than ever, the political edifice under construction requires another pillar capable of balancing economic interests and cultural activities, amongst which education occupies a privileged place. Intellectual development has shaped society since the Middle Ages: that is still true today, but will be even more so in the future, and universities are essentially charged with this formative role".

University historiography can be very useful to the shared European project today, by undertaking to examine in greater detail the common roots of universities across the European continent, a purpose it actually already endeavours to fulfil, so that, in the history of the first centuries of the new institution's activity, we can find objective situations, aspirations and solutions which even today enable light to be shed on the action of those who guide the choices in this vital sector.

Of all the institutions that developed in western Europe during the Middle Ages, the universities were among the most original created. Although it cannot be denied that other eras and other civilisations also produced forms of higher education (at Byzantium in the Roman Empire and in China), it is equally undeniable that universities did not develop from an earlier model but were clearly distinct from any past institution. Of course, that does not mean to say that they arose out of nothing. Quite the contrary. These were institutions the sole purpose of which was to preserve, develop and disseminate knowledge, and because they arose from that very calling, universities inherited a cultural tradition with origins rooted in antiquity. This tradition, defined by the disciplines taught and their acknowledged educative value, went back as far as the Greek philosophers, to Plato and Aristotle, and to their successors and Latin translators. In the late Empire, this cultural heritage was adjusted to meet essentially academic aims, while the first great Christian authors succeeded in combining this culture with Christian revelation by using it in the service of the latter. The fact that such a combination was not always complete and perfect is of marginal importance to us: suffice it to recall that in the sixth century, when ecclesiastical schools replaced lay schools, they assumed control of both schools and teachers whilst at the same time adopting the heritage of the old culture.

Universities also shared these elements of cultural continuity, but the origins of the new institution arose more out of a rift that developed, at first imperceptibly, throughout the twelfth and thirteenth centuries. This was played out on two particular stages, Bologna and Paris, soon followed by Oxford, Montpellier, Cambridge, Naples, Salamanca and Padua, and then others, through an uninterrupted process of association, which resulted in the creation of about 200 new foundations over six centuries.

In relation to preceding centuries, the rift involved a profound new change in educational methods as a result of the rediscovery of entire sectors of ancient knowledge which, having lain forgotten during the late Middle Ages, had reappeared, often richly supplemented with the contributions of Arab scholars. Then there was a rift encouraged by the growing number of students and teachers, which gave the universities a social influence not enjoyed by the ecclesiastical schools. The rift, however, was of a particularly institutional nature, separating the new schools from the monastic and cathedral-based organisation to which they had belonged for seven centuries.

Universities, on the other hand, represented stable structures devoted expressly to the dissemination of knowledge, and identified by a new legal concept, that of *studium generale.* In comparison to ecclesiastical schools which had limited jurisdiction, this concept granted them certain universal rights conferred individually on universities by a universal power, either the Pope or the Emperor, or sometimes both. The most interesting of these rights was the universal recognition of the degree, the *licentia ubique docendi,* namely the ability to teach anywhere without the need for the approval of particular authorities. This was due to the transnational character of the institution, which could consider itself outside the control of local authorities, both civil and ecclesiastical, to the extent that it was legitimised by universal authorities.

But the concept of *studium generale* referred back to other aspects: members of universities represented above all a separate section of society, recognisable by the fact that they enjoyed certain privileges. It was soon precisely because of this recognition as *studium generale* that universities were distinguishable from all other schools, since only the former enjoyed such recognition.

I want now return to the intrinsic meaning of the term *universitas* which, as we know, was used to describe a community of people. This required clarification as to whether it was a university of teachers, or students, or both. The success of the term, later used to describe the institution to which such specific communities of teachers and students referred, demonstrates the level of importance that the latter assumed.

"The university is built of men" wrote an important sixteenth century French legal expert, meaning thereby that the stability and success of the institution rested not so much on material structures, still in large part non-existent, but on the men who made it up, on the students and teachers who made it a living body, a legal entity, to use a modern term, capable of running itself, producing documents authenticated by its own seal, appearing before a court, endowing itself with statutes and commanding the respect of its members. This stage was reached in the thirteenth century when operational universities had already endowed themselves with their own statutes.

Identity factors were therefore strong and not merely the result of chance, but we can add others that indicate the extent of the uniformity which, beyond political or linguistic barriers, enabled those who belonged to a university to feel themselves members of a transnational community that furthered the migration of intellectuals and so the growth of a European cultural identity. Even now it is still rather astonishing to note how easy and usual it was to find intellectuals from different countries in the same university. Consider for example Paris in the thirteenth century, where there were the Englishmen Alexander de Hales and Roger Bacon, the German Alberto Magno, and the Italians Thomas Aquinas and Bonaventura. We can also emphasise the importance to European intellectuals of the *peregrinatio academica*, a custom which continued even when the network of universities had covered all of Europe and which did not stop until the middle of the seventeenth century with the great political and religious conflicts.

Emperor Frederick I's *Autentica Habita* had, since the twelfth century, established the principles of the privileged status of those who migrated to foreign towns to study *(facti exules amore studiorum)*, and for centuries students seeking to evade the jurisdiction of local authorities referred to this right. The disciplines making up the curriculum were the same from Krakow to Salamanca and from Prague to Montpellier, the *auctoritates* were the same and remained unchanged until the fifteenth century. The courses taught, the examination system and the conferring of degrees were identical, as were the teaching methods, which were based on scholasticism, and both oral and written communication were entirely in Latin.

This basic uniformity also applies to the buildings which, from the fourteenth century, began to host university activities, abandoning the casual nature of arrangements characterising early centuries. Firstly, there were the colleges, which had to welcome both students and teachers, then there were rooms for conferring degrees or the first libraries. As Michael Kiene has indicated to us, there is a significant uniformity in these buildings, seen in the gallery, courtyard, individual rooms, communal dining room, library and chapel. Consider Collegium Maius in Krakow, Collège San Clemente in Bologna or Saint Martial in Toulouse. It is not until later that we see certain defined typologies in university architecture, linked to individual institutional development.

Such uniformity was not only apparent but also represented one of the fundamental aspects of the unity of western civilisation in the Middle Ages.

We should not, however, think that there were no differences between the various universities. From the outset the first universities were constituted along different lines; Paris and Bologna are cases in point. Belonging to the same community did not cancel out differences, either among teachers or students. Social or geographical diversity remained, also hierarchical position within the same *universitas;* bear in mind that in universities organised on the Bologna model, only foreign students represented the *universitas scholarium.* This was not an indistinct entity: it hinged around national or regional sub-groups, each having its own judicial authorities and often enjoying particular privileges. In Parisian-type universities, there were faculties that combined schools of the same disciplines: choices were the preserve of individual assemblies and their implementation the preserve of a dean. There were still conflicts between faculties (between theology and philosophy, for example) and these became more marked during the Renaissance.

The colleges introduced another fundamental difference between the students. While initially created to help poor students, they soon transformed themselves into independent communities, with their own rules, their own hierarchy and individual objectives.

An even more important difference was that which arose between a large and a small university, and between universities with the established, general characteristics of an institution and new foundations wanted by towns or territorial sovereigns and which were based on these models but which often had no way of ensuring the quality of teaching, or a suitable number of faculties, or the continuity of financial support. Although the latter generally recruited locally, the former could claim a sphere of activity which had been international for centuries, and a reputation based on excellence of specialisation in one of the university disciplines, such as philosophy and theology in the case of Paris, or civil and canon law in the case of Bologna.

The combination of all the elements I have mentioned provides a glimpse on the one hand of a fundamental unity of purpose which made universities institutions with easily recognisable and codified characteristics, but on the other, gave them individual features which differentiated the various universities in terms of faculties or predominant disciplines, their recruitment characteristics and the varying influence exerted by local judicial or ecclesiastical authorities.

But individual, regional and then national characteristics also developed for a reason integral to the knowledge system and its transmission methods: these were based on dialectics, at the cost of any other intellectual system. Universities had to guarantee that new teachers had a perfect mastery of the contents of knowledge and methods taught, even at the expense of the ethical and social outcomes of education.

Real knowledge served truth, and this dimension was bound to appear too abstract, as the chancellor of the University of Paris observed at the beginning of the fifteenth century when he pondered: "What use is knowledge without action?"

From then on the conflict was felt to be irresolvable, and Rabelais summarised it brilliantly in his writing when he described the hilarious inability of Gargantua and the student from the Paris schools to communicate with each other.

The rigidity and limitations of school education never reconciled themselves to the new intellectual horizons of humanism. This caused a general hardening within the universities in defence of tradition, and beyond their walls occasioned the appearance of experimental study and research centres such as the academies, which, along with the universities, then became a meeting place for intellectuals.

From the fifteenth century onwards, another important phenomenon developed more and more explicitly: evidence of the control which the civil and ecclesiastical authorities always sought to exercise, with mixed results, over the universities increased considerably and gave rise to veritable "prince's universities", an expression which serves to emphasise the growing influence which political authorities assumed especially after the great Schism of 1378. As Jacques Verger has emphasised, the division of the Catholic world, by weakening the mediating and moderating function of the papacy, increased the pressure exerted by territorial sovereigns on already existing universities, or pushed them into creating new ones, these often being imitated by the grand feudal lords, for whom founding a university was a means of affirming their own independence.

This process was carried to its conclusion, and in practice the principle became accepted, whereby the right to confer academic degrees belonged to the *ius regale*, that is to say, the assignment of this privilege no longer necessarily came from a universal authority.

This new relationship gave rise to a new phase in the centuries-old university saga. Their history was increasingly linked to the choice of the sovereign, his court, and the centres of power, while their social and political function, even in the eyes of their members, prevailed over the objective search for knowledge. This was particularly evident in universities created during the first modern era, inside which from the outset the impact of social and political differences was felt more directly, the aspirations and intellectual results being more modest. However, we must not underestimate the importance of such universities to the extent that, like their predecessors, they contributed to the gradual and general progress of civilisation.

During this critical period, the invention and spread of printing diluted the effects of growing distinctions developing among universities by promoting knowledge and the circulation of scientific advances with a speed and a distribution previously inconceivable, and by promoting the network of relationships between the oldest schools and universities and the more recent schools in the Germanic and Slavonic world.

The often antagonistic relationship with the humanist movement did not, thanks to the movement itself, prevent links amongst intellectuals from growing and developing. The university authority enjoyed by certain humanists made their schools a meeting point for learned men of repute; suffice to mention the Guarino school in Ferrara, or the relationship which men such as John Colet, Rodolfo Agricola, Rotterdam's Erasmus and Antonio de Nebrija, to name but a few, had with the university world.

This situation redrew the geography of the great university centres of education: the prize now goes to establishments that had a secondary role in the Middle Ages or those that had recently appeared, as was the case with the college where we are today and which became a model for many other Castilian universities. Others include Montpellier's school of medicine, the Collège de Guyenne in Bordeaux, schools in Padua, Basel or Louvain, the *Academia Lugdunensis* in Leida and the University of Krakow, which proved very attractive on account of the quality of its astronomical and mathematical studies.

The breakdown in Europe's religious unity caused by the Reformation gave rise to a new and deep split in the world of European universities. Within the two coalitions, universities participated actively in the construction of the denominational state, whether they were Catholic universities influenced by the Jesuit *ratio studiorum,* or those within the orbit of the Reformation. Such activity prompted more widespread growth of university establishments, and during the century of great religious conflicts, about sixty new foundations appeared.

The intellectual unity of the university world was later thrown into crisis by ideological and religious divisions and prestigious members of the scientific world found better conditions for studying outside universities – Copernicus, Tycho Brahe and Descartes are well-known examples – and in the seventeenth century in general, universities were very slow to absorb the accomplishments of scientific thought.

The elements which bring European universities closer are recognisable today more in the function attributed to them from outside than in the spontaneous development of this function. The repression of teachers in Prague in 1602, and the repeated purges of teachers in Oxford and Cambridge during the civil wars of the seventeenth century demonstrate the desire to establish, even by extraordinary means, tight control over schools and university colleges and to allocate them a basic role, consisting in guaranteeing political conformity and religious orthodoxy, thus providing training for good pastors and capable bureaucrats.

Continuity and change are the two contradictory poles of development characterising universities as the culture of the Baroque period gave way to that of the Age of Enlightenment, which triggered the reversal of the traditional way of thinking which Paul Hazard has aptly called the crisis of European consciousness, accelerating the cultural revolution of the Age of Enlightenment. This change in cultural sensitivity made possible the re-appraisal and deepening of scientific developments, hindered time and time again by the latent conflict between theology and science, while the triumph of the Cartesian method opened the way to the successive stages in the history of science.

Continuity and change, we said: faced with tenacious opposition to any change in the university curriculum, the inability to embrace new disciplines or to promote new formative approaches, it is worth noting the instances of practical innovations in the academies at certain universities, cases in point being Halle or Göttingen.

During the Age of Enlightenment and even more so during the disorderly progress from the eighteenth to the nineteenth century, we saw successive reforms and legislative measures which completed the transformation of universities into "state institutions", reflecting the change from the point of view of political power which no longer considered the university as *pia causa* but as *res politica*. Beyond teaching activities, the selection of teaching staff, the control of students, curriculum and examinations, there also developed, amongst the tasks assumed by the state on behalf of universities, a much greater denominational tolerance, the progressive abolition of censure and the gradual affirmation of *libertas philosophandi,* that is to say freedom of research and teaching, to put an end, albeit somewhat slowly, to the way women were ostracised by universities.

This was the beginning of a radical revolt, a new phase in the centuries-old saga of this institution which, with the foundation of the university of Berlin arranged by W. von Humboldt in 1810, was to open the way to the university model which has predominated in the last two centuries, during which time universities have retained very few of the elements which characterised their life in the Middle Ages.

What still strikes us today from analysing this history, this recollection of the shared roots of present-day universities, is a message, which must touch the very nature of the university teacher. During its thousand-year history, the university has often aimed to affirm itself as an independent power, which may have weakened the basic function of the intellectual, namely exercising a critical mind, defending values relating to knowledge and its dissemination for the benefit of all society and not just as an instrument of personal power. As Jacques Le Goff has said, the great revolutionary principle of the medieval universities was of a social, cultural and intellectual kind; they introduced into our civilisation a means of progress and social advancement, based not on birth or wealth but on knowledge, effort and merit. University status has to be experienced as dignity and not as power. It is the dignity of a body which must legitimately manifest itself through a community symbolism, as in the Middle Ages, but which must also resist the temptation to form a caste. And then there are the students, and from their history we can draw elements that provide us with considerable food for thought.

For the lessons we can actually derive from it today, I want to conclude by recalling a custom amongst students, that is to say, from that part of the university body that we often forget when we talk about academia. It is a custom that spread rapidly amongst the students of central and northern Europe and which was very successful between 1550 and 1650, the period, which Henry Kamen has aptly described as "the century of iron". This involved students carrying with them throughout their studies, which often entailed travelling to different schools, university towns and European countries, a little book or album in which they asked teachers or friends to write a little motto or dedication. For them as adults, and also for their children and descendants, it acted as a souvenir of the schools they attended, the teachers with whom they enjoyed a friendly relationship and the friends with whom they had shared this intellectual experience. These albums tell the stories of bonds of friendship created in university rooms and uniting men of different countries and tongues. Significantly, they were called *libri amicorum* and bear witness to the extent to which sharing formative experiences and intellectual activities can become the most effective instrument for making common elements of identity and feelings of brotherhood and friendship prevail against ideological and religious divisions.

# Part IV

# The European dimension

# The idea of Europe through the history of universities: the European dimension as university heritage in the past, today, and in the future

*Paolo Blasi*

The ancient world, and in particular the agricultural society that characterised the period after the disintegration of the Roman Empire, did not feel the need and were not in a condition to provide institutions like the universities. At the end of the first millennium, European society was still fundamentally agricultural, and the seats of power and culture were mainly manorial castles and monasteries.

During the tenth and eleventh centuries, barbaric invasions came to an end, living conditions improved, there was more security, the population increased, the demand for goods became larger, hence the necessity of increasing agricultural production, as well as manufacturing and trade. Old towns, which had gradually lost size and had remained at a low ebb for centuries, found a new energy, introduced new forms of independent government, and tried new ways to ensure the pacific coexistence of the various corporations that had come into existence in the framework of their social and political structure. A substantial number of people left the countryside to find new life in the cities which grew bigger and bigger. The road system underwent a new development and ceased to be the preserve of solitary pilgrims and ruthless outlaws, and was open again to merchants, clergymen, and students.

This situation of population increase, of urban development, of improvement of road communication and trade, fostered the knowledge of law and science, and opened the way to new forms of vocational training – essential to the life of the towns, whose social and political structure was more complex and demanding than the one of the agricultural and feudal communities.

The teaching of liberal arts – the *trivium* (grammar, rhetoric, and logic) and the *quadrivium* (arithmetic, geometry, music, and astronomy) – could no longer satisfy current needs. The Byzantine and Arabic cultures became a new source of learning through the texts of their philosophers, mathematicians and astronomers, while works of Greek and Arab physicians, as well as texts of Roman law, drew general interest. This new trend could not be ignored even by theologians.

Hence the development of a demand for new learning and a new vocational training, which found an answer by the middle of the twelfth century with the first *universitates studiorum*, communities of students and teachers credited by the contemporary authorities – the Pope and the Emperor – and recognised as *studia generalia* with the authority of granting *licentiae ubique docendi*, ie the liberty of teaching everywhere. In this perspective, the university does not appear as the daughter of tradition, but the symbol of change and innovation, not responding to customary activities but an answer to new needs. A new cultural élite comes into being, and together with monks, clergymen, merchants and knights, would represent the driving force of the rising new Europe.

In the eleventh and twelfth centuries, universities came into existence through the spontaneous association of teachers and students. In Bologna, groups of students (*societates*) took the power of choosing teachers, of providing for their maintenance, and of planning learning (*universitas scholarium*). The most relevant field of study was Roman law, conceived as the proper instrument to develop a political theory independent from religious legitimacy. In this way, a process of secularisation of forms of government was started as a basis for the future separation of Church and State, which was to become the pivotal point of European politics.

In Paris the university stemmed from the initiative of clergymen *(clerici)* and was completely under the jurisdiction of ecclesiastical law, and therefore supervision was in the hands of a corporation of teachers.

Yet, the university was always well connected with the city, its activities and development; it represented the social and cultural meeting point of religious and secular interests, and helped the start of the commercialisation of learning and of the liberal arts. The very word *studium*, used as a definition of "university", emphasised the motivation and the intellectual efforts of the students, their active and reactive attitude to the challenges of a changing society and the new problems to be faced.

Ultimately, the young students were those who travelled around Europe to find in the universities the teachers they wanted, capable of opening their minds to the various fields of learning – theology, philosophy, law, medicine, and science.

As a result, universities became places where students of different nationalities, using a common language (Latin), lived together with the aim of learning. Communities that came into existence were lively and multifarious, with each member bringing in the peculiarities of his origin and culture, while getting to know and understand those of the others.

There was an independent, optimistic, occasionally hard-minded spirit, yet free from the conditioning of the two contemporary absolute authorities, the Pope and the Emperor.

In the universities of the Middle Ages  began those cultural, ethic, and civil values that, with the Christian ones, became the foundation of Middle Ages Europe and are today the common principles of European citizens.

Numerous universities came into existence in the thirteenth century. Some were autonomous institutions of their own creation. Others came into existence through what we call "migrations" from already existing universities. For instance, in 1224, Frederick II founded the University of Naples, the first institution in the world completely supported by the government. He claimed the necessity of training law specialists for his realm and, as he did not trust the University of Bologna, created a *studium* in Naples, providing directly for the maintenance of teachers, granting them the typical privileges enjoyed in other universities, corresponding to our "autonomy and academic freedom".

This was also his original answer to an edict of the Church which stated that "knowledge is a gift of God and must be imparted at no cost", and which had the aim of setting a limit to the ever increasing demands of higher salaries made by the teachers to the students, who had often protested. This marks the beginning of a typical European concept, the right to be educated, and at no cost.

At the same time, Alphonse IX, King of Castile, founded the University of Salamanca with the aims of legitimating his power and of reaffirming the Christian identity after the Arab invasion.

Various other universities came into existence as a consequence of the migration of students and teachers who left their own academy to establish another one in a more suitable location. This was the case of the University of Cambridge, which is a filiation of Oxford, of Angers and Orleans which derive from Paris, of Padua and Florence which owe their existence to Bologna, and so on.

The situation has a twofold aspect. On one hand, urbanisation increased more than ever, together with the development of the cities, which tried to get prestige and strength by being endowed with a university; on the other side the feudal monarchies were gradually getting stronger and, by creating autonomous universities, put up obstacles to the growing power of the town.

In fact, to balance the power of the cities and of their governments that took advantage also of the universities as an instrument of autonomous development, the Pope and several monarchs granted privileges to universities, strengthening their legal authority and their presence in the town itself.

In the fourteenth and the fifteenth centuries, new universities were founded in southern and northern Europe (for instance, Uppsala and Copenhagen). But very important are the universities that appeared in the cities of central Europe (in Germany, in Bohemia, in Poland, in Hungary), a consequence of the considerable economic, social, and cultural development of these areas and the prestige deriving from these institutions. It is important to remember that, particularly in Germany, monarchs would stress in their provisions the *autoritas* and the *potestas* of the crown.

In the fifteenth century, universities already existed in all the most important towns and they covered the European area. We can easy understand the interconnections between the various universities with the exchange of itinerant teachers and students, who spread information and ideas and, as a result, created a profitable intellectual interaction in the whole area. The Europe of learning, of trade, of arts was a reality.

It is also of primary importance to take into account the increasing power of feudal monarchies and their gradual transformation into absolute powers and the affirmation of regional powers in countries like Italy: these factors caused a considerable increase of the influence of political power on universities, and therefore a loss of autonomy and academic freedom could not be avoided, since universities had to adapt themselves and their programmes to the new situation.

Originally, universities appeared in a Europe with no borders inside and would attract students and teachers from anywhere, making possible a continuous mobility between universities that the Church and the Empire would favour and protect. In the constitution *Habita* of Frederick I, which was meant to be a *magna charta* of academic life, students were allowed to move around freely under the direct protection of the emperor. Foreign students were subjected to the only jurisdiction of the master or the bishop, and were explicitly exempted from the authority of the city.

Thus, in the first centuries of the past millennium, ideas would easily move around with the moving around of people, knowledge was free and innovation was pursued with enthusiasm. Dogmas were questioned, confrontation was encouraged and debate was a matter of fact.

The universities, which grew autonomously against this background, were a constant stimulus, a critical reality, a laboratory of ideas and initiatives; they hosted great scholars and students from everywhere. The university is actually an institution of European level and gives an essential contribution to the foundation of European civilisation, namely: respect and appreciation for each human being, importance of dialogue and criticism, legitimacy of political power separated from the Church, significance of knowledge and development of science.

Between the fifteenth and sixteenth centuries, the development of absolute governments stressed the importance of borders and of permanent residence. Mobility became less important: travellers were seen with a certain suspicion. The university was a symbol of royal power, an element of its territorial domains, hence its gradual loss of autonomy. It became a structure of the state, less European and more national and provincial. This process is facilitated by the dying out of individual and corporate freedom, and by the tightening of the control of subjects by the government.

It must not be forgotten that universities have always had contrasts and a difficult relationship with the cities. The great European towns (with the exception of Paris) as a rule did not have universities. This was the case with London, Rouen and Lyon, Palermo and Milan, Frankfurt, Hamburg and Munich, Antwerp and Amsterdam, etc.

In other cases, attempts to establish a university in a great town were doomed to failure. The University of Lisbon was transferred to Coimbra in 1537, the University of Florence to Pisa in 1472. The prince preferred to collocate the university in smaller towns: Milan favoured Pavia, Venice favoured Padua, Florence Pisa and so on. Academies not attended by students and controlled by the prince or one of his protectors were preferred in the bigger cities. Knowledge was more and more oligarchic and that was functional to the established power.

From the sixteenth to the nineteenth century universities were declining. They performed their duties, transmitting learning with dignity on the basis of traditional knowledge, but were no longer a vital element of society.

The Enlightenment and the Romantic Movement, the reforms of Napoleon and of other monarchs of the nineteenth century gave new life to universities defining their aims and social status. The university, particularly the Humboldtian kind, again became the most prestigious seat of free research and higher learning, with the aim of training an élite whose purpose would be the management and control of industrial and political structures of modern nations.

As a consequence, universities in their development conformed to national models that, however, showed a remarkable similarity of aims in all nations. We have the German model, the English model and the French model, differing mainly in the organisation and the degree of autonomy. Such models were be exported all over the world, ensuring a process of internationalisation of science and spreading methods of learning and research typically European.

It was only after the second world war and particularly in the most recent decades that the university situation underwent a radical transformation. The development of technology, the transition from an industrial society to a society of information and, right now, of knowledge, have made it necessary to make higher education available to an ever increasing number of people. Today, in Europe, between 40% and 50% of students of an age group go to university, and this creates what we call "the mass university".

European society has left behind the ideologies of the nineteenth century that imposed, rigid and inflexible models, blocked within the border of a political entity, and is now trying to cope with an age of great openings and great mobility, of the boundless availability of communication and the consequential phenomena of globalisation.

Therefore today, as at the beginning of the past millennium, we are bound to face new problems: we must deal with the complexities of globalisation while respecting the diversities; we must train citizens capable of surviving in a supranational reality where borders have the tendency to become hazy as in the first centuries of the past millennium; at the same time, communication between different cultures and different people is taking momentum.

In Europe, besides the economic and monetary community, we are trying to create a shared space for research and higher education, and therefore a common market of manpower and different cultural heritages. Initiatives such as Erasmus and Socrates, meant to encourage the mobility of students and teachers, imply a perspective similar to that of the constitution of *Habita* of Frederick I (Barbarossa), which prompted his famous saying still valid today: "Who would not feel sorry for those who have left their country for the love of science?"

Programmes such as Erasmus and Socrates must be encouraged and made available to other countries beside the fifteen of the European Union, to involve especially post-graduates and doctoral students.

We have to face two major problems to encourage mobility. First of all, full recognition of the work done in different universities must be assured for all students. For doctoral students and researchers, at the moment of their retirement, ways and means must be found to give recognition of their years of study and research spent in different universities. Young people are no longer craving for the permanent job to be safe for life, but they are right in asking not to be penalised for moving from one university to another.

Today's university has to define its role in the European and in the global context to be capable of meeting the challenge of the new millennium. The university has to play a main role in the present revolution, which is ethical and cultural. It is up to the university to give the man of today cultural and vocational values suitable to adjust him to the complexity of modern society, to make him master and use his own knowledge and capacity in favour of mankind.

Universities are acting in this perspective: in 1988, in Bologna, a *Magna Charta Universitatum* was signed, and an observatory has been now established to monitor the respect of its fundamental principles. We are again getting back the autonomy of organisation and management and are developing multifarious bilateral relations, in research as well as in education, and we are conforming our educational system to the principles of the Sorbonne Declaration as well as to that of Bologna, signed by twenty-nine European countries.

The challenge facing Europe is to establish a unitary government, able to represent it abroad, but respectful of the differences between the "domestic" countries, since such differences are a peculiarity and an important wealth of Europe. So it is necessary to refer to fundamental and shared principles, such as the respect of the human being independently from skin colour, culture and religion; dedication to learning and quest of justice; and finally, a deep awareness of the social relevance of individual behaviour. The culture of suspicion and external control must be replaced by the culture of individual responsibility and freedom, and the culture of rules must be replaced by the culture of results.

On these premises the orientation of Europe should, in my opinion, be: "fewer laws, fewer rules, and more education". Complexity cannot be managed by a multiplication of laws but by improving autonomy and individual responsibility. All this implies the adequacy and continuity of education.

Universities today are feeling the need to recover the unity of knowledge without interfering with the variety of disciplines and methods. They must be seen as laboratories experimenting the principle of subsidiarity, autonomy and responsibility. The political powers should pay attention to this laboratory.

The new planning (three years plus two years) of the higher educational system, the credit system, the disappearance of self-contained and isolated faculties, the increasing number of scholarships, traineeships, the spreading of tutorial facilities, more various and efficient educational programmes... all these provisions will deeply affect university education making it more open, more flexible and ready to satisfy social needs. To become actually European, the university should be transformed from a "teaching institution" to a "learning institution', a milieu where all its members, not only students and teachers, but also technicians and administrators, stay close together to learn. In a way, this means going back to the spirit of the medieval *studium*, individual efforts and the desire of learning will be encouraged. The universities will carry out their scope to create new knowledge, while preserving and transmitting the one of our heritage.

The student of today has a strong European identity, and strengthens it by travelling, becoming familiar with new environments, communicating and consorting with colleagues from other nations, and acquiring different languages. The university should help this European identity by rediscovering in our history and traditions our common origins, values and cultures.

The transformation of local universities into European universities is more advanced than the political union of the European countries. To facilitate this process it is necessary to promote mobility and co-operation, that is, to create the conditions needed for the development of bottom-up processes.

The past remains for all of us the common root on which we can build up a future of novelty and imagination. To reach the best quality of results, and to obtain a faster evolution, we basically need more co-operation, more autonomy and more resources.

Then, *"Cum tempore et labore omnia veniunt"*.

## Overview of the foundation of the earliest European universities

| | 11th-12th century | 13th century | 14th century | 15th century |
|---|---|---|---|---|
| France | 1170 Paris | 1229 Toulouse<br>1229 Angers<br>1289 Montpellier | 1303 Avignon<br>1306 Orleans<br>1332 Cahors<br>1339 Grenoble<br>1350 Perpignan<br>1365 Orange | 1409 Aix-en-Provence<br>1422 Poitiers<br>1423 Dôle<br>1437 Caen<br>1441 Bordeaux<br>1452 Valence<br>1461 Nantes<br>1465 Bourges<br>1485 Besançon |
| Italy | 1088 Bologna | 1204 Vicenza<br>1215 Arezzo<br>1222 Padua<br>1224 Naples<br>1228 Vercelli<br>1231 Salerno<br>1248 Piacenza<br>1276 R. Emilia | 1303 Rome<br>1308 Perugia<br>1318 Treviso<br>1321 Florence<br>1342 Pisa<br>1357 Sienna<br>1361 Pavia<br>1391 Ferrara | 1405 Turin<br>1412 Parma<br>1444 Catania |
| Great Britain | 1167 Oxford | 1209 Cambridge | | 1410 St Andrews<br>1450 Glasgow |
| Iberian Peninsula | | 1208 Palencia<br>1242 Salamanca<br>1254 Seville<br>1290 Lisbon | 1300 Lerida<br>1307 Coimbra<br>1346 Valladolid<br>1354 Huesca | 1430 Barcelona<br>1474 Saragossa<br>1499 Alcalá de Henares<br>1500 Valencia |
| Empire and Western Europe | | | 1347 Prague<br>1364 Kraków<br>1365 Vienna<br>1367 Pécs<br>1386 Heidelberg<br>1388 Cologne<br>1389 Buda<br>1392 Erfurt | 1402 Würzburg<br>1409 Leipzig<br>1419 Rostock<br>1426 Louvain<br>1455 Freiburg im Breisgau<br>1456 Greifswald<br>1460 Basel<br>1467 Pressburg (Bratislava)<br>1472 Ingolstadt<br>1473 Trier<br>1476 Tübingen<br>1476 Mainz |
| Scandinavia | | | | 1477 Uppsala<br>1479 Copenhagen |

# The university as the basis for a common European culture[1]

*José Luis Peset*

At its foundation 500 years ago, the University of Alcalá called on the services of Antonio de Nebrija, one of Renaissance humanism's leading masters. Humanism was a system of knowledge developed in Italy and France that reconciled the arts with the sciences and the past with the future. After studying in Salamanca and Bologna, Nebrija taught in Salamanca and Alcalá de Henares. He was privileged to witness – whether directly or indirectly – the Salamancan disputes over the discovery of America and the New World. His knowledge served the Columbus brothers' requirements since it demonstrated to "learned men and mariners" the feasibility of their proposals for reaching the spice lands by a westward route. What was needed was a good understanding of the ancients and moderns, both writers and scientists. Mathematics was therefore as indispensable as classical and modern philology since, in the words of Francisco Rico, "the use of the latest tools to approach the classics called for a new definition of space and time co-ordinates". Nebrija and Columbus were united by their emphasis on a knowledge of cartography, the measurement of distances and the charting of coastlines and cities. It is not surprising therefore, that Nebrija should have insisted on a study of the ancients, but from a modern point of view. He aimed to teach Castilian as a tool for teaching the classics and to use philology in order to shed light on the study of scientific treatises. Francisco Rico again: "Archaeological curiosity combined with scientific interests, dreams of conquest or missionary activity and commercial ambition. (...) The humanists did more than give a powerful initial thrust to geography in the modern age; in Italy and on the Iberian Peninsula they continued to contribute in writing and in thought to keeping alive the flame fuelled by the experiences of the navigators, the speculation of experts in the mathematical sciences and the need for expansion of a Europe which had become too small". Portuguese and Spanish expeditions paralleled the interest shown at the University of Salamanca in geography, mathematics and astrology. The humanists also sought in the public interest to explain the many discoveries of their predecessors. They sought to reconcile science with art, *res* with *verba* (Nebrija, *De Oratore*). The preserved vaulting in Salamanca University's Minor Schools portrays astrology alongside philosophy, art and philology. Geography and astronomy went hand in hand with the culture of an empire in search of a new view of the world.

The revival of interest in classical and modern languages was set in the context of a world in transformation. When Cisneros ordered an *auto-da-fé* of Arab writings after the conquest of the kingdom of Granada, he excluded books on philosophy and medicine. University libraries were opening up to knowledge of other lands and nations, and consequently to other cultures. Science in the modern world passed through a first phase of renewal in which culture was fundamental, although later, when it came to depend on observation and experimentation, the philological interest disappeared. Linguistic knowledge made it possible to rediscover the classics, whether Greek, Hebrew, Latin or Arabic. Languages became essential: a

---

1. Article presented at the first meeting of the project (Alcalá de Henares, December 1999).

knowledge of classical Greek was needed not only to read Aristotle, Euclid, Plato and Sophocles but also to understand modern culture and language. When Gregorio Mayans recommended to Pérez Bayer that he read Arias Montano's translation of the Song of Solomon, he was entering not only the field of religious tradition but also that of European culture, linguistics and poetry.

Alcalá was emerging both as a city and as a university town. In the past, as archaeological excavations have shown, its academic interest lay in the importance of the Roman city. Of equal note, however, was the existence of a palace belonging to the Archbishop of Toledo, which was frequented by his influential prelates. It is not surprising that Cardinal Cisneros should have reawakened the old interest in founding schools. His university, which was set up to provide a sound education for the clergy, boasted faculties of philosophy, ecclesiastical law and theology. For a number of reasons he also founded a faculty of medicine. The Renaissance was coming back to an appreciation of the human body, believing that medicine – as the Greeks had affirmed – was necessarily complementary to the nurture of the soul. It is not surprising that Alcalá de Henares should have had a college named *Madre de Dios* housing doctors, theologians and philosophers, who held discussions and shared their knowledge in all these fields. Again, this was not surprising, since medicine was considered to be the knowledge of nature, which in turn was the knowledge of divine wisdom. The sacred texts contained information concerning the salvation of the soul and the body, while secular books spoke of divine power. It was in this context too that Francisco Valles, a leading Alcalá physician and Hippocratic reformer with an interest in anatomy, was capable of combining sacred and secular thought. In his book *De Sacra Philosophia*, Valles sought to penetrate the secrets revealed by the Bible to medicine, just as he saw scientific texts as arguments in support of revealed knowledge. He was renowned as a doctor, and certain of his works, such as the *Controversiarum Medicorum et Philosophicarum Libri Decem*, were published and republished in Spain, Italy, Germany and France. In this book he harmonises philosophy with medicine, the discussions with his fellows in the college having proved fruitful here. The modern world was not yet divided between the two cultural viewpoints.

It was a culturally very rich world dominated by European humanism and the exchanges, which it fostered. The trilingual college and its professors trained competent linguists, and language was to serve in the hands of the early humanists to improve Biblical exegesis. Classical language experts were brought in, and the possibility of visits by such figures as Vives and Erasmus was mooted. This was a rich world not only in terms of its cultural life, but also in terms of the social life that grew up around it. While the shared life of the lecture halls and colleges was important, that of the streets and theatres, gaming-houses and taverns was no less so. This meant not only drinking, gaming and sex, but also rivalries and disputes, which were sometimes of a violent nature. As Miguel Angel Castillo has pointed out, the city took shape around the University in the same way as the streets and neighbourhoods existed to serve the Cardinal. The beauty of the Renaissance was embodied in Gil de Hontañon's University façade. The Crown, brawling students and the University and city authorities vied for control of the streets. The University of Francisco de Quevedo's *El Buscón* was the route to the Church, Parliament, the hospitals and the courts, yet also to the jailhouse and to America.

Michel de Montaigne – a man far removed from the university – called for a noble system of education, yet he knew well what Renaissance humanism was about. Concerning the education of noble children, he recommended respecting and encouraging their natural disposition. It was important to listen to one's pupils and place oneself in their situation. Since all men were different though equal, one must not seek to form identical minds. Pupils must be taught meanings rather than words and shown how to put what was taught into practice. They must learn about the diversity of views and opinions, the world at large and nature, love for one's parents and one's nation, fortitude, temperance and justice. Montaigne stressed the importance of experience, practical action, travel and familiarity with customs, conflicts, peoples, languages and nations. It was essential to focus on the entire being rather than nurture body or soul alone.

However, Montaigne also spoke in defence of pure rather than utilitarian study. He was doubtless dissatisfied with universities and cast a wary eye on the jurists and physicians employed to teach there. This reaction was shared by later humanists, such as the Englishman Robert Burton, who watched with dismay as the former interest in classical languages, mathematics, poetry or learning was adulterated by the new taste for profitable employment. True, a good understanding of Latin and Greek was required for both law and medicine, but the pure enjoyment of language *per se* was lost. Never again would universities be free of the debate between knowing and doing, pleasure and utility. The universality implied by a general education comprised a juxtaposition of very different areas of knowledge between which the University was torn. It was difficult for it to decide on balance whether theoretical, scientific or technical learning should take precedence. Society, business, government and the University administration all contributed to this debate. While too much utility was undesirable, certainly, so too was the failure to recognise the interests of society. López Pinero's warning that science in Spain was harming itself by its stubborn insistence on utility could be applied to Spanish universities, which were converted in the nineteenth century into vocational institutions for lawyers and doctors. Technical subjects were lost but found their place in the *Politécnicas*.

Spanish universities – the University of Alcalá is a case in point – suffered greatly at the end of the ancient regime. By 1800 the wealthy humanist universities had gone into decline. Their finances were being run down or wasted, their academics lacked dedication and theological disputes were rife. Besides, the rise in new forms of instruction brought new scientific, technical and vocational institutions. The universities were ruined by the Crown, certain of them being dissolved or transferred elsewhere. The University of Alcalá moved to Madrid, where it became a university for doctors and lawyers. Its treasures were sold and its buildings were put to alternative uses, changed hands or fell into disrepair. Today it stands as a monument to its success in reviving the city's cultural pulse, restoring buildings, attracting students and becoming the home of intense scientific activity. It is significant that the University has been the city's salvation, in return for the townspeople's restoration of the *Colegio Mayor* of San Ildefonso after the move to Madrid 150 years ago. This is a worthy example for those returning old universities to use.

Also very interesting is the German university model, which was originally developed in the nineteenth century by Wilhelm von Humboldt and Friedrich Daniel Ernst Schleiermacher. Their purpose was to achieve the rational freedom advocated by Immanuel Kant through the union of reformed religion with freedom of study, in terms of both curriculum development and independence from the authorities. German academics devoted themselves to the continuing quest for natural laws and self-knowledge and to seminar and laboratory-based research. As Walter Rüegg recently pointed out, the aim was to maintain the partnership between scientific research and humanism. In combination with philosophy, science made it possible to comprehend the pattern of nature and attain the heart of all things by moving beyond Kantianism. The dangers of the French model, with its suffocating bureaucracy and professionalisation, were successfully avoided. For German universities, it was essential to combine teaching with research and autonomy with freedom. As for the universities of Oxford and Cambridge, they never had a vocational role but were constructed around colleges and learned societies, with the consequence that science and humanism came together in a shared universalistic atmosphere.

Since the Renaissance, universities have struggled to maintain a difficult balance between the arts and the sciences, utility and learning, theory and practice, pure and applied science, vocational training and culture. In the new European Community, however, a further awkward balance is necessary between European knowledge and that from outside Europe. There are challenges on the one hand from the USA and Japan, and on the other from the Third World. In the case of Spain, the longstanding relationship with Latin America has always been necessary and beneficial. Immigrants have frequently brought Latin American culture to our cities and countryside. Another element in this full and complex picture is the conflict between official European culture and the cultures of the various nationalities that are becoming apparent as Europe takes shape. There is no question that Europe has fewer states than national cultures or that there are more peoples demanding their own cultural identity than there are different passports, the number of which, moreover, is in decline. However, in order to build an authentic Europe, it is essential to respect citizens' rights to their own identifying characteristics. To achieve the aim of sustaining a universal culture, it is vital that universities investigate local and national cultures. Study and research carried out in university lecture halls and libraries must take account of all cultures, whether Western or oriental, state-based, national or regional, and whether specific to indigenous populations or recent immigrants, majorities or minorities. The cosmopolitanism beloved of Montaigne, Vives and Paracelsus is crucial if old and new concerns alike are to be assimilated. Old-style humanism, with its tolerance and open-mindedness, must be revived, and to this end all efforts to promote teacher and student exchanges between European universities are significant. One positive piece of information in this connection is that the European Union has approved the second phase of the Socrates programme, increasing its duration from five to seven years and doubling its budget. Socrates comprises the Comenius programme (for schools), Erasmus (for university students), Lingua (focusing on languages) and Minerva (focusing on specific technologies). In addition, the Leonardo and Youth programmes will be expanded to reach a broader social spectrum.[2] For its part, the Spanish government is setting up a Foundation for Postgraduate Studies in Latin America, which will rely on national and European (CREU) grants to promote doctoral programmes in America.

Books are the principal instruments for communication in universities. Whether on parchment, on paper or in digital form, they have been crucial to developing and sustaining the intellectual heritage. Initially they were very hard to obtain, and scribes were employed to copy them for students and professors. Printing helped enormously with the dissemination of written culture, and computer methods today are beyond all imagination. Books preserved, created and propagated knowledge. The publication of textbooks brought modern scholarship into university lecture halls. Leading scholars' writings were exported, imported, sold, lent, reprinted and translated – allowing an extremely fertile exchange of ideas in Europe at a time when travel and communication were difficult. It is for this reason that magnificent university libraries exist as centres of knowledge, which must be preserved, restored, rebuilt, reopened and made accessible. Since university book collections are not always in perfect condition, substantial investment is necessary in the areas of infrastructure, restoration, binding and printing. A possible future development will be the indirect consultation of books, with computer technology allowing them to be printed and downloaded from remote locations. Although we shall have to give up the touch of paper, on-screen display is flexible, rapid and saves on money, materials and space. In any case, large collections must be handled with care, and at a time when antiquarian books are prized by collectors it is essential that an effort be made to keep rich university libraries in good condition. The same could be said of separate collections in fields such as art, anthropology, science, natural history or the health sciences, and of university archives, which contain the most precious records of the institution's life. Science museums in particular are of interest for the future. What is more, they are simple to set up because universities and other research bodies have been major purchasers of scientific equipment, which is now in danger of being destroyed, plundered or sold at a loss.

Books also continue to be a fertile source of culture. Universities have always concerned themselves with publishing good textbooks for use in teaching various subjects. This is a practice, which will never be discontinued. It is in the publication of such books that culture is exchanged and innovated. In order to promote European awareness, therefore, it is essential to develop international co-operation in the publication of course books. Their pages must reflect the image of a Europe of similarities and differences, and thus there is a need for a partnership of nations as specialists to ensure that the unifying and distinguishing characteristics of separate cultures are not forgotten. The task of re-examining the history of the extremely interesting last 500 years, from the religious wars to the second world war and the upheaval in the Balkans, is a very complex one. The rise, suppression and rebirth of European national currents – and the difficult relations between them – comprise a theme, which calls for international interdisciplinary study. Colloquies, exchanges and joint projects are indispensable to the aim of achieving a better understanding of

---

2. *El País*, 29November 1999 and *Gaceta Universitaria*, 29 November 1999.

Europe. The similar cultural movements, which have arisen in all European nations, must be analysed for their links, parallels and family resemblances.

In this connection, it is important to note the major project being run by the CRE[3] to draw up a history of European universities. A number of volumes have appeared as a compilation of exhaustive studies on the history of the University in Europe from the Middle Ages to modern times. A comparative approach is used to address the main themes of university history. A panorama is provided of university life in each period, with information about schools, teachers, students and subjects taught. There is also a separate volume containing a bibliography. University history is tackled from the point of view of relations with society and with other cultures. Concerning relationships with other countries, special attention is given to the connection with America. The project has led to plans for a history of European culture. This would be a humanistic, cosmopolitan history avoiding insularity and emphasising intercultural and interethnic relations. I believe that this same aspiration was responsible for the most brilliant studies contained in the history of European universities to which I have just referred.

Yet this effort must be applied not only to creating culture but also to transmitting it. Until recently it was difficult in Spain to obtain books published by universities. These days, outlets exist for Spanish university publications, but they are still not universally available in Europe. Links must be established between all university publishers from the Cambridge University Press, which claims to be the oldest in the world, to the publishing houses of institutions founded more recently. It is also essential to set up joint editorial projects, which can function as key channels for scholarship. Themes such as European art, law, science, philosophy or politics could be addressed through university projects with the support of academic departments, faculties and publications. There is a need not only for national cultural projects but also for projects on European culture, which should be considered a part of national culture. The problems facing university teaching could constitute a further inter-institutional and international topic of discussion. Themes of key importance for culture and science in every country include university independence, administration and teaching practices.

Europe today is facing doubt over whether to close in on itself or open up to the world. The only thinkable course is the latter, since it is impossible to ignore either the first world – USA and Japan – or indeed the developing world. Both Europe's relations with the outside world and the nature of life in European cities are compelling reasons to open up. As Mircea Eliade has so aptly observed: "Western civilisation will run the risk of declining into an emasculating provincialism if it neglects or disparages dialogue with other cultures. (...) The West will have to get to know and understand the existential circumstances and cultural universe of non-westerners. (...) Moreover, this confrontation with 'others' will enable westerners better to understand themselves. (...) It is quite possible that new civilisations will emerge from this vast process of syncretisation, just as Europe emerged from the disintegration of the ancient world". Europe is being shaped by the collapse of walls

---

3. Editors' note: on 31 March 2001, the CRE – Association of European Universities was merged with the Confederation of EU Rectors' Conferences to form the European University Association (EUA).

and frontiers, the reconciliation of the churches and the union of capital and industry. Yet culture is just as much a factor. The masses devour culture, albeit culture in its broadest sense, which includes cinema, music and fiction. Teilhard de Chardin and Julian Huxley speak of the "noosphere" of ideas, which emanate from society but in turn inspire humankind. I shall close with the words of Roland Stromberg, who writes as follows: if the most pressing task ahead of us is to organise our ideas so as to use them creatively, and if these ideas are indeed the "invisible forces governing mankind", the systematic study of ideas with some bearing on life – namely, in the social and historical context – will not be the least significant of the many studies that are currently in progress. Yet much remains to be done. It is in this way that life may continue in a Europe, which produced many of the best ideas of humankind, such as democracy, tolerance and freedom.

# The role of universities in developing a democratic European culture[1]

*Alain Renaut*

It is no simple matter, even for European citizens themselves, to define what the European identity might be. This is largely due to memories, which are still too close for comfort, memories which every nation has of past rivalries or enmities and of the suffering that all so often went with them. If not for historians, at least for the individuals and groups living in Europe, if this body of peoples is to have a specific identity which could unite it as a genuine community, that sense of identity can clearly not yet be based on the past, nor on the memory of that past. It is therefore important to pay special attention today to every factor that may help to create such an identity or at least make people aware of it once more. It is here that the role of universities might well prove vital and deserves to be made the subject of theoretical discussion at institutional level.

## The European origins of universities

In many respects, if there is any institution that Europe can most justifiably claim as one of its inventions, it is the university. As proof thereof and without wishing here to recount the whole history of the birth of universities,[2] it will suffice to describe briefly how the invention of universities took the form of a polycentric process of specifically European origin. The very first university was founded in 1088 in Bologna, followed only a few years later by Paris and Oxford, but their respective foundations were the result of different procedures in each case, a fact that renders the emergence and development of universities in Europe more complex than has often been supposed.

For a very long time, the history of universities was described as a continuous process starting in the thirteenth century, as if a single model (generally identified as the "Paris model") had continued uninterruptedly to spread from the French capital throughout the rest of Europe.[3] If this were the case, the "renaissance of the European vocation of universities"[4] might be understood purely and simply as a reactivation of the original and supposedly unique model. As much as I believe it necessary to reaffirm the "European vocation of universities", I am equally

---

1. This article was written for the Higher Education and Research Committee (CC-HER) project on European Studies for Democratic Citizenship. It was published in *Concepts of democratic citizenship*, Council of Europe publications, ISBN 92-871-4452-4, December 2000. The article was submitted to the first meeting of the Ancient Universities Route.
2. Relevant studies include: J. Verger, *Les Universités au Moyen Âge*, Paris, PUF, 1973; R. Chartier, D. Julia, J. Revel (chief editor), *Les Universités européennes du XVIe au XVIIe siècle*, Paris, Ed. de l'EHESS, 1986-1989 (2 vols.); G.P. Brizzi and J. Verger (chief ed.), *Le università dell'Europa*, Milan, Silvana, 1990-1993 (4 vols.); H. de Ridder-Symoens (ed.), *Universities in the Middle Ages*, Cambridge, CUP (volume 1: *History of the University in Europe*, 3 further volumes planned).
3. See for example J. Minot: *l'Histoire des universités françaises*, Paris, PUF, 1991, in which the author endeavours to show that the type of institution founded in Paris in the 12th century was subsequently adopted by all universities.
4. *Op. cit.*, p. 120.

convinced that the ways and means of achieving this cannot be conceived in such a simplistic fashion, for the idea of an alleged Paris model having spread throughout Europe is largely a myth.

Moreover, the legendary aspect of this idea does not only concern the actual place where universities were first invented. In the course of this "European" rather than "Parisian" process,[5] it was, I repeat, Bologna that came first, whereas the Parisian students and teachers began only some ten years later to form an association whose first articles were not adopted until 1215; and it was also at the same time that a number of teachers in Oxford, who had begun to form a group in about 1200, succeeded by 1214 in obtaining papal privileges confirmed by the king shortly afterwards, thereby guaranteeing the autonomy of what from then on established itself as a "university".

This geographical diversity was accompanied above all by the variety of universities that were set up. To quote a particularly significant example, namely Bologna, the creation of the university took the form of a struggle for its recognition by the municipal authority that governed the city at the time. While the very remote suzerain, Frederick Barbarossa, had granted privileges in 1158 to the teachers and students, the local authority or Commune had unceasingly interfered in academic affairs (not only the award of degrees, but also in an attempt to enrol the teachers as municipal employees): this produced a series of conflicts between the municipal authorities and the university, the latter supported by the pope, which lasted until 1321 when the Commune finally recognised the university's independence. In the course of this struggle, punctuated by strikes and the flight of academics to take refuge in other towns, the system finally established was characterised by the fact that the staff were not part of the university, which became institutionalised in the form of a society or company of students. The University of Bologna therefore grew initially out of quite a different concept than the one that accompanied the institutionalisation of the Sorbonne.

In the Paris of the late twelfth and early thirteenth centuries, the primary aim had been to ensure that the budding *universitas magistrorum et scholarium Parisiensium* would enjoy independent status, *vis-à-vis* the power of both the Church and the emergent state, as clearly demonstrated in the charter in which Robert de Courçon defined its privileges in 1215. In the Latin of the time, the term *universitas*, which in ancient Rome had the meaning of "totality", had become synonymous since the Justinian's Digest with a collective body organised according to joint principles with a view to protecting its interests: the Parisian university was therefore first of all a corporation composed of teachers and students, set up not so much to demonstrate the unity of their knowledge as to defend their common interests, against the contemporary backdrop characterised by the beginnings of a centralised monarchy, in other words the constitution of the future modern state.

---

5. Though the institution created in Paris did sometimes inspire similar establishments: when German students were prevented during the Hundred Years' War from going to Paris, the Pope decided to found a University in Heidelberg "modelled on the University of Paris".

We must therefore be very wary of idealising, by dint of a kind of retrospective standardisation, the birth of European universities by deriving from their imagined homogeneous nature the conviction that, in the various social and political contexts in which it appeared, the university was conceived in identical terms from the outset, and thereby represented a kind of pole towards which we would merely have to return today, once geographical unity has been achieved, in order to resuscitate the European vocation of universities.

If one wished to pinpoint the time at which a particular universal model became dominant in Europe and acted as the focus for the major efforts to develop a system of higher education, one would have to redirect one's gaze from the Middle Ages towards modern times, by drawing attention to two really defining moments in the process of creating a sense of identity for European universities.

## A European university identity

Paradoxically, the first phase in the formation of this sense of identity was negative in tenor. In the majority of European countries it corresponded to a crisis in – if not indeed the demise of – the Medieval university heritage.

In 1789 there were twenty-two universities in France but a large number of their faculties were moribund, with sometimes barely a score or two of enrolled students. The institution therefore seemed on the verge of extinction to such an extent that, in Germany, threatened with a similar crisis, a decision to close all universities was even called for by certain representatives of the political and intellectual world who went as far as declaring that universities were suffering from an incurable disease. As an alternative, they proposed a new concept of science that the traditional universities would be unable to cater for and according to which knowledge should be productive and its utility measured in terms of the efficiency of its practical applications. Accordingly, there appeared throughout the eighteenth century in Germany certain "specialist" and "higher vocational" institutions (*Spezialschulen*, *Fachhochschulen*), which dispensed a totally different version of what was claimed to represent higher education. This process was paralleled in France over the same period with the appearance, after the collapse of the Ancien Régime, of "specialist colleges" designed to train civil engineers, mining engineers, etc. (examples being the Ecole du Génie de Mézières, the Ecole des Ponts et Chaussées, etc.). In response to these parallel crises in France and Germany therefore, establishments were set up which gave more priority to specialist training of immediate social utility, rather than to the comprehensive aim that universities had pursued since their origins, namely training students both to acquire knowledge and at the same time to build on and expand that knowledge.

In the eighteenth century then, Europe was marked by the weakening of the university institution, which it had itself invented five centuries earlier. Nevertheless another defining moment in the formation of a European university identity occurred almost simultaneously to counterbalance the disastrous effects of the former. Just as revolutionary France, confirming as it were the *de facto* decline of the universities, proclaimed in 1793 their *de jure* abolition (on the grounds that, being corporations, they were Ancien Régime institutions) and thereby paved the way for the rise of the

123

specialist colleges (*grandes écoles*), simultaneously, the eighteenth century crisis triggered a response in Germany whereby the nineteenth century became the golden age of German universities.

We shall not dwell in detail on how this unexpected resurgence can be traced back to a policy of reconstructive modernisation: the policy concerned, symbolised by the founding of Berlin University in 1809, was inspired by Wilhelm von Humboldt and was directed against both the utilitarian ideology embodied by the specialist colleges and the pre-existing universities. For our present purposes, it is much more crucial to draw attention to the fact that the Humboldt reform, by putting a stop to the utilitarian trend without rehabilitating the obsolete traditional model, forged a new idea of the university around which most of the hopes placed in universities in Europe and even elsewhere were able to crystallise.

The compromise proposed by Humboldt was undoubtedly an extremely skilful formula. It confirmed the role of universities as the depositories of pure knowledge (the search for truth), but without excluding the "practical" aspect, in the conviction that acquiring knowledge is in itself an educational process: a university education which trains students to acquire knowledge while at the same time seeking to produce new knowledge amounts to promoting education by means of knowledge or forming students by informing them (*Bildung durch Wissenschaft*). Because these universities, contrary to the specialist colleges, are intent on the acquisition of theoretical knowledge as such, they are assigned the exclusive task of dispensing the most authentic brand of practical training, namely educating the whole person: this entails educating people for personal liberty, and this liberty is best acquired by a university education in assimilating knowledge through an "autonomous activity" in which it finds its self-justification.

Because university institutions were thus able to respond to the criticisms of the inadequacy of its training compared with practical requirements, the Humboldt model became the major point of reference for academic identity in Europe for a century and a half. During the Victorian era the principal protagonists of the debate on British universities (J. H. Newman, Matthew Arnold, T. H. Huxley, John Stuart Mill, etc.) expressed their unceasing admiration, despite certain differences in emphasis, for the formula proposed in Germany since the early nineteenth century. Britain even served as a relay in the partial export of the German model to the United States, whence numerous experts came to Germany throughout the nineteenth century to take stock of a European concept of universities, which was to have a strong influence in their own country, from 1860 onwards, on the movement to create and expand higher education. In the case of France, it was Victor Cousin, by publishing a report on German universities in 1833 which caused a sensation, followed after 1870 by a good number of other academics who visited the higher education establishments across the Rhine (Renan, Dreyfus-Brisach, Fustel de Coulanges, Lachelier, Seignobos and others), who undertook to explain to their colleagues the specific nature of the German model. The upshot was that the Third Republic, after renovating the education system on the basis of state provision, crowned its efforts by enacting the law of 10 July 1896 whereby higher education was to be reorganised by uniting all the faculties existing in the same town into a single "university". In this process, the creation of universities "like those in

Germany", to quote Louis Liard (director of higher education and, as such, the main architect of this policy), was the major objective of the recomposition of French higher education.

There can be no question of claiming that all European universities, including those in France, effectively succeeded in evolving according to the Humboldt model; nevertheless, it was around this model that a lasting university identity was formed, sharing the same high ideal and defending common values – first and foremost the principles of disinterested research, the antithesis of out-and-out mercantile professionalism, and the autonomy of knowledge *vis-à-vis* its various practical applications. Undoubtedly, of course, with this ideal as the starting point, national traditions played their part by diversifying its application and, today, France realises only too well the ground lost in its universities by attempting to circumscribe the aims of Humboldt within an institutional framework, which, on account of excessive centralisation, was in reality barely compatible with the model. The fact remains that it was the German concept of higher education that succeeded in haunting the minds of several generations of academics as an indispensable point of reference.

The formation of a European university identity in this way also helps one to understand, almost two centuries after Humboldt's compromise solution and now that it is itself beginning to prove problematic and is even threatened by disintegration, how this identity has since been exposed to difficulties which are curiously similar from one country to another – a trend which no doubt calls for a new change in the said identity, beginning with self-examination.

**Universities as depositories of culture**

There are at least two arguments in favour of the belief that, unless they are to find themselves marginalised, European universities must make a fresh start today.

Firstly, thanks to what is sometimes (in Germany) called the "opening up" of universities and sometimes (in France) described as the mass acceptance of students ("massification"), an increasingly large proportion of a particular age group is henceforth destined to spend a certain number of years attending higher education establishments. This proportion, although it certainly varies from country to country, is tending to become standardised[6] at such a high level that, in any case, there is currently no other institution in Europe which can bring together such a large percentage of those people who, at an age where their basic education is complete and they are acquiring full citizenship through the right to vote, are destined to become the élite which their respective countries need.[7] If, therefore, it were deemed a good idea to enrich the intellectual and cultural education systems specific to each country by adding a common element through which, as part of the learning process, a number of values and principles could be shared, universities would seem to be the most apt institution to fulfil this function – provided, however, they were

---

6. It is over 40% in Germany and France. Although traditionally lower in Great Britain, it is increasing rapidly and now stands at 32% (cf. the Dearing report on higher education, released in July 1997).
7. There are now an estimated 11 million students in the European Community (including 2 million in France, 1.85 million in Germany, 1.67 million in Italy and 1.5 million in Great Britain).

able, in line with their original vocation, not only to offer access to increasingly specialised knowledge, but also to teach students to appraise knowledge as such, whether fundamental or specialised.

Secondly, it is also conceivable that, by helping to shape this European identity, our universities could also rediscover part of their own identity. It is commonplace, but nevertheless it touches on the real-life situation of universities today, to note the extent to which they are finding it increasingly difficult to define their own specific place in the multifaceted world of higher education that now exists in different countries. Threatened perhaps by *grandes écoles* (in France) or Hochschulen (in Germany), contemporary universities, where the teaching of humanities and social sciences is constantly growing in importance (currently accounting for 40% of students in France), are desperately wondering what role they might still play in a world where education is governed more and more by the need to teach vocational skills, which is hardly the traditional function of universities. A new and constructive way of appeasing this concern, which is perfectly justified, could be to consider how universities might be able to help set up a genuinely European body of knowledge and culture.

Since the first universities were founded in the thirteenth century, the word "university" has meant unity in diversity (*uni-versitas*). Originally, this unity was that of a body composed of teachers and their students (at least in the French tradition). The first university revolution[8] took place in Germany at the beginning of the nineteenth century, as explained above, and was symbolised by the great name of Humboldt and by the foundation of the University of Berlin. Once the unity of the existing universities had been broken up by the individualism of modernity, their very existence was threatened and indeed they only survived because the traditional model was sacrificed and a new one emerged, based on the notion of "uni-versity" as a centre of learning which embodied and revealed the essential unity of science (*universitas scientiarum*). The formula conceived by Humboldt consisted in education through knowledge, which, as we have already indicated, enabled universities to stand up to competition from special or vocational institutions (*Spezialschulen, Fachhochschulen*). This was consistent with the conviction based on the philosophical principles of German idealism, whereby rationalism can only become a dynamic force when knowledge is channelled and shaped into a system: in other words, if the knowledge dispensed by the university has an educational value it is because, contrary to the specialist training in vocational institutions, knowledge is not communicated in a compartmentalised form without regard to the links between the different elements of a subject considered as a self-contained whole, or to the factors linking the various subjects within knowledge as a whole, but rather according to a systematic pattern based on principles. Whereas the acquisition of a particular technical skill confines the individual learner within one narrow field, the only real way to train students to fulfil their destiny (which is none other than individual freedom) is to provide access to a more comprehensive body of knowledge inspired with the ideal that everything is ultimately derived from a single original principle – that is, the scientific ideal such as it has always been understood

---

8. I have analysed the reasons for and impact of this in: A. Renaut, *Les révolutions de l'Université. Essai sur la modernisation de la culture*, Paris, Calmann-Lévy, 1995.

within the context of German idealism, charged with the energy inherent in the system. Understood in this way, the reform of European universities undertaken by Humboldt consisted in reinterpreting the term "university" itself, abandoning the (mediaeval) meaning of *universitas magistrorum et scholarium*, in favour of the (modern) meaning of *universitas scientiarum*: higher education could therefore continue claiming to be truly "uni-versal" in so far as it remained faithful to the ideal of forging unity out of multiplicity – a unity which, compared with the specialisation induced by the demands of more immediate professional or vocations aims, postulates human knowledge as an unfragmented whole.

For these reasons, whether demographic (due to the changing face of the university population) or epistemological (linked to the modern phenomenon of increasingly compartmentalised knowledge[9]), this model, which captivated academics in every country of the world for more than a century, has probably now had its day. Occasionally viewed with nostalgia, the Humboldt model could never be redesigned to meet contemporary needs.[10] Does this mean that, because these two successive models are no longer valid, the very idea of a university should be considered out of date or even that "the end is nigh" for universities?[11]

It could be regarded as one of the most fundamental tasks for a European identity – in so far as there is a historical duty to maintain its university heritage as one of its essential components – to help avert such a pessimistic prospect by conceiving a possible new transformation, or even revolution, in the "uni-versity" aspect of higher education. Contrary to what occurred in the North American context, where the *universitas scientiarum* concept imported from Europe rapidly degenerated under pressure from the demands of vocational training into a "multiversity" designed to train students in specialisms corresponding to their pre-selected careers[12], there is no reason why higher education in Europe should not avoid the fate of being entirely devoted to providing a mere juxtaposition of specialist training modules for all sectors of social activity. In the United States, where it has greatest currency, this situation has sparked controversy owing to the adverse side effects of ultra-professionalism, such that the cause of an authentic "uni-versity" has emerged with a new lease of life. Nevertheless, the real question today in the attempt to reconstruct a university where the subject matter no longer depends on the demands of the economy is how to define the exact nature of the "unity" composing the university, since it can certainly no longer be the former idea of a corporation, nor the now purely hypothetical concept of human knowledge in its entirety. It is precisely on this point that our self-reflection on the European university identity can enable us to imagine, on the threshold of the twenty-first century, a means of conferring new significance on the "uni-versity" as a concept by proposing that the

---

9. For example, J. Mittelstrass, in a research paper on German universities (*Die unzeitgemässe Universität*, Frankfurt/M, Suhrkamp, 1994), states that more than four thousand different specialist fields are currently taught by German higher education establishments.
10. This was made perfectly clear by J. Habermas as far back as 1963, in *Theorie und Praxis*, Hermann Luchterhand, vol. II, ch. 10.
11. Mittelstrass, *op. cit.*, p. 49.
12. For arguments in support of the transition from university to "multiversity", see Clark Kerr, *The Uses of University*, Berkeley, 1963.

unity which constitutes the aim and purposes of the university since its invention by Europe could be reinterpreted today as being that of a culture.

In his speech on 20 November 1964, on being awarded an honorary doctorate by the University of Strasbourg, Léopold Sédar Senghor said that the term "*universitas*" actually comes from the word "*universum*" in the sense of what is universal and of values that are capable of universality.[13] This is undoubtedly an impressive ideal that should be taken into consideration, at least for its regulatory potential. However, an approximate, more modest and more realistic version could, in our countries, be based on the concept of an institution whose "uni-versity" aspect was based on the common values which underpin European cultures. If Europe, as is often repeated these days, is not to be confined to the euro, one way of enhancing the existing economic and financial union and making it less soulless could be for our universities to make a genuine contribution to the establishment of a common European culture.

Of course, certain measures which are forerunners of such a task are already in place. They have so far mainly consisted of the Erasmus and Socrates exchange programmes which (in 1998) are providing travel grants for some 200 000 students (31 000 of them from France) in twenty-three different countries. But what are 200 000 students out of a total of 11 million, and does helping young people to travel and live insecure existences abroad provide a sufficient guarantee for the dissemination of culture? Although it is certainly a welcome sign to witness the introduction of various mechanisms designed to harmonise curricula[14] or to foster the development of research leading to a doctoral thesis placed under the joint auspices of two European universities, these innovations are nevertheless still far from corresponding to the declared aim. Other avenues are now being opened up which will have to be more thoroughly explored in the coming decades: the creation of European university poles combining existing universities located close to one another but in neighbouring countries; the urgent founding of at least one fully fledged European university, for its symbolic value, to be managed by the Community institutions (Strasbourg University has sometimes been considered for this purpose); and the development of a high-powered computer network linking the databases of many different libraries. All of these ideas reflect in one way or another a determination to enable universities to contribute to the development of European citizenship. No matter how fruitful these strategies may prove to be, however, it is likely that they will only constitute the first stage in a more far-reaching transformation affecting not merely the formal operation of universities, but the subject matter and culture transmitted by academic institutions: to put it bluntly, has the time not come to include in at least the first phases of higher education the cultural requirements necessary to create a European citizenship?

Everything today points to the need to undertake a thorough reform of the early stages of university education that have felt most keenly the effects of

---

13. L. S. Senghor, *Négritude et civilisation de l'universel (Liberté III)*, Paris, Éd. du Seuil, 1975.
14. This reorganisation was strongly advocated in the joint declaration issued in Paris, at a colloquium organised in the Sorbonne in May 1998 by the German, British, Italian and French Ministers of Education. The same aim has also been confirmed in France in the report by the Commission chaired by J. Attali "Pour un modèle européen d'enseignement supérieur", Stock, 1998.

"massification". This calls for a clearer vision of the role that these first terms should perform in providing first-year students with the extra general knowledge that is the necessary grounding for every subsequent course of specialist training. The historic opportunity should not be missed for incorporating within all national universities and their curricula the indispensable foundations for building up a common culture. This opportunity has scarcely been realised so far, except in the important – though limited, or at least preliminary – form of the systematically intensified learning of European languages. But we need to go much further and give thought to devising training programmes in European culture and history, and to the functioning of the European institutions and incorporating them into the curricula. Clearly, if all these proposals are to be implemented, an extensive review of what is now taught in universities and of the current structure of degree courses will be necessary. Will universities, whose courses are generally already too specialised to accommodate with ease even a common "national" culture, be able to make room for a common European culture?

There are certainly many difficulties and obstacles. It will be necessary to pinpoint them and to devise ways of solving or getting round them. Generally speaking, the prospect of a truly European university platform will never become reality unless every country brings its universities up to date. It is absolutely vital that undergraduate courses, which currently specialise far too early, be restructured with greater emphasis on aspects of general culture, particularly in the humanities which are so popular, if European culture is to be a significant part of what, after all, should be a general education. The undertaking therefore is immense. At stake is not only whether Europe can be more than just a single market, but also the very future of our universities – and all this at a time when the need for universities to co-exist with other types of higher education establishments and scientific institutions is prompting them to move away from simply providing sound knowledge in a clearly defined field.

# Part V

# The cultural heritage of European universities

# Case studies and examples

# The University of Bologna, its Student Museum and Historic Archives[1]

*Gian Paolo Brizzi*

## The University of Bologna

Rather than venturing into the intricate labyrinth of the origins of Bologna University, I shall simply point out that 1088 is conventionally taken as its year of birth. At this time Irnerio (*lucerna iuris* as his disciples called him), who founded our school of law, was already teaching civil law on the basis of Roman legal texts that had been transferred to Bologna from Ravenna, the former imperial capital. From that date onwards the Bologna Schools gradually built up a solid reputation and its "doctors" and "laws" took on an authority which influenced many European countries, providing the basis for ordinary law, the new universal code for public and private relations, and the method of organising economic, social and political relations.

Fruitful symbiosis quickly sprang up between the university and the city: in the twelfth century Bologna acquired the titles of *dotta, culta, mater legum,* and *mater studiorum.* It came to represent the ideal laboratory for testing the newly emerging schools, which differed from their forerunners in many respects.

The public university of Bologna was above all a lay institution, or what we would now call a secular university. After several centuries of Church monopoly on teaching, Bologna administered a new type of knowledge, civil law, which was aimed not at increasing human understanding of divine revelation but at meeting the requirements of the new urban communities and the novel state structures.

For a long time, as we know, law was the centre of gravity of the Bologna schools. Civil law was renewed by the "rediscovery" of Roman law, Justinian's *Corpus iuris civilis*, particularly the extremely important *Codice* and *Digesto.* These texts were then constantly updated and extended by means of a complex system of marginal notes, glosses, which were used both for studying the meaning of the text and for applying it to specific cases coming before judges and lawyers in the course of their professional duties. The school of glossators produced such masters as Bulgaro, Azone, Odofredo and Accursio, whose doctrines gained fame throughout Europe thanks to their students, who became promoters of the new legal civilisation.

Canon law, which was essentially studied and taught through the *Decretum,* was also fostered by the Bologna academics, foremost among whom was Graziano, a professor whose name still adorns the monumental compilation classified and completed in Bologna, from whence it was disseminated throughout Europe. Again,

---

1. The first part of this article was presented at the first meeting of the project (Alcalá de Henares, December 1999), while the second and third parts were presented at the third meeting (Bologna, July 2000).

the Bologna school seems almost invariably to have had a hand in updating legislation produced prior to the *Decretum*, thus indicating that the University had a kind of permanent "observatory" ensuring the updating of the whole field of canon law.

Any description of the University of Bologna must include a mention of its students, who contributed decisively to the originality of the new schools, constituting a new social category that consolidated itself as the universities' role came increasingly into focus. The *universitas scholarium* had a special status based on the privileges which were bestowed in 1158 by Frederick I Barbarossa on the Bologna students and professors, which were subsequently confirmed by successive Emperors and Popes, and which constituted the legal foundation for the whole statutory tradition of the European universities.

While the University of Bologna gained rapid worldwide fame on the basis of its legal studies, the range of subjects taught broadened to take in literary and scientific disciplines, and eventually even theological courses. The medical faculty was particularly important. Its teaching staff included Thaddeus Alderottus, a specialist in Galen and Hippocrates; the anatomist Guglielmo da Saliceto; and Mondino de'Liuzzi, the author of an anatomical treaty *(Anatomia)* which was for centuries to remain the principal work of reference on the subject in the major European faculties.

In the thirteenth and sixteenth centuries the University of Bologna also played a pioneering role in the academic world by nurturing new establishments and proposing a series of statutes and regulations that provided the basis for the development of numerous universities. Bologna continued to recruit students from many different countries throughout the early modern period, and the renown of its schools attracted not only such young students as Copernicus but also such established figures as Erasmus of Rotterdam.

On the scientific and teaching front, the early modern period saw the decline of the law schools, which had remained true to their traditional methods. Philological studies and the exact and natural sciences began to take on greater importance, and the anatomical and surgical schools made considerable progress.

The doctrinal and political controversies of the sixteenth century inhibited cultural exchanges and thus encouraged the regionalisation process in the University of Bologna, a trend which intensified under the influence of the Thirty Years' War. It was not until the early eighteenth century that the first unequivocal signs were noted of a scientific and cultural revival, based primarily on the experimental method and the *libertas philosphandi*: the setting up of the Science Institute in 1714 at the prompting of Marsili and, remarkably, supported first by Clement XI and then by Benedict XIV, gave decisive impetus to cultural and scientific life in the city and reinvigorated the University.

The first degree conferred on a woman, Laura Bassi, was the sign of an irreversible turning point.

134

The Institute adopted the latest research methods and trends and divided them up into the following sectors: sciences, astronomy, mechanics, experimental physics, natural history, chemistry, optics, military architecture, geography, nautical science, gynaecology, anatomy and surgery. Each sector was excellently equipped and possessed modern instrumentation which prompted renewed interest from foreign observers. Charles de Brosses visited the Institute's collection in 1739 and pronounced it the most interesting in Europe at the time, and thanks to the Institute's scientific studies and laboratories Bologna once again benefited from intensive cultural exchanges with the other scientific research centres.

The scientific renewal movement prompted by the Enlightenment lent fresh prestige to the University of Bologna, which Napoleon designated as one of the two main seats of the university system of the Republic, later to become the Kingdom, of Italy. The city's decline during the Restoration period was accompanied by the gradual impoverishment of the university, and it was not until after Italian unification that it recovered the leading role that it had occupied for centuries.

Nowadays, with 103 000 students, Bologna is the second largest Italian university, and holds a unique position within the Italian university system. Nine centuries of academic activity constitute an extremely important heritage, and it is precisely in its own past that Bologna has rediscovered a specific role and mission in the current university set-up.

During the Middle Ages the University of Bologna fostered the understanding and integration of European cultures thanks to the presence of students and teachers from a variety of origins, who were granted intellectual freedom in their research ventures at Bologna. Now, nine centuries later, our University has decided to retrace its own history with a view to triggering a resurgence of European cultural unity.

This initiative was launched at about the same time as the Erasmus Project, and was based on a consensus that removing political barriers and customs frontiers was insufficient to ensure full unity among the European countries. The nations of Europe had and have to be placed in a position to understand themselves, to share a common destiny, and to recover and enhance our shared cultural heritage, which is very obviously deeply rooted in our European awareness.

The whole university has a frontline role to play in this project, educating new generations for integration of the European peoples, concentrating on young, lively intellects. The university, as the top cultural institution, has the onerous task of implementing an educational approach capable of promoting a European awareness that is the *sine qua non* for creating a Europe of the peoples and the citizens. For all these reasons, the University of Bologna decided to produce a kind of university *magna charta* incorporating and affirming the basic values of autonomy and freedom of research by providing pointers to the appropriate present and future options and thus helping inaugurate a cultural Europe.

On 18 September 1988, during the main ceremony for the 9th Centenary of the University of Bologna, several hundred university rectors from Europe and elsewhere signed the *Magna Charta Universitatum*, which had been drawn up by a committee consisting of the Rectors of the Universities of Bologna, Paris-Sorbonne, Louvain, Utrecht and Barcelona and the President of the CRE.[2] In June 1999, it was in this spirit that the University of Bologna hosted the meeting of European Ministers of Education. This even was an active contribution to the process of unifying the European university system, which provides for standardising curricula and academic degrees, aims which have been legitimated by past experience.

The next phase, which is currently being prepared, will be to set up a European observatory of academic freedoms in our university, aimed at guaranteeing protection for anyone noting infringements of certain inalienable rights in the university framework, ie the right to study and freedom of teaching and research.

This endeavour is directly in line with our academic past.

**The Student Museum**

On 12 October the first two halls of the Student Museum will be opened,[3] and the whole structure should be operational by the first quarter of 2001. The museum, which our rector agreed to house in a section of the university's *Palazzo Centrale* museum, was designed by a number of specialists and a whole host of enthusiastic volunteers, with financial assistance from the university. As the oldest European university and the headquarters of the first *universitas scholarium* (university taking in lay students) in the world, the *Alma Mater Studiorum* decided to promote a cultural initiative to encourage study and knowledge of the student world, capable of evolving into a permanent documentation centre on the history of the European student.

The plan for the museum emerged about ten years ago when a number of historians who were studying the university student phenomenon met up with some representatives of associations of former students. The initial idea necessitated specifying the aim to be attained: after the original hypothesis of an exhibition of items dating back to last century's *goliardia* (students' associations), a more ambitious objective came to fruition, namely a permanent museum centring on the student figure from the beginnings of the university to the present day, with particular stress on the European experience. In order to deepen our knowledge we held a series of seminars and colloquies, the first results of which, including the volume *Gaudeamus igitur* and the study by A. Mola on the international student association *Corda Fratres,* are already available, with further publications following hot on their heels.

The question naturally arises: what is the current importance of the history of students in the eyes of historians of collective attitudes, political scientists, specialists in the formation of the ruling classes and historians of customs, manners and society? Another question we have addressed is how best to circumscribe the

---

2. Publisher's note: on 31 March 2001 the CRE – Association of European Universities and the Confederation of European Union Rectors' Conferences merged to form the European University Association (EUA).
3. Publisher's note: the inauguration took place on 12 October 2000.

student identity in a manner that is necessarily a representative summary. There are many precedents for university museums with sections on the student presence (from Leipzig through Utrecht to Würzburg), but we felt that none of these adequately portrayed the whole student phenomenon.

We also knew that we would be judged by the academics, who would then decide whether or not to support our aims. We remembered how Charles Haskins had begun his introductory speech at a conference on the mediaeval student: "university would be a most pleasant place if it weren't for the students", he said, reflecting the majority view of his professorial colleagues. Haskins' observation was more than a mere rhetorical device, and we know that this opinion was still applauded seventy years later. The extensive historiographical lacunae that can be noted in the numerous tomes of university history implicitly confirmed this fact. The students themselves have often helped maintain this point of view: they have always liked to promote a self-image exaggerating the more wayward aspects of their existence. This attitude, which stems from the basic solidarity of youthful friendships, has helped maintain the image of students as a "potentially dangerous class", an opinion which has gained momentum at a time of mass university admission and widespread student protests. Personally we had already weighed up these points of view and did not feel unduly influenced by them.

On the other hand, we did ponder the appropriateness of the museum formula: the very word "museum" is redolent of the past, and to the common mortal suggests the idea of something established and defined in human knowledge and in the function assigned to it scientifically. The student condition is a transitional phase in an individual's life, an age that leaves few traces that can be used as museum exhibits. We also know that many forms of youth behaviour are generated in order to join a group, to reinforce this group's identity and strengthen its solidarity. Seen from the outside these forms of conduct often take on a meaning that the person originating them would never have recognised.

The concepts of research laboratory or documentation centre might possibly have been more appropriate, but we eventually opted for "museum" because it assigned the student figure the respect it merits as an essential component of the university world.

Finally, there was a consensus that this museum should be located in Bologna, where students, for the first time in history, secured an autonomous organisational structure, a system of self-government thanks to the regular election of rectors, who were also students and who were for centuries the supreme authority of the *Studium*. It is also the origin of the myth of student power as proclaimed by students during the events of 1968. This is the origin of some of the basic features of the student identity which has come down to us through its continual metamorphoses and adaptations. The museum as we saw it was to highlight not only this leitmotiv stressing the continuity in student history, but also the differences emerging over time in the various countries and universities, throughout nine centuries of university life.

We did not stop in the face of the many difficulties we encountered, as we were increasingly convinced that our aim could bring immediate institutional benefits. Restoring a collective memory that has often proceeded in fits and starts could guide the choices of those in daily contact with students.

The exhibits soon began to flood into the future museum's storage rooms thanks to the generosity of many benefactors and to purchases on antique markets throughout Europe. Concurrent work was carried out on the organisational aspects, especially on the guidelines for the requisite choices and the optimum means of representing a historiographical concept or pathway by selection and exhibition of a given item.

The first problem was a methodological one involving the categories of items to be collected. We began by defining a schematic profile of the student. The student emerged as a new social figure in the twelfth century, in Bologna, Paris and Oxford, and in 1158 was granted legal recognition by Frederick I Barbarossa, providing the basis for future dispositions by emperors, popes and sovereigns defining the student's identity and social status. For centuries the collective identity of this figure might be summarised as follows: the student is a young unmarried male person varying in age from adolescence (in the case of arts faculties) to adulthood (especially for theology). Regardless of his actual age, the student is "institutionally young", a condition which induces him to engage in conduct that might be described as "Rabelaisian", practical jokes, pranks and carnival disguises. Over the last two centuries this stereotype has changed considerably because of increasing female representation (women are now in the majority), the greater stability of this age bracket and the under-representation of foreigners in the student community.

Furthermore, the presence of the student as a figure has always been confined to urban societies, a status dictated by material and intellectual exigencies. The town was the ideal breeding ground for an increasingly secularised kind of knowledge. Now as then the urban environment facilitates encounters with other intellectuals, teachers or students from other schools with whom to exchange points of view and engage in ongoing comparison of experiences and ideas.

So students live in towns and cities. However, for several centuries they remained completely separate from the other urban social groups, particularly their own age bracket. For centuries students were a foreign body in the town, protected by laws, privileges and norms alien to the local customs. Some division between the student body and the urban population was therefore inevitable, and set the scene for potential "town and gown" conflict. This dividing line has survived in the collective subconscious, and even today it produces an aloof, sometimes suspicious attitude to students, albeit under circumstances very different from those prevailing in the past.

This led to the need for various forms of mutual aid, with specific regulations and a separate university judiciary to put up a common front in times of danger and tension which, often going beyond the anecdotal, repeatedly marked the history of this social group. Student associations (from the mediaeval *nationes* and *universitates* to the modern *Burschenschaften*) are extensively illustrated in the museum.

The relationship of conflict which has often subsisted between students and the authorities is another of the museum's central themes, including the gradual evolution of this aspect over time, culminating in the anonymous hero on Tiananmen Square.

There is nevertheless obvious continuity, even in the socialisation mechanisms, transcending any formal differences from era to era.

It emerges that students were generally immigrants, but from the sociological and cultural angles they were unlike most other immigrants in that they never lacked roots. Their group of belonging has always laid down its own social rules and produced original cultural expressions which identify all group members and with which they can identify, above and beyond the specific place where they make their provisional abode.

This "meta-language" is universal, shared by the whole student world regardless of territorial boundaries, facilitating student exchange. Moreover, this does not apply solely to the past, the era of *peregrinatio academica:* today it is still one of the preconditions for the success of student mobility programmes.

Student initiation rites are a classic example of these social rules. These rites have evolved over the ages in accordance with cultural changes, but some of them have deeply marked the whole of society.

I am thinking of the *depositio*, which is currently fashionable in various universities, and which used to consist of a specific "liturgy" as described in a series of printed booklets. The *matricola* (fresher) and *beanus* were considered as foul beasts who had to submit to a rite of purification: imaginatively reproduced horns, claws, manes and fangs were filed, cut and blunted. The novices had to gulp down large doses of salt and quaff considerable quantities of wine in order to purify their innards, celebrating their admission to the group. The metaphor of the "beast to be emancipated" highlights the esteem in which students hold their own special status and the group's "otherness" *vis-à-vis* the rest of society.

I think that even today all *goliardi* would recognise this ancient mediaeval ritual which continued up to the sixteenth century, the forerunner of a rite which the modern *goliardia* practised right up to very recent times.

I have gone into some detail on the ideas behind our preparatory work in order to show our determination to lay an accurate historiographical foundation for the museum.

However, founding a museum also involves selecting the exhibits, choosing an appropriate exhibition method and organising the establishment in accordance with the concepts to be transmitted.

Every generation of students and some individual student groups have produced their own symbols, their distinctive signs, but the transient nature of the student condition has made it difficult to preserve the evidence of these symbols.

Another task on which we are still working is to recover the traces and endeavour to interpret them. This operation will enable us to weave the fabric of continuity and change within which to describe the multiple expressions of student life. This article is not the place to analyse the hundreds of relics that we have collected on the basis of the thousands of testimonies that have come in from students of all eras. I shall simply mention a number of them in order to highlight their diversity: they range from paintings to statues, from posters to engravings, from diplomas to postcards and clothes, from codices illustrated with miniatures dating back to the thirteenth century to masses of silver and gold that belonged to a Renaissance student rector, symbolising his high office. Further items include a fifteenth-century register of students featuring Nicolaus Copernicus, a series of *libri amicorum* that belonged to various German students, a cockade made for two revolutionary students decorated with the colours of the future Italian national flag, films of mid-twentieth-century student parties and photographs and documentaries on the student protest years. There are also literary works, from Villon to Rabelais, plays, satirical and political journals, cartoons and musical compositions such as the *Carmina Burana, Carmina Cantabrigiensia* and the Montpellier Motets, right up to the 1930s, when student creativity, the students' capacity to innovate and anticipate on new cultural trends, was at its height.

Each exhibit was selected on the basis of its potential for representing modes of behaviour and cultural expression in the student world. Items from the nineteenth and twentieth centuries are obviously more abundant: traditional costumes (eg Spanish *Tunas* and the parade costumes of the German *Burschen*) and *mensur* (ritual duel) sabres. All the exhibits are objects and symbols with metaphorical qualities, created for use in specific, albeit temporary circumstances: the student who used these insignia or wore these costumes lived inside a system of living relations and contexts which must be appropriately interpreted and represented in the museum.

The establishment is to comprise a number of itineraries drawing on the students' social and institutional role to follow their development over nine centuries of history, stressing specific points in time or such particularly significant themes as student mobility (from the mediaeval wanderers to the Erasmus Project), relations with urban societies, initiation rites, relations with the authorities and political powers, student songs, theatre and poetry, the presence of women in the university, the themes of intellectual and then vocational training, the social components of the university, etc.

For the time being I would like just to show you the plan of the museum, which I hope you will be able to visit in the near future, just as I hope that in the coming years it will be possible to create a travelling exhibition based on our museum, touring all the capitals of European culture.

**The Historic Archives of the University of Bologna**

Bologna has one of the best university archives in Italy where both the continuity and completeness of the holdings and their intrinsic interest are concerned. The older university archives have experienced much adversity: dispersal, damage, theft, and even the destruction of some archives owing to wars, fires or earthquakes (as happened in Naples and Messina). Sometimes all trace has been lost of the earliest documentation (as in most universities where the Jesuits were active); furthermore, the documentation is usually stored on a site separate from the university: depending on the body responsible for university activities, it might be stored among the files of town halls, bishop's palaces, professional boards of lawyers, judges or physicians or ministerial departments responsible for supervising university activities. Italian unification and the incorporation of the universities of the pre-unification states into the new national university system was also a very difficult time for these documentary archives: many universities chose to hand over their earliest documentation to the newly created national archives, even though they were under no obligation to do so. Pending the establishment of universally applicable regulations, some of the archives were gradually absorbed by the Central Archives of the Kingdom of Italy, at first in Turin (where the files on our university dating back to the period of provisional government are stored) and subsequently in Rome, in the Central State Archives. This dispersal of historic documents regularly brings up the problem of whether the documents produced by the universities before Italian unification and stored in the national archives to the present day are being held on "transfer" or on "deposit". This is an important technical/legal point, because if the former is true the current situation is irrevocable, whereas in the latter case the storage order could be cancelled at the request of the university in question.

It must be said that in most cases the consignment of the universities' historic archives to the state vaults has safeguarded the earliest documentation, as the universities have not always been careful and competent enough to ensure the requisite conservation and protection. The situation varies greatly from one university to another, not only because of the size and value of the documentation in question but also in terms of the status of the various historic archives: most of them lack competent staff (university technical staff includes very few qualified archivists), while others have recruited "archivists" with dubious professional qualifications (eg librarians with a specialised diploma in archiving). The physical dimensions of the material directly conserved in the universities' historic archives are also an indication of the importance formerly attached to personal memories. The Ministry of Cultural Assets has so far conferred "particularly important" status on the archives of only three Italian universities, namely Bologna, Padua and Palermo. This is further direct evidence of the importance of the holdings and the state of conservation in which they have come down to us.

Let us now look at the specific situation in Bologna. The historic documents have been split into two sections. In 1892, all pre-unification documents, with very few exceptions, were handed over to the National Archives, where they are still held in a special separate section. On the other hand, the documents issued by the university in the post-unification period are stored in the University's Historic Archives. The archives have been reorganised as an educational and scientific resource centre, giving it the same degree of independence as a university department, with its own technical, administrative and auxiliary staff, its own budget, and its own director, who is backed by a scientific board and a management board responsible for programming the budget.

In connection with the specific qualifications required for managing "particularly important archives", the conditions of protection and operation in our archiving department are ideal thanks to its specialised staff and the board of scientific researchers responsible for planning the work. Of course there are some problems, including logistical and organisational obstacles to the scientific board's programmes. One of the problems is the fact that large sections of the historic archives are still stored in the place of issue of individual academic papers (this applies, for instance, to students' files, which are still held by the various Faculty offices), while other archives are in temporary storage in the various administrative sections, although this also applies to the archives consigned to individual research bodies (especially the documentation held by the Department of Astronomy, some items of which date back to the seventeenth century). Moreover, some documents were purchased on the antique market or were donated, including the historically unique archives of the German nation, which were donated to our university in 1956 and comprise documentation dating back to the thirteenth century. The latter consists of several codices richly illustrated with miniatures, and also such extremely interesting documents as register entries for students who were later to gain fame, eg Nicolaus Copernicus and the future Emperor Ferdinand II. The historic archives have a photographic annex with a number of collections of major historic and artistic value. There is also an architectural section, which is already one of the biggest in the whole sector in terms of documents collected.

Beyond these specific aspects, I would also like to mention a number of orientations which will have an immediate effect on the status and organisation of the Bologna historic archives and which also bear witness to the growing attention being paid to this issue at the international level. I would remind the reader that in 1992 the International Council on Archives set up a section on university archives that pools the various university resources with a view to tackling common problems.

In short, our University Archives department is in a constant state of flux, requiring new skills alongside the traditional specialisations: for instance, document conservation techniques must increasingly be combined with modern computer technologies. However, the main challenge is the exponential growth of the archives. According to the first results of an inventory we are currently running of all the historic archive sections scattered around the research offices and centres, five-and-a-half kilometres of shelving would be required to house all the documents. This is the most intractable problem facing our university on the archiving front. We must now take a number of long-term strategic options, because the foregoing comments have concerned the university as it was in 1960, that is to say with some 16 000 students and 630 teachers, assistants and technical, administrative and auxiliary staff. The historic archives department must now be adapted to the current state of the University of Bologna, with its 103 000 students and about 6 000 staff working as teachers or in other capacities.

This is a tricky matter, which will confront us with the problem of selecting and/or destroying papers as a matter of absolute priority, an area where the interests of historians and archivists are always liable to diverge.

142

In this connection, the option of appointing a history teacher to direct the historic archives was intended to stress one particular difference between such archives and those of any other organisation. I am referring to the special status of university historic archives which, unlike other archives, have persons qualified to exploit them on hand, namely teachers of archiving techniques, university historians and science historians. However, the archives are also increasingly being consulted by sociologists, economists and political scientists wishing to identify an historic context for their research endeavours. Accordingly, when providing the requisite instruments for this "laboratory", we must learn to look beyond the archives produced by academic institutions in the strict sense of the word "archive", to transcend the mere safeguarding of documents produced by the institution (minutes of the governing board's meetings, regulations, accountancy documents, student files, etc.), but also to understand the university in its original role as a centre dedicated to research (as described in the history of science), as a forum for organising encounters and promoting cultural life, and as an initial and further training institution. The university generates many complex associations and bodies which are hardly ever mentioned in the conventional archive documents (eg the university colleges and student and teacher associations in past centuries). We have tried to recover evidence of these associations for inclusion in our archives, creating an annex to contain scientific archives belonging to researchers who have worked in our university. In another connection, we have also taken systematic stock of documents from the Bologna university college archives, a project which has involved investigating many public and private archives from Brussels to Zagreb and from Vienna to Naples or Turin.

I would like to conclude by stressing that the university's historic archives must be seen as a research laboratory, in all the acceptations of the term, which means also considering their management and management strategy aspects. They are not a mere storage area for papers produced and received by the university, but rather a dynamic element, a growth factor capable of helping identify specific conditions and directions for the institution's further development. They should constitute an effective instrument for the university governing bodies and for anyone wishing to compare their research work with past experience. The historic archives must retain their whole institutional vitality, as a laboratory not only for historiographic research but also for learning about self-awareness and self-organisation. This is vital for an institution that is constantly seeking to strike new balances that are now dictated and governed by the principle of self-government, which derives its prerogatives and procedures for self-realisation precisely from its historic memory.

# The University of Coimbra and its traditions at the beginning of a new millennium[1]

*Maria da Fátima Silva*

Over the 710 years of its existence, the University of Coimbra has built up a collection of traditions that link up the various stages in its history. Today, these traditions constitute a precious heritage, an amalgam of age-old practices and innovations, or simply attempts to reconcile the two by an institution that is sensitive to its past yet looking eagerly forward, in a flexible frame of mind, to whatever the future may bring.

A brief summary of the decisive stages in the University of Coimbra's history is necessary if a number of its practices are to be made clear. At the close of a period during which the town had been a medieval political centre and the seat of government – the twelfth and thirteenth centuries – the University of Portugal, officially founded in 1290 by King Dom Dinis, entered the first phase of its existence. Although the university was originally established in Lisbon, it was moved to Coimbra a few years later, as the site seemed to offer obvious advantages as a place of study in addition to its central geographical position in the country. The first faculties of the Arts, Law, the Canons and Medicine date from this period. From its very beginnings in Coimbra in the fourteenth century, the university was involved in the huge religious advances made by the cathedral and, especially, Santa Cruz monastery, which was particularly active in the cultural and educational life of the city. This cultural activity was, in fact, a decisive element in obtaining royal approval.

After a number of successive moves back to Lisbon and then back again to Coimbra, the university finally settled in the town on the Mondego in 1537, where it occupied the old palace as it still does today. A long period then followed, from the Renaissance to the nineteenth century, during which the town became the leading university centre of Portugal. While the university was establishing itself and a number of colleges were being built around the old palace, a reform of the curriculum was undertaken, an attempt was made to renew the educational activity of the Church and the most distinguished and stimulating thinkers in Europe were encouraged to teach there.

However, this long period of four centuries was marked by contrasting climates: an initial period of liveliness followed by a state of crisis and monotony, for which the Portuguese Inquisition was largely responsible. This state of affairs was finally brought to an end in the eighteenth century by the Court, through the famous minister of the realm, the Marquis of Pombal. The so-called Pombaline reform curbed the Jesuits' influence on the university, while the curriculum was modernised, with a marked priority being given to the exact sciences, which until then had been far from receiving the academy's favours. This reform led to a great

---

1. Article submitted to the third meeting of the project (Bologna, July 2000).

deal of building work: the Physics Room, the Natural History Museum and the Chemistry Laboratory, among others, all of which are now part of the university's remarkable architectural heritage.

In the last century, the Coimbra Academy had to face domestic competition resulting from the founding of several other schools of higher education, after the universities of Lisbon and Oporto, and all the events that marked the political and social history of the country. But the new conditions that were imposed on the University of Coimbra, which had for centuries been the only Portuguese university, also helped to give it its unique identity and made its ancestral practices and traditions an undisputed model for all its Portuguese rivals.

Three main forces forged the University of Coimbra's identity over the seven centuries of its existence: the Court, which left an obvious mark on the buildings that are still used and their decoration, and determined the successive reforms of the schools' curricula; the Church, which had a decisive influence on the university's cultural development and many of its traditions; and, lastly, international contributions, which for centuries opened the university to outside influences, made it a partner of other European institutions and guaranteed its vitality and constant modernisation.

The celebrations and ceremonies that yearly renew the university's bonds with its traditional calendar of events and are an integral part of university life – what are called the *praxe*, a term that covers all the customs that illustrate the unique experience of belonging to the university community over the centuries – can be divided into two categories: institutional customs, so called because they were introduced by the university authorities, and events organised by the students' association. Both categories of events are also civic celebrations, although in different ways, because the town, in particular, and representatives of other universities, and even of the Portuguese government, take part.

Let us begin with occasions of an institutional nature, among which attention should be drawn to the celebrations that accompany the solemn opening of the academic year in October, and the *honoris causa* doctorates that are frequently conferred, though at no particular time of year. What is notable about these ceremonies, apart from the speeches giving accounts of the previous years' activities and plans for the year that is just beginning in the first case, or eulogies of the new doctor and his or her paranymph in the second, is their visual aspect. Both events require that the lecturers wear their ceremonial costumes, that is to say their *capa* and *batina*, with their elaborately embroidered and colourful insignia, and their *borla* and *capelo*. As everyone knows, each faculty can be identified by its colours. At these university ceremonies, the rector, as president of all the colleges, must abstain from wearing the colours of his own faculty and appear only in plain black academic dress. The whole university community – the rector, the lecturers and their distinguished guests (representatives of other universities, candidates for *honoris causa* doctorates and members of the government) – forms a procession in the old library or one of the rooms of the rector's office, depending on the specific circumstances, and sets off for the deeds room. The procession is accompanied by university guards and the *charamela*, a band of musicians playing traditional tunes. The order in which the

146

different groups take their places depends on the seniority of the faculty and, within each faculty, the hierarchy of professors. This means that the rector takes his place in the upper gallery, with the professors of the Arts Faculty, the oldest faculty, on his right and those of the Faculty of Law, the second oldest, on his left. They are followed by the professors of Medicine and Science, who represent the university's beginnings and its development through to the eighteenth century. Then come the three recent Faculties of Pharmacy, Economics and Psychology, and, last of all, the Faculty of Sports Sciences.

The solemn doctorate award ceremony in particular has a ritual that has preserved some of the ingredients of medieval chivalry: the *borla* is placed on the candidate's head in the presence of a page and a paranymph, a ring is placed on his or her finger and then he or she fraternally embraces each lecturer in turn. Furthermore, some of the ritual phrases pronounced at points in the ceremony are still in Latin. Many scientists working in the most varied specialist fields and public political figures have, over the years, been rewarded with this distinction, which is also a major element of prestige for the university.

The students also have their own celebrations, especially at the beginning and end of the academic year. Today, the beginning of the academic year is greeted with a range of events in the individual faculties and a joint party for the new students, which has all the characteristics of an initiation ceremony whose origins are centuries old. The oldest students gather in organised groups, called troupes, and engage in some of the practices that marked academic life in the Middle Ages to welcome the new students and guide them through their first steps in the, to them, unknown universe of the Academy, but also to punish the "offences" committed by the newcomers as is the university guards' traditional prerogative. Misconduct such as walking in the streets after it is fitting that students should be at home (6 p.m. according to a code that is considerably dated!), or wearing the students' costume in some non-regulation manner (with brown stockings instead of the traditional black, for instance) could meet with punishment like having one's hair cut or one's fingernails rapped. A whole range of practices by which a student's status could be identified according to his or her place in the university hierarchy has been almost completely forgotten, except for those that mark special occasions in the university calendar, like the beginning and end of the academic year, and only serve as a means of entertainment. However, the official code of the *praxe* can still be consulted in a volume that dates from the eighteenth century, *The metric toothpick*, or, in a more recent version dating from the middle of the last century, *The Praxe Code*. A scholar's costume of medieval design and occasional examples of application of the *praxe* code are the last remaining vestiges of an ancient tradition.

October, the month when the new students arrive and the year's studies begin, is also the time when one of the most significant student celebrations is held, the *latadas*. The word comes from the Portuguese word *lata*, which means tin and, by extension, tin cans and boxes, the sound of which has signalled the arrival of new students and the beginning of university activities since the middle of the twentieth century. Before that, the tradition was that, on the contrary, these sounds should signal the end of lectures and accompany another ceremony that remains famous today and still marks the end of the university year, the burning of the ribbons. The *latadas* go at least as far back as the middle of the nineteenth century, although some sources claim that they date back as far as the sixteenth century, when noisy events were forbidden by the king. On *latadas* day, the students form a procession, the older students wearing their scholar's costumes and the new students, or *caloiros*, dressed in ridiculous clothing according to the imagination and whim of their seniors and dragging tin objects behind them, walk through the main streets, where curious townspeople gather to watch the young people's celebrations. There is singing and general high spirits, and students carry placards bearing slogans taunting their lecturers or satirising prominent national and international political or social events. At times when the political situation is particularly difficult, as it was during the Salazar government in the mid-twentieth century, or when an educational reform policy is being challenged, these slogans can be extremely scathing.

The close of the academic year is also celebrated in solemn fashion, which in student terms means gaily and irreverently. Events of a more personal nature take place when students reach the end of their courses. As soon as they have passed their last exam, their comrades tear their costumes to shreds in public, leaving the students wearing only their *capa*. This practice seems to have existed for at least a century, but it is not known exactly when it originated.

The end of lectures is also the time when the biggest annual student celebration is held: the *Queima das Fitas*, the burning of the ribbons, which takes place every May before the exams. All the other Portuguese universities have more or less faithfully adopted this practice, imitating Coimbra's tradition without attaining its authenticity. At the end of the nineteenth century when it began, the celebration took the form of a *tourada* in a square on the university campus in which the part of the bulls was played by the *caloiros*, after which the ribbons were burnt in a chamber pot to symbolise that a stage in the students' lives was over. These narrow ribbons were used to bind books, papers or the famous *sebenta* at a time when few could afford portfolios. Burning them marked the successful completion of a first stage of university studies, the award of the baccalaureate, which was followed by a final year during which students were entitled to carry the portfolio of honour, with its much wider silk ribbons, some of which were highly decorated as can be seen from the examples on show in the university museum. By 1904, however, the *tourada* had become a real *tourada*, in which the animals faced spontaneous performers, the students themselves. At the same time, the celebration began to grow longer, spreading over several days and involving a whole range of cultural and sports activities and concerts. It now lasts for seven days and all the branches and bodies that make up the Students' Academic Association help to organise it.

It has to be acknowledged that this collection of cultural events is not the first of its kind. The nineteenth century already had its regular *Récita de Despedida*, meaning final performance, which was devised, written and performed by final year students and belonged to a longstanding theatrical tradition in the university. This tradition continues in the form of today's *tourada* and ribbon-burning ceremony. A procession has been held since 1899 and is the most famous and public event in the programme. Coimbra is filled with visitors from all over the country and abroad at a time of year when the town is already enjoying a certain amount of tourism. The presence of delegations from other Portuguese and foreign universities, especially from neighbouring Spain or even – in this year celebrating the discovery of Brazil – from South America, and of former students of all generations with their families and friends is the general rule. Normal daily life in Coimbra comes to a halt on this day, when its inhabitants fill the streets to cheer their students. After burning their ribbons in their respective faculties, the students walk through the streets or drive through them in cars decorated with the colours and symbols of each faculty.

Placards taunting the university lecturers or parodying current events are to be seen everywhere. The students and townspeople thronging the pavements exchange flowers or traditional souvenirs of the occasion, typical examples being booklets containing descriptions and caricatures of all the final year students in each faculty, a tradition that dates back to 1912. Inevitably, a number of former students, some of whom are now quite elderly, join in, their decorated cars leading the procession. The opening of the festivities is a very special moment: a serenade on the cathedral steps attended by a crowd that fills the surrounding square. Old *fados* are sung and guitars are played in the traditional Coimbra style.

The pleasure of singing in the streets at night is one of the old traditions of student life. Songs are sung in tribute to a lady, a fiancée, or simply for the sake of sharing a few moments' relaxation with comrades. Although modern living conditions do not lend themselves easily to traditions of this sort, they are still observed occasionally. Songs are also sung at celebrations, or as a tourist attraction, especially during the summer programme of events. But the songs known today as Coimbra *fados* only appeared in the nineteenth century. They are somewhat melancholic songs that generally tell of love, of student life in Coimbra, the town and its surroundings (the river and the places traditionally frequented by students) and the sadness of leaving. *Fados* are sung by male voices only, accompanied by a guitar. The first great *fado* singer was Hilario in the second half of the nineteenth century, and the tradition has gone from strength to strength since then. And although the essential quality and tone of the *fado* is still present, it is also true to say that since the 1950s, new life has been breathed into it by a number of innovators, in particular José Afonso. He lived in Coimbra during the university crisis years and used his songs to deliver political and social messages from the early 1960s.

The *fados* also bear witness to the fact that most Portuguese writers and poets spent some time in Coimbra, where they were filled with inspiration and left traces of their stay. From the Middle Ages on, to Camões and Antero de Quental, António Nobre, and, very recently, Manuel Alegre, to mention only a few of the most outstanding among them, Coimbra has sung through the voices of its poets, who are also the nation's voices. The music has been subject to a number of changes since the beginning of the twentieth century without losing its unique tone that is passed on from one generation to the next.

A few words should be said about the Coimbra Academic Association, founded in 1887, which over the years has become the hub of student life. Besides its sports clubs, especially football, which have made it famous throughout the country, it comprises prestigious cultural groups, the most notable being the "Academic Orpheon" – the Coimbra choir, which has celebrated its first centenary – the Students' Theatre (TEUC), the *Tuna*, or orchestra (TAUC), the Group of

Ethnography and Folklore of the Academy of Coimbra (GEFAC), the Fado Club, and many others. The various activities they conduct throughout the year depending on the circumstances and occasions, in addition to the special events they organise for the major celebrations, have made them popular both in the town and all over the country. As a result of the international contacts they have established, and which increase with every passing day, they have become important ambassadors for the university's activities today.

It is obvious from this summary of the university's celebrations that the nineteenth century was an important period. Although the Coimbra university community already knew that many of its customs dated back to the early days, it was during the second half of the nineteenth century especially that a range of events began to be held regularly and extend to the university as a whole.

All these century-old events, the fundamental purpose of which is to mark the major stages in the university year, calling upon the talents of the creators of the most significant forms of expression of university life, are sometimes supplemented by new initiatives, as is only right and proper for an institution that wishes to remain lively and creative. Another event that was launched only recently, but whose future is promising, is the Cultural Week held in March, a month when all the university bodies are particularly active. The aim of this event is to involve the whole community and give demonstrations in the university, the town and throughout the country of the cultural activities that are part of the university's daily life. It also celebrates the anniversary of the foundation of the university on 1 March. The programme for the week's events, which are open to the public free of charge, includes contributions from the artistic groups of the Coimbra Academic Association, the faculties, museums and all the other university bodies. All the events are co-ordinated by the Rector's office and make up a varied programme of information meetings, exhibitions, theatrical and musical performances, guided tours, competitions and prizes for creativity, which help to bring the cultural world and the general public closer together.

One institution bears witness to all this heritage, which survives in the Portuguese people's memory and thanks to its active participation: the Coimbra Academic Museum, the only museum of its kind in the country. Run jointly by the Rector's office and the directorates of the Academic Association and the University of Coimbra Former Students' Association, the museum is the home of a vast collection of material and objects that document the most varied aspects of university life. The collections are mainly the result of private gifts and each is in some way unique. As well as offering the Portuguese public and foreign visitors an interesting journey through the university's past, the museum possesses documents that are of use to scientific research on several aspects of the country's university life and society.

In conclusion, I should like to quote a few words that a poet who is well known in modern Portugal (Eugénio de Castro) dedicated to Coimbra and which, in my opinion, aptly describe the town's character:

"Coimbra is like certain women who, having suffered the worst ravages of time and destiny, preserve in their old age traces of the beauty, which, as young women, they obviously possessed."

# The medieval university: the example of Montpellier

*Béatrice Bakhouche*

To address the subject of the intellectual heritage of universities during the Europe, a Common Heritage Campaign, which saw the creation of the Ancient Universities Route, I thought it would be a good idea to return to the beginnings, ie the emergence of the universities in the Middle Ages, for our image of that era is inaccurate, and solid links were forged in the Middle Ages with other European centres, some of which are represented here today.

The first universities date from the beginning of the thirteenth century. The emergence of these new institutions went hand in hand with a new socio-economic development, and while it is true that the differences between universities are linked to a specific social context, it will be interesting to consider the specificity of Montpellier University in its early days[1] before moving on to our plan to highlight our intellectual and cultural heritage.

It should be noted, first of all, that the old curricula of the Carolingian reformers, focused on the liberal arts (literary and scientific disciplines) and on religious studies, were upset by the renaissance of the twelfth century when, from around 1130 onwards, a flurry of translation from Arabic and Greek opened up vast swaths of previously unknown Greek culture. Then the generally buoyant economic and social situation led to the emergence of new disciplines, such as law. Meanwhile the monastic schools were in decline, giving way to the cathedral schools, which sprang up, from the end of the eleventh century. New schools like the canonical schools were also open to outside students, but there were far fewer of them in the south of France.

## Montpellier before the university

Arts schools probably existed (teaching literature and rudiments of philosophy), as did scripture schools like the one where Alain de Lille taught around 1190 during his stay in Montpellier. The most original, however, were the secular schools of law and medicine.

In law a founding role was traditionally attributed to various exiled doctors who came from Bologna to teach in Montpellier. In fact, the very presence of Rogerius in Provence and Lower Languedoc around 1162 is purely hypothetical. And although Placentin, another legist from Bologna, taught in Montpellier in 1166 and 1192, there is no evidence that he founded a lasting school. Lesser known native teachers, trained in Italy, may have taught law periodically at about that time or even earlier (around 1130) in various towns of south-east France. There is no trace, however, of an institutionalised tradition of law teaching.

---

1. Based on the book by J. Verger, *Histoire des Universités en France*, Paris, 1999.

In the medical field, in contrast, from 1137 onwards Montpellier enjoyed a reputation as a centre of teaching and treatment (although it was less well regarded than Salerno in southern Italy). While the city may conceivably have served as a centre for contacts with the Jewish doctors in the region and with neighbouring Muslim Spain, we do not know how the teaching was organised. We do know, however, that several of the first Christian doctors known to have worked in Montpellier were trained in Salerno. The first written reference was the charter of Count Guilhem VIII, dated 1181, stating that no one could be granted a monopoly on the teaching of medicine in Montpellier. This meant that anyone who so wished could open a school, indicating that there was already a well-established tradition.

The new economic and social context was conducive to an open outlook towards the outside world, as a result of which "private" schools flourished in the twelfth century, often poorly controlled by the civil or church authorities. They were pleased to serve as privileged homes for the newly translated texts and for disciplines – such as dialectics, law and medicine – that were generally viewed with suspicion. This denotes a thirst for knowledge, a great curiosity that the master, often an itinerant scholar, tried to satisfy. While certain centres that shone before 1150 subsequently declined, others, like Montpellier, continued to thrive, as the major centres of learning tended to develop in places where urban growth was particularly dynamic. The main cities of southern France were open to exchanges with Italian and Spanish thinking. One should also bear in mind the cultural specificity of southern France, not only in terms of Occitan language and literature but also in scientific learning. From the twelfth century, under the influence of local or non-local legists, all trained in Italy, Roman law began to compete with local custom, imposing its procedures and its vocabulary, penetrating ever deeper into the very fabric of social relations.

The Church soon reacted to these schools, which escaped its authority. Pope Alexander III generalised the term "licence", or authorisation to teach *(licentia docendi),* which the "scholaster" or his equivalent issued to any teacher wishing to open a school in the diocese. In this way the Church controlled the opening of new schools, but the schools of law and medicine in the south of France were secular schools and consequently outside its reach. The lack of control and harmonisation was a danger, however. The birth of the university seemed like a sensible, lasting solution.

**The University of Montpellier**

For most of the thirteenth century there was no real higher education or university to speak of in Montpellier except in medicine. In 1220 Cardinal-legate Conrad granted "the University of doctors, both masters and students, of Montpellier" statutes which doubtless merely endorsed the existing situation, indicating a fully-fledged institution which had perhaps existed since the beginning of the century: the licensing system was introduced for medical schools, requiring all applicants to spend a prior six-month period with a local practitioner, and the duty of mutual defence and assistance that linked masters and students was officially acknowledged. The statutes concerned (which formed the institutional framework for universities until the end of the Middle Ages) introduced the post of dean, responsible for organising the teaching, and placed the University of Medicine under the protection and jurisdiction of the Church. So it was the bishop of Maguelone or his representative, the chancellor (chosen, it is true, from among the doctors), who issued the licence and judged the members of the University, whose status changed from that of laymen to clerics, symbolised by the wearing of the tonsure. This is a very clear illustration of the popes' determination in the early thirteenth century to extend their control over the whole university world.

For a long time the other schools in Montpellier were much less well organised and were barely distinguishable from all those, active and not so active, that existed in the different cities of southern France. Theology was taught only in the mendicant convents and the priory founded in Montpellier by the Cistercians of Valmagne. In 1242 the arts schools were issued with deceptively fine-sounding statutes by the bishop of Maguelone, very different from those of the medical university. Unlike legists, doctors considered it essential that their students should previously have studied the arts. They were too convinced of the importance of the epistemological links between the "arts", particularly natural philosophy, and medicine to dispense their students from training in the arts. Many doctors in Montpellier in fact held masters degrees in the arts, and not necessarily from Montpellier. In spite of this, it is unlikely that the statutes of 1242 sufficed within a short period to turn the very modest schools of grammar and the arts that existed in Montpellier at the time into real faculties.

In law teaching the situation long remained the same as in the twelfth century, ie legists held an increasing role in society, introducing Roman law to the detriment of custom and even occasionally producing knowledgeable and relatively original commentaries on the *Corpus iuris civilis*, but without creating any regular teaching of law. Although they were of local origin, they were almost all trained in Bologna. When they returned home they would occasionally, at their own initiative or at the request of a lord or a city, give a few lessons in law; examples of "law schools" are documented here and there, such as Bertrand Dorne's *studium* in Montpellier. For a long time, however, none of these schools were regular or illustrious enough to rise to University rank. Only in the last third of the thirteenth century in Montpellier, a political and economic capital, did the group of doctors of law grow large enough to provide regular classes, form a university-type community and obtain privileges from the higher authorities that signalled official acknowledgment. A university of law was established in the last decade of the thirteenth century and the arts schools more or less became a part of it. The university soon prospered, around 1300, with renowned teachers lecturing on a permanent or less regular basis: in canon law, Bertrand de Deaux, Pierre Bertrand and Jesselin de Cassagnes; in civil law, Pierre Jame d'Aurillac, Guillaume de Nogaret and Guillaume de Plaisians (the future "legists" of Philippe le Bel). The statutes of 1339 placed the running of the university in the hands of a rector and twelve councillors, elected by the nations (Catalonia, Provence, Burgundy), who could not (in theory) be doctors.

The development of the universities in Montpellier at the end of the thirteenth century doubtless precipitated the decline of neighbouring centres, like Béziers or Narbonne, where a certain amount of teaching may have gone on at some stage during the thirteenth century. In the fourteenth century, as more new universities were created, like the one in Perpignan in the kingdom of Aragon (1350), the universities came increasingly under the control of the civil authorities rather than the Church. They all tended to conform to the same institutional pattern and to privilege the teaching of law. The French university network was also strengthened in the late Middle Ages by the opening of new schools of theology: Toulouse in 1360, Avignon in 1413 and Montpellier in 1421, in an effort to end the monopoly, which Paris had enjoyed until then.

## Courses and careers

The arts faculties (which were the least well known and the least prestigious) in principle taught grammar and the "arts", ie logic and a little philosophy, and were intended for students from 14 to 20-years-old, while the higher faculties were for men aged 20 to 25. Doctorates usually came later, and in theory one had to be 35 years old to be a master of theology in Paris.

The precise mandatory duration of courses was set in the statutes. It was generally long: ten to thirteen years for a degree in civil law, and ten to eleven years for one in canon law. Medical studies were shorter – five to six years in Montpellier – but, unlike law students, medical students were required to have studied the arts first. In practice the length of studies varied at the master's discretion.

Students, like teachers, were not necessarily recruited locally, far from it. Staff and students at the university of medicine, although modest in number even in its heyday, came from far afield. In 1378, for example, the fifty-six masters and students came in more or less equal proportions from the southern half of the Kingdom of France (naturally enough), from the Low Countries and from Germany and Prussia (seventeen, ten and ten respectively). Another nine came from Spain, three from the north of France, and the origin of the remaining seven is unknown. It is quite plausible that certain brilliant German, Dutch and Spanish doctors were trained in Montpellier.

Having completed one's studies, what did one do with a degree in the Middle Ages? The university's main role was to contribute to the training of leading administrators and judges, who played an increasingly important role as the monarchy grew stronger and bureaucracy took hold of the Church.

The Avignon Popes (who had all studied and sometimes taught theology or law) were systematically favourable to the universities in their policies, particularly those in the south of France. In Montpellier, for example, they founded various colleges, including Saint Benoît and the "Douze médecins", founded in 1368-69 by Urban V. The most eminent of the pontifical legists assembled at the Hearing of Causes of the apostolic palace, the "Rota", the supreme court of the Roman Catholic Church. And many bishops and their auxiliaries had studied at university.

In the civil sphere, particularly in southern France, people with university degrees could work for the cities, teach or engage in private activities.

Doctors could combine medical and teaching activities. Surprisingly, however, developing their private practice does not seem to have been the main concern of many doctors in Montpellier. They preferred either to teach or to serve as court physicians. The popes and cardinals in Avignon attracted them in large numbers in the fourteenth century, mainly on a full-time basis and mostly from Montpellier. This partly explains the prominence of Montpellier at the time. From Arnaud de Villeneuve to Jean de Tournemire, through Guy de Chauliac and Jean Jacme, Montpellier's most famous regents of the day placed themselves at the service of the popes.

Doctors from far-off lands could also have successful local careers, like Jacques Rotschild, known as *Angeli*, from Kolberg in Pomerania, who was chancellor of the university from 1433 to 1455, wrote a medical encyclopaedia and several treatises, was interested in alchemy and the occult sciences and, when he died, left his sons Jean, a doctor of law, and Antoine, a physician, a sizeable fortune in real estate.

**Yesterday and today**

And so the university went on. It has developed and changed over the centuries but has it changed beyond all recognition? Not really. It still faces the same problems.

From *licentia docendi* to doctorate, diploma, master's degree, the names change but not the underlying realities. Paradoxically, the mediaeval university I have briefly described above could serve as a model of student and teacher mobility. Nowadays we need programmes like Erasmus and Socrates to attract our (all too sedentary) students to new pastures. Students were much more mobile in the Middle Ages! The mediaeval dynamic contrasts with modern-day immobility, or at least a tendency to compartmentalise knowledge that is prejudicial to its circulation.

What attitude should we take towards yesterday's university model? We should make the most of the heritage that lies hidden in our libraries, so as better to grasp how knowledge has evolved.

If we look at the Middle Ages alone, the intellectual heritage is meagre, it is true, as far as the faculty of arts is concerned, whose masters hardly left any trace. If Ramón Llull taught, and wrote some of his key works on logic, during his various stays in Montpellier, this was more likely to have been in the convents than in the university's schools of the arts. The medical university, on the other hand, as we have said, was renowned and scientifically advanced, as witnessed by the extensive writings left by its members: the works of sixty Montpellier doctors have come down to us over the centuries.

The institutional characteristics of the university have been highlighted, as has its general historical development, but so far little has been said about its intellectual heritage proper. While it is true that we do not have all the works of all the mediaeval masters, the Medical School Library, the Municipal Library, the Archives and even the Inter-University Library have enough works in stock to warrant a research programme spanning several years!

The broader culture of the university masters, extending far beyond the limits of the disciplines in which they specialised, is also worth studying through their writings. Most of their texts have yet to be published – preferably in two languages – in order to reveal the taste these men of yesteryear had for philosophy in particular and also for esotericism (alchemy, astrology, etc.). The study of their libraries would also be very revealing. These are all paths researchers could follow up.

This research into and highlighting of the heritage should not be confined to the Middle Ages or to Montpellier, however. In view of the relations forged from the outset with other centres, and the origins of certain academics, it would be interesting to tighten the links between the old universities of the Mediterranean arc in order to derive maximum benefit from what is largely a common heritage.

Today a group of academics from the three modern-day universities in Montpellier is setting up a research programme on "memory and heritage", to study the intellectual heritage from the mediaeval university onwards, ie the transmission and transformation of knowledge through the four main branches of learning – theology, medicine, law and the arts (in the sense of the "liberal arts", making it possible to incorporate the three traditional dimensions of literature, science and philosophy).

With this research the Ancient Universities Route would not be a route to travel without stopping, but on the contrary an opportunity to get to know one another and pool our complementary resources. It is quite obvious that the spotlight cannot be turned onto our intellectual heritage without the co-operation, in particular, but not exclusively, of Bologna and Spain.

# The European dimension of the historical heritage of the University of Santiago de Compostela: a view from Santiago de Compostela[1]

*Antonio López Díaz*

Before considering the European dimension of the historical heritage of the University of Santiago de Compostela we must first be clear about what we mean by Europe. Europe can be considered as a great mosaic where numerous cultures, religions and peoples live side by side. Certain basic principles common to all those who compose the European identity are superimposed on this cultural, ethnic and religious plurality. They include democracy, pluralism, tolerance and respect for minorities.

This picture of Europe has been arrived at without a doubt by constant exchange and mobility conducive to such a fusion of cultures, faiths and ethnic groups. Like the pilgrimage to Santiago de Compostela, building Europe was a step-by-step process and now new information and communication technologies are opening up new channels for the ongoing exchanges that are the essence of Europe.

In this process of cultural fusion, the European universities have played, and continue to play, a major role as beacons beaming out the cultures of the host societies in their different forms (language, art, etc.). This role as living witnesses to different cultures becomes all the more important in the case of an institution that has existed since the Middle Ages, that has witnessed the birth of states and still looks on today at the sweeping changes affecting civil society as the supranational integration process gathers momentum. The University as an institution and, in particular, broad-spectrum universities, as the oldest civil institutions, are vast repositories containing the traces of all the different stages through which the surrounding cultures have passed.

Europe is the result of dialogue between cultures. More than mere cultural warehouses, universities have been instrumental in disseminating culture. Exchanging ideas has always been at the root of progress in human knowledge. This is why the universities, which generated the knowledge, have always encouraged communication between their members. These exchanges and the dissemination of culture were revolutionised when printing was invented and books became widely available, and they are undergoing a new revolution today with the development of the new information and communication technologies, with universities once again spearheading the process as pioneers of innovation.

The new technologies are also providing new channels – such as networking – for the cultural dialogue between universities that is at the heart of the European idea. The spirit of co-operation, the exchange of experiences and the search for solutions to common problems are bringing our higher education institutions together in

---

1. Paper presented to the fourth meeting of the project (Krakow, 23-24 October 2000).

networks and understandings to help them rise to the challenges of globalisation. Even if globalisation does override all geographical barriers and have a universal vocation, the formation of groups at the highest level becomes easier when the members share common features that bind them together. It is only natural, therefore, that without losing sight of this global dimension, we should give consideration to the immediate environment of the universities, which in this particular case is Europe. One has only to observe the political integration process to realise that the greatest successes have been obtained through momentum developed at the regional level (European Union, MERCOSUR[2]).

Moving from the general level to that of the individual university – in this case Santiago de Compostela – in order to assess its European dimension, we must first look at the circumstances of the country in which it is located. The European outlook of the surrounding society clearly affects the university's own attitude towards Europe.

From this point of view Spain is truly a paradigm; the events of this century have vastly changed our country's vision and position with respect to Europe. After the essential role played by Spain in the European events under Habsburg rule, Spain gradually focused its attention on the new continent, to the extent that the loss of its last colonies in Cuba, Puerto Rico and the Philippines at the end of the nineteenth century was a national disaster that marked a whole generation of intellectuals known as the "Generation of '98".

Spain's isolation from Europe continued through part of the twentieth century. While Europe was the theatre of two major wars that marked the contemporary history of the old continent, Spain waged its own conflicts in North Africa and engaged in a fratricidal civil war that marked the ensuing years. Its isolation continued in the post-civil-war period, under a non-democratic regime, when Spain once again turned towards Latin America and remained aloof from the European reconstruction projects and the integration process that were to lead to the European Union.

Not until after the fall of the Franco regime and the democratic transition of the last twenty-five years of the century did Spain turn once again towards Europe as a natural destiny, joining in the integration process that was already under way and uniting its destiny with that of the old Europe, sharing its principles and its projects.

This historical background also conditions the attitude to Europe in a community such as a university and indeed in the institution itself. It can safely be said that European awareness in the university, as in society at large, is going through a critical phase that affects university staff in general and teaching staff in particular. However, it is with the transition to democracy that the university community is opening itself to Europe, aware of the need to go beyond geographical boundaries and eliminate barriers to science and knowledge. Although all sectors of the university community are involved in this process, the intensity of their awareness

---

2. Editors' note: Latin American regional organisation composed of Argentina, Brazil, Paraguay and Uruguay, with Chile as associate member.

of the European dimension differs, because of the volume of exchanges and travel involved, which tends to make this awareness much stronger among teachers and students than among the administrative staff. The higher level of training, exchange programmes and knowledge of other languages are highly instrumental in this awakening to the European idea.

If we go back to the origin of our university we must not forget to place it in context. The Santiago de Compostela Route was and still is a meeting place for people from different regions. They developed into a propitious setting for building a European identity and awareness through the exchange of ideas, knowledge and experience. It is not surprising, therefore, that both the Council of Europe and the European Commission found them interesting enough to proclaim them the first European Cultural Route, or that Unesco, at the same time, declared Santiago de Compostela a world heritage site. Its context has logically helped to shape the university's attitude to Europe since its foundation in 1495. Its location in the city, at the arrival point of the cultural and religious route, has undeniably influenced the European and even universal vocation of the Compostelan *alma mater*. This vocation is encouraged by the presence of thousands of pilgrims arriving in Santiago, moved by faith and penitence, who bring with them their culture, their skills and their knowledge, all of which have left their stamp on our architecture and in our writings and our libraries.

Continuing our historical journey, we find other signs of this permeability of our university towards the outside world, particularly to things European. In the mid-sixteenth century, for example, Saint Patrick's Irish College was founded in Santiago de Compostela, where, as in other such institutions, Irish nobles came to study following the Reformation and Henry VIII's proclamation as King of Ireland. From that moment on, Irish teachers and students officially existed in Santiago de Compostela.

Another example of the university's European dimension is the use of Latin for teaching and learning until around the mid-eighteenth century. Latin, in which quite a few European languages originate, imposed itself as a lingua franca that reached beyond geographical boundaries and placed the university and the academic community on a common footing. The introduction of Castilian into academic activities in the eighteenth century and of Galician at the end of the twentieth century reinforced the university's role as a bastion of the culture of the society it represents.

Concerning the essential values of Europe, our university has been directly affected by a good number of the factors that have helped to build western Europe. Various periods of its life, for example, have been marked by the Church, be it its hierarchy – Pope Julius II's 1504 papal bull allowing the university to issue diplomas, presence of local bishops or clergymen (Alonso III de Fonseca, Diego de Muros III) – or its different religious orders (Jesuits, Dominicans, Benedictines). The university has also been sensitive to the influence of political power, especially since the Enlightenment and the formation of the modern states, which gradually took on new roles *vis-à-vis* the universities. All these factors have helped to forge the European identity.

The universities have also contributed a great deal to such basic principles of the European edifice as democracy and pluralism. From the mid-sixteenth century a constitution was in force at Santiago de Compostela that imposed the annual election of the rector or president of the university by the teaching staff at an assembly, which also debated the adoption of measures of great importance to the university. At a time when the sovereign power of governments was at its most virulent, the university was organised on a collegiate basis and elected its rector annually. There is no denying, however, that there was a certain amount of outside interference of a political or religious nature.

Also worth noting is the part played by the university's autonomy in the academic but also the organisational and economic realms. Its autonomy was a source of freedom to carry out research and teaching and, in spite of the more sombre episodes when this autonomy was seriously undermined, it was a guarantee of progress in science and knowledge as recognised in the Bologna charter.[3]

There is also the matter of the future role of universities in the building of Europe and the definition of its essential values.

– First of all, if Europe and its culture can be defined as a vast and dynamic mosaic and the different cultures, religions, ethnic groups, etc., are the pieces, the universities, particularly those with a long history, can help to put those pieces in place. Their architectural, scientific, bibliographic and documentary heritage bears witness to a whole range of human activity that leaves the stamp of what we call culture. One example is the *Ex libris universitaris* exhibition organised by the Network of Spanish University Libraries. This collective heritage, which includes the University of Santiago de Compostela Archives and its Pharmaceutical and Natural History Museums, constitutes what Pierre Nora calls the basis of the spontaneous collective memory. In addition to this spontaneous memory, European construction also calls on the premeditated or conscious memory made up of commemorations, celebrations, etc. which tend to strengthen the feeling of unity, of being part of a common project.

– Training is another front on which universities can contribute to European construction. Considering the high proportion of people who have access to higher education (40%), the impact of this education is hardly surprising. Several lines of action must be highlighted here:

- First, together with the strictly academic training contained in the curricula leading to various diplomas, universities must provide training on a more human level, to familiarise students with the values on which European construction is based, which are also, as we have seen, values found in the university itself. This is without a doubt the way to greater social awareness of these values and their European dimension.
- Secondly, in addition to these values, universities can provide another kind of training to help people understand the European idea and put it into practice, by

---

3. Editors' note: *Magna Charta Universitatum*, adopted by European university rectors in 1988 on the occasion of the 900th anniversary of the foundation of Bologna University.

providing essential language teaching, making it easier for people to travel in Europe and thereby strengthening their European awareness.

- And thirdly, every branch of university teaching – economics, political science, law, social sciences, etc. – must include subject matter designed to give students a better picture of the reality we call Europe.

– Universities must encourage their members – teaching and non-teaching staff and students – to travel, acknowledging the value of the exchanges thus generated and providing the necessary financial support. These journeys and exchanges can take place at different levels. The most ambitious are the schemes already in place at the international level (such as the European Union's Socrates and Erasmus projects). It is worth noting that in the 1999-2000 university year the University of Santiago de Compostela hosted 450 foreign students under these schemes. On a smaller scale there is travel at the national level. The Seneca grants (Becas Séneca), for example, help students move from one Spanish university to another; and there is also the Peregrino programme run by several universities in the Compostela Group. This mobility and exchange between universities brings the people concerned into contact with new students, new cultures, fuelling the ongoing dialogue between cultures upon which Europe is founded. Awareness of the reality of Europe and of the scheme for Europe is the first step towards commitment to its construction.

– A fourth line of action is commitment to the university integration process, a field where the University of Santiago de Compostela is aware of its early European outlook. The strengthening of the institutions that represent European universities – the European University Association (EUA), for example – is a demonstration of this integration at the regional level, which can make a valuable contribution to European construction.

In Santiago de Compostela we also have great faith in the Compostela Group of Universities, an initiative launched in 1993, a holy year in Santiago de Compostela, when the university began to make contact with other higher education establishments located along the Santiago Route in order to build a network enabling the universities concerned to work closely together to safeguard the historic and cultural heritage that has risen up all along the pilgrimage routes that have brought pilgrims from all over Europe to Santiago de Compostela since the ninth century.

After the initial contacts, fifty-seven European universities met in Santiago de Compostela from 2 to 4 September 1993 to map out the initial lines of action to set up this new university network, whose aims are:

– to strengthen channels of communication between the member universities;
– to organise activities involving the study and discussion of European issues;
– to foster mobility and travel as a means of learning European languages and studying European cultures.

This project is clearly motivated by a deep-rooted awareness of Europe and the European dimension of the higher education establishments involved, which now number more than eighty in thirteen of the fifteen European Union member states and also in the Czech Republic, Slovak Republic, Hungary, Malta, Norway, Poland, Russia and Switzerland.

Our university's international outlook also extends further afield, to Latin America. Many bonds, including language and culture, link Spain with Central and South America. In the case of Santiago de Compostela this alliance is even stronger because of the huge numbers of Galicians who emigrated to Latin America from the late nineteenth century to the mid-twentieth century. Spain's universities and in particular the University of Santiago de Compostela, can thus serve as a bridge between these two cultural realities which are at once so far apart and so close.

As stated in the document *Bases for a strategic plan for the University* (1998), "the University of Santiago de Compostela prides itself on being an open university. For this reason its strategy includes openness to the innovations of every order – not only technological innovations – that will be occurring in the university environment in years to come, and openness to contacts and exchanges, preferably with Europe and the Americas, for obvious historical, cultural and geographical reasons. The University of Santiago de Compostela must take advantage of its peripheral location to make the most of the vast opportunities offered by contacts with other universities and centres and participation in projects and networks using the new information and communication technologies".

# Part VI

# Conclusions and the way forward

# The heritage of European universities: the way forward

*Nuria Sanz and Sjur Bergan*

The Europe, a Common Heritage Campaign has been brought to a successful conclusion, but the results of the campaign will be felt for quite some time to come. The end of the project on the heritage of European universities is not the end of our concern with this topic, but on the contrary that the project has discerned much material for a potential follow up. The concluding article of this volume, then, aims to draw on the experience of the campaign and the project on the heritage of European universities, as outlined in this volume, and offer some thoughts on possible further developments.

We hope to have established that the heritage of universities is an essential part of the European heritage. First of all, universities are essentially European by their origin and their values. While the university institution originated in the southern and central parts of western Europe, it rapidly spread to most other parts of our continent[1] so that more than almost any other institution currently surviving, the university is a European institution. This point is further underlined by the establishment of universities on other continents, starting with Mexico in the 1550s, that were either established by European migrants or built on the tradition of European universities.

This is, of course, not to say that high level training, education, writing and inventions were unknown in other parts of the world, but the university as a model for the organisation, development and dissemination of knowledge as well as a way of conceptualising education and research as an essential component of civil society, starting in the Middle Ages, is of European origin. It has been sufficiently successful to be adopted in just about any other part of the world. In an age of globalisation, the university must surely be one of the best examples of globalisation on the part of Europeans – and we would even venture to say that it is one of the best examples of beneficial globalisation.

Secondly, the university tradition is European in its orientation and outlook, and the only "dilution" of this outlook has been in the direction of a broader world view – not towards an exclusive focus on what is national, regional or local, even though individual universities may of course play important roles in the national, regional or local communities of which they form a part. On the contrary, universities have often played an international role through their teaching and research and as places of freedom of expression. Examples may be found both in the formative period of European universities, such as eleventh to thirteenth century Bologna and Montpellier, and in recent times, such as nineteenth to twentieth century Tartu, Cluj or the Agricultural University of Wageningen. Even where the subject matter is national or regional, such as Armenian literature, Icelandic history and culture or the

---

1. Cf. the list of universities established in Europe before 1600 included in H. De Ridder-Symoens (editor), W. Rüegg (general editor): *A History of the Universities of Europe*, vol. II, (Cambridge 1996: Cambridge University Press), pp. 90 ff.

Pyrenean flora, the methodology is established internationally, some of the researchers come from abroad and the results are published for an international community of peers.

Beyond doubt, institutions like the universities of Europe are preeminent examples of continuity and it is precisely this continuity that has created the necessary framework for shaping one of the most interesting *patrimonia* evolving from a cultural institution. These *patrimonia* also implied a skill in the practice of conservation both implicit (archives, libraries, collections) and explicit (transmission of knowledge). Universities are important because they span the whole range of heritage, both material and immaterial. Some university buildings are among the most valuable built heritage in Europe, both for their architectural value and for the traditions and values they represent, by themselves and as part of the urban environment to which they belong. The *aula magna* of Bologna, the Collegium Maius of Kraków, the whole complex of the old university in down town Vilnius or the Alta – *quartier universitaire* – of Coimbra come to mind in this context, without forgetting examples from San Ivo alla Sapienza (Rome), Padova or Weimar.

Material and immaterial heritage are useful categories of classification, but sometimes the twain meet and the distinction is less than obvious. University museums, collections, libraries, archives and botanical gardens may be housed in historical buildings, contain valuable objects and at the same time be intimately linked with the immaterial heritage of universities through the achievements of their teaching, learning and research. This heritage is added to generation by generation. While parts of it fall into disuse because of achievements in learning and teaching, other parts of the university heritage remain relevant through centuries because they are necessary independently of new advances in science. Universities have museums, collections and botanical gardens in the first place because these are important to teaching and research, and this was possibly even more true before the advent of advanced instruments and computers refocusing much research, eg in natural sciences, outside of collections.[2] Books and documents may have considerable material heritage value, but their main importance in an academic context nevertheless lies in their contribution to the immaterial heritage of universities.

This immaterial heritage is exceedingly difficult to define in any precise manner, but it comprises elements such as:

– the traces and achievements of teaching, learning and research within higher education institutions and bodies;
– the history of higher education institutions and bodies, including their written traces contained in archives, libraries and collections;
– the traditions and methods of teaching and learning and student/teacher relations;
– the concept and methodology of transmission and development of knowledge;
– the identity of scholars, teachers and students as an "imagined community" and the traditions and customs, rules and regulations of the academic community;

---

2. On this point, see P. J. Boylan in the present volume.

– the values and ethics of higher education institutions and bodies, and of the academic community, including openness, tolerance, respect and acceptance, and a critical attitude;
– the freedom of academic teaching and research as well as of thought, belief and expression.

The very degree systems of higher education are an important part of this heritage, and the fact that they are currently being reformed in the framework of the Bologna Process[3] does not change their role as living heritage, because reforms are also a part of the university heritage. Edmund Burke's dictum on changing the form in order to preserve the essence and the values also applies to universities. Other examples of the immaterial heritage of universities include the discovery of the DNA molecule, the theory of transformational-generative grammar, the tradition of student exchange, the doctoral dissertation followed by public defence and higher education autonomy and governance, but also university festivals and solemn occasions and manifestations of student life such as the *tunas* of Spain and Portugal.

One part of the university heritage that is perhaps in danger is that of the academic community of scholars and students. This "imagined community"[4] cuts across academic disciplines, national boundaries and centuries. While more research would be needed to establish whether an educated guess is also a fact, our impression from the texts and questionnaires of the project is that the multiple pressures, loyalties and identifications of students and staff along with an increasing emphasis on the immediately utilitarian function of higher education and the use of business jargon to designate students as "clients" cannot but reduce their identification with the academic world. This is not to say that students and staff should be exclusively academic, or that higher education institutions should seek to isolate themselves from society. Multiple identities are the rule rather than the exception,[5] and the ivory tower is not a viable university model. Nevertheless, an essential part of the university heritage would be lost if the academic community cannot recognise itself through its education and in the university heritage. If it recognises itself as a community, it will also more easily assume responsibility for its heritage. Then, its traditions and festivals will not be seen as pageants but as a natural part of university life providing a link between the past and the present, and – through its students and its heritage – also to its future. There is no contradiction between being a citizen of Europe and identifying with the academic community. Quite to the contrary, it would be unnatural for a member of the academic community not also to identify with the strong European dimension of the university heritage. Even if conditions in

3. Reproduced in the appendices to the present volume.
4. The term "imagined community" is normally used in discussions of nationalism and was coined by the political scientist Benedict Anderson in his *Imagined Communities: Reflections on the Origin and Spread of Nationalism* (London 1983: Verso), but the term is fitting also for other kinds of communities.
5. Most people identify with some entity outside of their immediate surroundings. Thus, people can identify with their local community, their region, their continent and feel like citizens of the world, all at the same time. A poignant illustration is given by Dominique Baudis' slogan for his 1995 campaign for the European Parliament: *toulousain – français – européen*. Nor does identification with a layer of territorial entities preclude simultaneous identification with, say, a place of work, a church, an organisation (eg the Red Cross or Amnesty International), a school (cf. the English "institution" of the "school tie" or US alumni associations) or a range of other entities.

US society are different from those of European societies, could the example of US alumni associations be worth pursuing and adapting to the European context?

These considerations lead us to a further point that has been emphasised in this volume, namely that heritage continues to be heritage only if it is transmitted to new generations who identify with it and keep it alive. The major question arising from the project is: how can the university heritage be preserved and made relevant both to the world of higher education and to wider society? The answer to this seemingly simple question is, as we have attempted to show, manifold in terms of both activities and actors.

Through the work undertaken and our conversations with rectors and other university representatives, it is clear that there is a need to identify what constitutes the heritage of each university in setting out to define a true policy for university heritage. While some elements of this heritage are evident, as in the case of an *aula magna* or a historical library, a definition of the content and an overall management of this heritage are largely lacking. In other words, we believe there is a need to invent or to reformulate an integrated conservation policy for the heritage of universities.

A key decision process in university life, is the planning process, whether it goes by the name of "medium term", "long term", "strategic", "global" or any other label. Essentially, it is a plan for the future development of the university, so we shall refer to it as the development plan. It will contain elements on the main priorities for the future development of the institution, including a mission statement presenting the institution's view of its own role, the academic areas that should be expanded, perhaps those that should be decreased, the institution's goals in terms of the quality of its teaching and research, its relations with the local community, its communication strategy and often its physical development. Here it is also important that the university heritage be given specific consideration. Only by being made a part of the overall university development can the university heritage continue to live. If it is considered as something apart, to be given consideration only on solemn occasions as places of memory, and if the budget allows, the heritage will die and cease to be heritage. Again, the point is not that the heritage should block all development, but that the development of a higher education institution should take specific account of its heritage. Heritage transforms tradition into an everyday reality.

An important step would be to take account of the heritage in university decision-making and development. The main "routine" development decision is the adoption of the university budget,[6] generally on an annual basis, but our material indicates that specific consideration is rarely given to the university heritage in the elaboration or adoption of the budget, nor do many universities actually know how much they spend on their heritage.[7] A first step would therefore be to define the financial

---

6. Or budget proposal, where the final budget is adopted by bodies external to the university, such as national or regional parliaments or ministries responsible for higher education.
7. See our article on the Cultural Heritage of European Universities in the present volume.

systems in such a way that it is possible to identify how much is spent on the university's own heritage.

This knowledge should then be applied in the budget process, which is not to say that heritage concerns have an automatic claim on priority in the university budget. However, they should be one of the many factors that are taken into account when the budget is adopted. We can think of no other policy process that takes into account the various interests, concerns and priorities of higher education institutions to the extent that the budget process does. This process is the archetypical example of overall policies of checks, balances and compromise, and it is disturbing to see that heritage concerns too often do not weigh in the scales. The funds for the preservation of university heritage can come from both the regular university heritage and from other sources, such as foundations, from visiting tourists, from copyright fees or from percentages of business transactions, such as the example mentioned by the University of Zagreb, where the university receives a commission on transactions by alumni using a special credit card. There is no reason why heritage should be an exception to the trend towards greater diversification in financing which characterises other parts of higher education activities – nor should possible external funding be an excuse for reducing heritage appropriations under the regular institutional budget.

Decision processes involve decision makers and managers, many of whom combine a responsibility for the overall management and development of their institution with a particular responsibility for a part of it. Deans in charge of specific faculties are obvious and almost universal examples, but there are many others, depending on the structure of the university: vice rectors responsible for institutional development or international relations, directors of finance, or heads of technical services. From our material, it is far from obvious that responsibility for the university heritage is clearly defined. In view of the lack of specific consideration of heritage in the financial information systems, budget decisions and development plans, it would even have been surprising to find a clearly defined responsibility for heritage. There are of course head librarians and museum directors, but their responsibility is in a sense punctual rather than overall. The future of the university heritage would be much more secure if an elected officer or career manager had specific responsibility for co-ordinating it, in co-operation with those who take care of specific parts of it. We have found some examples of this kind of integrated co-ordination, notably the University of Salamanca and the Universidad Autónoma de México. Could a University Heritage Board chaired by a vice rector and with representatives of museums, collections, libraries and archives as well as of the larger academic community be a path worth pursuing?

In the same way that higher education institutions need to establish an overview of their heritage and to integrate it into their institutional planning process, they need to reinforce their efforts at awareness raising. Only through targeted awareness raising can both staff and students, residents of the local community and those further removed from the institution get to know and identify with the university heritage. In this context, it is important that this awareness raising include two aspects: it should be concerned with both the specific heritage of the institution and place this in a comparative perspective. If no man is an island, this is even truer of the

171

quintessentially European institution that is the university. Any presentation of the heritage of a specific university would be incomplete without placing it in its proper context of the European university tradition. Through the project, each participant has found a number of points of comparison with other universities.

Target groups could usefully include the institution's own students and staff, members of the local community, visitors and various kinds of specialised audiences, including foreign academics. Institutional awareness raising strategies should be transversal undertakings involving heritage specialists, historians, communication specialists and institutional decision makers, and the strategies should take account of the needs, interests and starting point of each target group. Many study systems give students the opportunity to take a number of elective credits as a part of their degree, and the reforms of the Bologna Process could provide such an opportunity to students that cannot make use of it today. Why could not one or more elective courses focus on the university heritage and give credits that count towards a degree, even for students not specialising in heritage? One things is certain: awareness raising cannot be used as propaganda on occasions such as anniversaries, when the past is glorified and any attempt at critical analysis is left at the doorstep of the *Aula Magna* where the main ceremonies are likely to be held.

Schoolchildren are a particularly important target group in that they provide a valuable link to the local and prospective members of the academic community, and this at an age when attitudes are formed. In our survey, only Coimbra reported specific activities aimed at schoolchildren. Organised visits for schoolchildren of different ages with an adapted programme that sought to build awareness of the university heritage and how it is reflected in the university of today would be an inestimable investment in the future of the university and its heritage, as schoolchildren develop not only into future students but also into future citizens that will decide the priorities of society a generation further down the road. The means of reaching today's adult citizens are certainly diverse, spanning from brochures and publications to TV programmes and Open Days. All of these methods are already in use, and the competence and relevance of university staff is widely recognised, even if the general public would tend to consider some specialties as irrelevant.[8] Would it not be worthwhile to use these methods not only to focus on the university today but on the foundation on which it rests – its heritage? Why not a University Heritage Day or Heritage Classes? Is there a TV producer with the competence and the courage to do for the university heritage what David Attenborough has done for the world's natural heritage and Basil Davidson for the history of Africa, through their television series? The student museum, as exemplified by the one in Bologna,[9] is another way of making a part of the university heritage come alive. Publications, as in the case of the University of Kraków, or institutional gifts, as in the case of Vilnius University, can also contribute to making the university heritage known.

---

8. Although even such disciplines can meet with interest and recognition. One example among many was the TV series *Fråga Lund* ("Ask Lund [University]"), in which specialists from one of Sweden's two oldest universities answered questions from the public covering the whole range of academic fields in such a way as to make their expertise accessible to the general public.
9. See Gian Paolo Brizzi's article in this volume.

That there is great need for awareness raising and information is also illustrated by a small experiment: an Internet search by the present authors for "European university heritage" with two large search engines brought forth all of two links, both of them to the Council of Europe web sites for the Europe, a Common Heritage Campaign and the higher education sector. Broadening the search to "university heritage" increased the number of links dramatically, but among the first seventy-five listed, only some five were relevant, and some of these were from North America. The search, incidentally, also illustrated that the term heritage is sometimes used in ways which have little to do with the more technical definition of the term, or at least with the most conservationist use of it.

These considerations bring us to the domain of publications, where Hilde de Ridder-Symoens[10] has shown the dominance of what she calls "jubilee publications", which are too often the antithesis of modern scholarship without necessarily being good examples of successful popularisation. Through the CRE/EUA, European universities have risen to the task in terms of describing their own history through a multi volume work of serious scholarship.[11] A similar effort on heritage terms would be highly desirable, and it should be matched both by descriptions of the heritage of individual universities and by a popularised overview. There is in fact no contradiction between serious scholarship and popularisation. Rather, the latter is only possible if it can build on serious research, but research results must be popularised to reach beyond the readership of specialists.

Therefore, both teaching and research on the heritage of universities from a transdisciplinary perspective should be encouraged. The academic freedom of researchers choosing their own focus is of course a key component of the university heritage. Nevertheless, research interests can be stimulated and encouraged, both through awareness raising and by setting up research programmes with funds for which interested researchers can apply and compete. Research programmes can be set up and financed by individual higher education institutions, research councils, academies, ministries responsible for higher education, foundations or other bodies, and through international programmes such as those of the European Union. A research programme on the university heritage encouraging the setting up of transdisciplinary research teams taking a comparative approach would be of immense value, and we would even dare to say it would be a natural complement to the Bologna Process.

Research programmes must be matched by research training on heritage, not just in individual disciplines that are of relevance to heritage. This point has two aspects: on the one hand, it concerns how universities train specialists to work on their own heritage, on the other hand it concerns the function of higher education institutions in training a range of heritage specialist, most of whom will later work on other parts of the common European heritage. While many individual academic disciplines of relevance to heritage are well covered by European universities, there seems to be a need for advanced training with a transdisciplinary heritage approach. Here is a

10. See her article in this volume.
11. Walter Rüegg (general editor), Hilde de Ridder-Symoens (editor), published in four volumes, English edition published by Cambridge University Press.

major challenge for higher education institution: adapting their current structures and programmes to provide professionals that will be adequately trained today to make the heritage of yesterday accessible and relevant tomorrow.

The status and professional recognition of heritage professionals within and outside of higher education institutions is another important point. Academic careers are built above all on research merit and to some extent on competence in teaching. Therefore, academics with career ambitions will mainly focus on writing publications and running research projects, whereas establishing, taking care of and improving museums, collections, archives and libraries will count less for career advancement, even within heritage related disciplines. While heritage specialists may do a part of their research in museums and contribute to collections through their research, eg through excavations in the case of archaeologists, this does not make them experts on museums, whether in terms of management or the conception of exhibitions for a broader public. Universities and competent public authorities would be well advised to reconsider the career structure and criteria for academic advancement in heritage and related areas to take adequate account of the whole range of skills required for the profession. As we have repeatedly underlined, universities constitute veritable heritage laboratories to work in an integrated manner with both training and management.

All of these considerations bring us back to the European dimension of the university heritage. While the heritage of each higher education institution has its intrinsic interest, its value is greatly enhanced by putting it in its proper context – that of the European university tradition. Teaching, learning, research and awareness raising focusing on the university heritage must take a comparative, European perspective, and must use all available opportunities such as international research and student and staff exchange programmes. These are too numerous to be mentioned extensively, but they include, in addition to the European Union programmes, smaller and larger scale programmes such as those of the Nordic Council of Ministers for the Nordic countries as well as for the Baltic countries and north-west Russia, CEEPUS (the Central European Exchange Program for University Studies) for a number of countries in central Europe, the Community of Mediterranean Universities (CUM) for all parts of the Mediterranean and EUCOR for the Upper Rhine.[12] Where these programmes could include topics related to the university heritage, the possibilities should be used to the full.

However, academics and higher education institutions should not work in isolation. Networking is particularly important for academic fields which may be small within each institution, but which are nonetheless part of a larger European and international community, and in disciplines with a clear European and international dimension. EUCOR, CUM and the Nordic Agricultural University[13] are only three examples of successful inter-institutional co-operation in specific disciplines. In EUCOR, students can attend courses at any participating institution and have them

---

12. For more on regional cooperation in higher education, see the report of the conference arranged jointly by the Council of Europe and the Nordic Council of Ministers in Reykjavík in September 1997, issued as Regional Cooperation in Higher Education, TemaNord 1998:533.
13. *Ibid*.

recognised towards their degree at their home institution, while the Nordic Agricultural University is not an institution at all, but the name of a very close co-operation between the agricultural universities of the five Nordic countries in which a good number of specialities are taught at only one institution for students from all universities without regard to their origin. The term CUM Schools designates a system of intensive advanced courses of limited duration held at one of the CUM universities in co-operation with at least two further institutions from different countries. Of the many topics covered so far, examples include Law in the Mediterranean Countries (held in Lebanon), Conservation of Monuments (Italy), Mediterranean Architecture (Israel), An Introduction to Desalination Technologies (Libya) and Mediterranean Ecotoxicology (Malta).[14]

All three examples provide viable models for co-operation between European universities interested in promoting their own heritage and/or in the training of heritage specialists. Inter-institutional co-operation provides opportunities for joint use of scarce resources and above all for broadening the perspective of both staff and students by giving access to a wide range of examples and cases and by offering a comparative perspective. While the three examples quoted concern regional co-operation, ranging from the relatively small area of the Upper Rhine valley through the five Nordic countries to the whole Mediterranean Basin, similar networks could be established at European level.

What we have outlined is a vast agenda that has to be addressed by higher education institutions, heritage professionals, public authorities, local communities, international organisations, whether governmental or non-governmental, foundations, volunteer associations[15] and certainly many other bodies. The agenda is as vast as the university heritage, and while it will not be completed in the immediate future, it is urgent that we begin addressing it. It may well be argued that Rome was not built in one day, but it should also not be forgotten that Rome was built because someone started building and others followed suit.

The heritage of European universities is a heritage of the past and a heritage for the future in accordance with the exercise of transmission, which is the essential objective of this institution. It has proven its importance and value by surviving for centuries, by adapting to new circumstances and not least by becoming a point of reference also for other areas of society. The greatest threats to the survival of the university heritage are perhaps on the one hand the danger of it being taken for granted since universities have been a fixture on the European scene for centuries, taking into account that the university is a privileged setting for discovering and rereading the common history of Europe. On the other hand, universities and the traditions and values they represent are coming under increasing pressure from societies that seem to be loosing their capacity to think and plan beyond the immediate horizon, whether this is the upcoming election, the budget year or tomorrow's headline. Universities are important institutions in society precisely because they are able to put at society's disposal today knowledge, skills and

---

14. http://www.iqsnet.it/universita/html/cum_ing.html.
15. See the Declaration on the role of voluntary organisations in the field of Cultural Heritage adopted at the Fifth Conference of Ministers responsible for Cultural Heritage, Portorož, 6-7 April 2001.

competence that have been developed over years of hard work. In the same way, they will contribute to solving the problems of tomorrow and at the same time help us evolve as human beings.

The university heritage is not a story of immediate gratification, nor is it one of constant and unfailing success. Its importance is of a different order: the heritage of European universities is one of the most consistent and most important examples of sustainable success and achievement that Europe has ever seen. The university is a part of our heritage, and its future is decided now. We hope this volume and the project on which it builds will in some small way contribute to securing the future of the heritage of European universities, and to strengthen the link between this heritage and the important and necessary reforms of the Bologna Process.

Our reflection on the university heritage coincides with a time when cultural heritage policies are no longer only identified with a typology or with a prescriptive approach to tangible and intangible resources, but they are also aimed at valorising problems of heritage policies that also have to do with filiation and affective ties (cultural, sociological, confessional, territorial). From these ties a specific kind of current relationship to the ways of establishing memories can be defined, based on what is lived today, on my family, my neighbourhood, my city or village, or my understanding of citizenship and my civic culture that accompanies the approach to what everyone considers his or her own heritage.

Heritage could be considered as everyone's "inner voyage" in his or her everyday life. In this sense, who has the right to decommission heritage? How can the political and technical responsibility be reconciled with the subjective filiation with everyone's heritage, in accordance with the fundamental right to self-defined identities? How is society able to share responsibilities and make concerted decisions on heritage enhancement, protection and definition? Which mechanisms can ensure that all voices are heard, and how can a plurality of approaches be managed in a given conflict context, that may be academically incoherent or politically undemocratic. How can heritage be defined as European and which responsibilities does it involve? How can all the socio-cultural agents be made to participate adequately in consultation and decision-making processes affecting heritage?

Who defines what is valuable, and according to which values? This is a question that mere technical experience is probably insufficient to answer. A lot of questions combine to form a single panorama, the significance of which is plural by nature, a panorama in which simultaneously one generates a diversity of perception and, hopefully, a respect and responsibility for this diversity. Today, it seems clear that the protagonist is the subject of heritage policies and not only the beneficiary of these policies, and an institution like the Council of Europe should take account of this when it comes to preparing a reference instrument on the considerations of the possible heritage of each individual.

In this context, the duality of heritage and university is of particular interest. Each one of the meanings conveyed by the intellectual heritage of values of the university is a key to interpretation, verification or analysis that could well help to prevent conflicts of all kinds, whether political or confessional, near or far away, one's own or someone else's, and thereby put into practice the contribution of the university to a model of society educated in its own values.

The university is defined as a place of confluence, as an interface, as a space in which, without losing the essential asset of one's own heritage, one could be able to establish shared categories of respect through innovative daily practices where meanings and feelings will be driven by universal values.

This project has been carried out through a close co-operation between two committees and with substantial support from the European Commission, and not least with the participation of institutional representatives and heritage specialists from all parts of Europe. They have all borne witness to an increasing interest in the heritage of universities as an important part of our common European heritage. The Council of Europe campaign, in this sense, provided an indispensable platform for an integrated approach and for a well constructed beginning. The project has continued to grow and to define various areas of interest throughout 2001. The interest in co-operation and the enthusiasm of the participants have proven that the project is in good health.

# List of contributors

## Editors

Nuria Sanz, a university professor specialised in heritage training, was seconded by the Spanish government to co-ordinate national and transnational projects of the Europe, a Common Heritage campaign (1999-2000).

Sjur Bergan, writing from the perspective of an educational policy maker, is head of the Council of Europe's Higher Education and Research Division.

Together, the editors of the present volume co-ordinated the project on the heritage of European universities.

## Contributors

Béatrice Bakhouche is Professor of Classical Languages and Literature (Latin) at the University of Montpellier III – Paul Valéry, director of the transdisciplinary programme "Mémoire et Patrimoine", with contributors from all three universities in Montpellier.

Paolo Blasi is Full Professor of Laboratory Physics at the University of Firenze, of which he was Rector 1991-2000. He is a member of the Administrative Board of the International Association of Universities (I.A.U.), Higher Counsellor of the Bank of Italy. He was a member of the Board of Directors of the National Council for Scientific Research (C.N.R.) 1998-2001 and Vice President of the CRE (Association of European Universities) 1991-2000. His scientific activity has resulted in more than eighty publications concerning the properties of the atomic nucleus and reactions between nuclei.

Patrick J. Boylan is a geologist and historian of science by academic specialisation. He directed major local authority arts, museums, heritage and archive services across England for twenty-two years before joining the Department of Arts Policy and Management, City University, London as Professor and Head of Department in 1990. Since his official retirement at the end of 1999 he continues to work in the Department part-time with the title of Professor of Heritage Policy and Management. He has served as Centenary President of the Museums Association (UK), Vice President of the International Council of Museums (Icom) and as an advisor on cultural and heritage policy, management and professional training to Unesco, the Council of Europe, the World Bank, and more than a dozen governmental authorities around the world.

Gian Paolo Brizzi is Full Professor of Modern History at the Universities of Sassari and Bologna, where he presently teaches at the Faculty of Cultural and Heritage Studies. Currently he is president of the graduate course in archive and library studies and secretary general of the Inter University Centre for the History of Italian Universities as well as the Italian member of the International Committee for the History of Universities. His research on the history of Universities and, more generally, the history of education, has chiefly focused on the educating and training of the ruling class (*La formazione della classe dirigente in Italia nel Sei-Settecento*, 1976; *La "Ratio studiorum" . Modelli culturali e pratiche educative dei Gesuiti in Italia tra Cinque e Seicento*,1981; *I collegi per borsisti e lo Studio bolognese, 1984; Il catechismo e la grammatica*, 1985-1986). Co-editor of a six-volume work with Jacques Verger on the history of the European Universities from their origins to the Napoleonic age (*Le università dell'Europa*, Milano, 1990-1995). Director of the review "Annali di storia delle università italiane".

Antonio López Díaz, Vice Rector for the Co-ordination of the Compostela Campus, University of Santiago de Compostela

José Luis Peset, CSIC – Consejo Superior de Investigación Científica

Alain Renaut, Professor of Philosophy, University of Paris IV

Hilde de Ridder-Symoens is Professor of medieval history at the Free University of Amsterdam and the University of Ghent. She has been editor of volumes 1 and 2 of *A History of the University of Europe*, published by the European University Association (Cambridge UP, 1992, 1996). Since 1995, she has been president of the International Commission for the History of Universities.

Walter Rüegg is Professor Emeritus of Sociology at the Universities of Bern and Frankfurt. He was Rector of the University of Frankfurt in 1965-70 and is general editor of *A History of the University of Europe*, published by the European University Association.

Maria da Fátima Silva is Vice Rector for Culture of the University of Coimbra and tenured Professor in the Faculty of Letters, specialist in Ancient Greek Literature. She has published in the field of theatre (tragedy and comedy) and historiography (Herodot). At present she is co-ordinating a group elaborating an overview of representations of Greek and Latin theatre in Portugal.

Claudia A. Zonta, doctoral student in History, Stuttgart.

# Appendices

# Appendix I

## The *Magna Charta Universitatum*

### Preamble

The undersigned Rectors of European Universities, gathered in Bologna for the ninth centenary of the oldest University in Europe, four years before the definitive abolition of boundaries between the countries of the European Community; looking forward to far-reaching co-operation between all European nations and believing that peoples and States should become more than ever aware of the part that universities will be called upon to play in a changing and increasingly international society,

Consider:

1. that at the approaching end of this millennium the future of mankind depends, largely on cultural, scientific and technical development; and that this is built up in centres of culture, knowledge and research as represented by true universities;

2. that the universities' task of spreading knowledge among the younger generations implies that, in today's world, they must also serve society as a whole; and that the cultural, social and economic future of society requires, in particular, a considerable investment in continuing education;

3. that universities must give future generations education and training that will teach them, and through them others, to respect the great harmonies of their natural environment and of life itself.

The undersigned Rectors of European Universities proclaim to all states and to the conscience of all nations the fundamental principles which must, now and always, support the vocation of universities.

### Fundamental principles

1. The university is an autonomous institution at the heart of societies differently organized because of geography and historical heritage; it produces, examines, appraises and hands down culture by research and teaching.

To meet the needs of the world around it, its research and teaching must be morally and intellectually independent of all political authority and intellectually independent of all political authority and economic power.

2. Teaching and research in universities must be inseparable if their tuition is not to lag behind changing needs, the demands of society, and advances in scientific knowledge.

3. Freedom in research and training is the fundamental principle of university life, and governments and universities, each as far as in them lies, must ensure respect for this fundamental requirement.

Rejecting intolerance and always open to dialogue, the university is an ideal meeting-ground for teachers capable of imparting their knowledge and well equipped to develop it by research and innovation and students entitled, able and willing to enrich their minds with that knowledge.

4. A university is the trustee of the European humanist tradition; its constant care is to attain universal knowledge; to fulfil its vocation it transcends geographical and political frontiers, and affirms the vital need for different cultures to know and influence each other.

**The means**

To attain these goals by following such principles calls for effective means, suitable to present conditions.

1. To preserve freedom in research and teaching, the instruments appropriate to realize that freedom must be made available to all members of the university community.

2. Recruitment of teachers, and regulation of their status, must obey the principle that research is inseparable from teaching.

3. Each university must – with due allowance for particular circumstances – ensure that its students' freedoms are safeguarded and that they enjoy conditions in which they can acquire the culture and training which it is their purpose to possess.

4. Universities – particularly in Europe – regard the mutual exchange of information and documentation, and frequent joint projects for the advancement of learning, as essential to the steady progress of knowledge.

Therefore, as in the earliest years of their history, they encourage mobility among teachers and students; furthermore, they consider a general policy of equivalent status, titles, examinations(without prejudice to national diplomas) and award of scholarships essential to the fulfilment of their mission in the conditions prevailing today.

The undersigned Rectors, on behalf of their Universities, undertake to do everything in their power to encourage each State, as well as the supranational organisations concerned, to mould their policy sedulously on this Magna Charta, which expresses the universities' unanimous desire freely determined and declared.

# Appendix II

## Joint declaration on harmonisation of the architecture of the European higher education system

Paris, Sorbonne, 25 May 1998

The European process has very recently moved some extremely important steps ahead. Relevant as they are, they should not make one forget that Europe is not only that of the Euro, of the banks and the economy: it must be a Europe of knowledge as well. We must strengthen and build upon the intellectual, cultural, social and technical dimensions of our continent. These have to a large extent been shaped by its universities, which continue to play a pivotal role for their development.

Universities were born in Europe, some three quarters of a millennium ago. Our four countries boast some of the oldest, which are celebrating important anniversaries around now, as the University of Paris is doing today. In those times, students and academics would freely circulate and rapidly disseminate knowledge throughout the continent. Nowadays, too many of our students still graduate without having had the benefit of a study period outside of national boundaries.

We are heading for a period of major change in education and working conditions, to a diversification of courses of professional careers, with education and training throughout life becoming a clear obligation. We owe our students, and our society at large, a higher education system in which they are given the best opportunities to seek and find their own area of excellence.

An open European area for higher learning carries a wealth of positive perspectives, of course respecting our diversities, but requires on the other hand continuous efforts to remove barriers and to develop a framework for teaching and learning, which would enhance mobility and an ever closer co-operation.

The international recognition and attractive potential of our systems are directly related to their external and internal readabilities. A system, in which two main cycles, undergraduate and graduate, should be recognized for international comparison and equivalence, seems to emerge.

Much of the originality and flexibility in this system will be achieved through the use of credits (such as in the ECTS scheme) and semesters. This will allow for validation of these acquired credits for those who choose initial or continued education in different European universities and wish to be able to acquire degrees in due time throughout life. Indeed, students should be able to enter the academic world at any time in their professional life and from diverse backgrounds.

Undergraduates should have access to a diversity of programmes, including opportunities for multidisciplinary studies, development of a proficiency in languages and the ability to use new information technologies. In the graduate cycle, there would be a choice between a shorter master's degree and a longer doctor's degree, with possibilities to transfer from one to the other. In both graduate degrees, appropriate emphasis would be placed on research and autonomous work.

At both undergraduate and graduate level, students would be encouraged to spend at least one semester in universities outside their own country. At the same time, more teaching and research staff should be working in European countries other than their own. The fast growing support of the European Union for the mobility of students and teachers should be employed to the full.

Most countries, not only within Europe, have become fully conscious of the need to foster such evolution. The conferences of European rectors, University presidents, and groups of experts and academics in our respective countries have engaged in widespread thinking along these lines.

A convention, recognising higher education qualifications in the academic field within Europe, was agreed on last year in Lisbon. The convention set a number of basic requirements and acknowledged that individual countries could engage in an even more constructive scheme. Standing by these conclusions, one can build on them and go further. There is already much common ground for the mutual recognition of higher education degrees for professional purposes through the respective directives of the European Union.

Our governments, nevertheless, continue to have a significant role to play to these ends, by encouraging ways in which acquired knowledge can be validated and respective degrees can be better recognised. We expect this to promote further inter-university agreements. Progressive harmonisation of the overall framework of our degrees and cycles can be achieved through strengthening of already existing experience, joint diplomas, pilot initiatives, and dialogue with all concerned.

We hereby commit ourselves to encouraging a common frame of reference, aimed at improving external recognition and facilitating student mobility as well as employability. The anniversary of the University of Paris, today here in the Sorbonne, offers us a solemn opportunity to engage in the endeavour to create a European area of higher education, where national identities and common interests can interact and strengthen each other for the benefit of Europe, of its students, and more generally of its citizens .

We call on other Member States of the Union and other European countries to join us in this objective and on all European Universities to consolidate Europe's standing in the world through continuously improved and updated education for its citizens.

Claude Allègre
Minister of National Education, Research and Technology
(France)

Luigi Berlinguer
Minister of Public Education, Universities and Research
(Italy)

Tessa Blackstone
Minister of Higher Education
(United Kingdom)

Jürgen Ruettgers
Minister of Education, Science, Research and Technology
(Germany)

# Appendix III

## The European higher education area
## Joint declaration of the European Ministers of Education
## convened in Bologna on the 19 June 1999

The European process, thanks to the extraordinary achievements of the last few years, has become an increasingly concrete and relevant reality for the Union and its citizens. Enlargement prospects together with deepening relations with other European countries, provide even wider dimensions to that reality. Meanwhile, we are witnessing a growing awareness in large parts of the political and academic world and in public opinion of the need to establish a more complete and far-reaching Europe, in particular building upon and strengthening its intellectual, cultural, social and scientific and technological dimensions.

A Europe of Knowledge is now widely recognised as an irreplaceable factor for social and human growth and as an indispensable component to consolidate and enrich the European citizenship, capable of giving its citizens the necessary competences to face the challenges of the new millennium, together with an awareness of shared values and belonging to a common social and cultural space.

The importance of education and educational co-operation in the development and strengthening of stable, peaceful and democratic societies is universally acknowledged as paramount, the more so in view of the situation in South East Europe.

The Sorbonne declaration of 25th of May 1998, which was underpinned by these considerations, stressed the Universities' central role in developing European cultural dimensions. It emphasised the creation of the European area of higher education as a key way to promote citizens' mobility and employability and the Continent's overall development.

Several European countries have accepted the invitation to commit themselves to achieving the objectives set out in the declaration, by signing it or expressing their agreement in principle. The direction taken by several higher education reforms launched in the meantime in Europe has proved many governments' determination to act.

European higher education institutions, for their part, have accepted the challenge and taken up a main role in constructing the European area of higher education, also in the wake of the fundamental principles laid down in the Bologna Magna Charta Universitatum of 1988. This is of the highest importance, given that universities' independence and autonomy ensure that higher education and research systems continuously adapt to changing needs, society's demands and advances in scientific knowledge.

The course has been set in the right direction and with meaningful purpose. The achievement of greater compatibility and comparability of the systems of higher education nevertheless requires continual momentum in order to be fully accomplished. We need to support it through promoting concrete measures to achieve tangible forward steps. The 18th June meeting saw participation by authoritative experts and scholars from all our countries and provides us with very useful suggestions on the initiatives to be taken.

We must in particular look at the objective of increasing the international competitiveness of the European system of higher education. The vitality and efficiency of any civilisation can be measured by the appeal that its culture has for other countries. We need to ensure that the European higher education system acquires a world-wide degree of attraction equal to our extraordinary cultural and scientific traditions.

While affirming our support to the general principles laid down in the Sorbonne declaration, we engage in co-ordinating our policies to reach in the short term, and in any case within the first decade of the third millennium, the following objectives, which we consider to be of primary relevance in order to establish the European area of higher education and to promote the European system of higher education world-wide:

Adoption of a system of easily readable and comparable degrees, also through the implementation of the Diploma Supplement, in order to promote European citizens employability and the international competitiveness of the European higher education system

Adoption of a system essentially based on two main cycles, undergraduate and graduate. Access to the second cycle shall require successful completion of first cycle studies, lasting a minimum of three years. The degree awarded after the first cycle shall also be relevant to the European labour market as an appropriate level of qualification. The second cycle should lead to the master and/or doctorate degree as in many European countries.

Establishment of a system of credits – such as in the ECTS system – as a proper means of promoting the most widespread student mobility. Credits could also be acquired in non-higher education contexts, including lifelong learning, provided they are recognised by receiving Universities concerned.

Promotion of mobility by overcoming obstacles to the effective exercise of free movement with particular attention to:

– for students, access to study and training opportunities and to related services;

– for teachers, researchers and administrative staff, recognition and valorisation of periods spent in a European context researching, teaching and training, without prejudicing their statutory rights.

190

Promotion of European co-operation in quality assurance with a view to developing comparable criteria and methodologies

Promotion of the necessary European dimensions in higher education, particularly with regard to curricular development, inter-institutional co-operation, mobility schemes and integrated programmes of study, training and research.

We hereby undertake to attain these objectives – within the framework of our institutional competences and taking full respect of the diversity of cultures, languages, national education systems and of University autonomy – to consolidate the European area of higher education. To that end, we will pursue the ways of intergovernmental co-operation, together with those of non-governmental European organisations with competence on higher education. We expect Universities again to respond promptly and positively and to contribute actively to the success of our endeavour.

Convinced that the establishment of the European area of higher education requires constant support, supervision and adaptation to the continuously evolving needs, we decide to meet again within two years in order to assess the progress achieved and the new steps to be taken.

# Appendix IV

## Towards the European higher education area

Communiqué of the meeting of European Ministers in charge of Higher Education in Prague on 19 May 2001

Two years after signing the Bologna Declaration and three years after the Sorbonne Declaration, European Ministers in charge of higher education, representing 32 signatories, met in Prague in order to review the progress achieved and to set directions and priorities for the coming years of the process. Ministers reaffirmed their commitment to the objective of establishing the European Higher Education Area by 2010. The choice of Prague to hold this meeting is a symbol of their will to involve the whole of Europe in the process in the light of enlargement of the European Union.

Ministers welcomed and reviewed the report "Furthering the Bologna Process" commissioned by the follow-up group and found that the goals laid down in the Bologna Declaration have been widely accepted and used as a base for the development of higher education by most signatories as well as by universities and other higher education institutions. Ministers reaffirmed that efforts to promote mobility must be continued to enable students, teachers, researchers and administrative staff to benefit from the richness of the European Higher Education Area including its democratic values, diversity of cultures and languages and the diversity of the higher education systems.

Ministers took note of the Convention of European higher education institutions held in Salamanca on 29-30 March and the recommendations of the Convention of European Students, held in Göteborg on 24-25 March, and appreciated the active involvement of the European University Association (EUA) and the National Unions of Students in Europe (ESIB) in the Bologna process. They further noted and appreciated the many other initiatives to take the process further. Ministers also took note of the constructive assistance of the European Commission.

Ministers observed that the activities recommended in the Declaration concerning degree structure have been intensely and widely dealt with in most countries. They especially appreciated how the work on quality assurance is moving forward. Ministers recognized the need to cooperate to address the challenges brought about by transnational education. They also recognized the need for a lifelong learning perspective on education.

### Further actions following the six objectives of the Bologna process

As the Bologna Declaration sets out, Ministers asserted that building the European Higher Education Area is a condition for enhancing the attractiveness and competitiveness of higher education institutions in Europe. They supported the idea that higher education should be considered a public good and is and will remain a public responsibility (regulations, etc.), and that students are full members of the higher education community. From this point of view Ministers commented on the further process as follows:

*Adoption of a system of easily readable and comparable degrees*

Ministers strongly encouraged universities and other higher education institutions to take full advantage of existing national legislation and European tools aimed at facilitating academic and professional recognition of course units, degrees and other awards, so that citizens can effectively use their qualifications, competencies and skills throughout the European Higher Education Area.

Ministers called upon existing organizations and networks such as NARIC and ENIC to promote, at institutional, national and European level, simple, efficient and fair recognition reflecting the underlying diversity of qualifications.

*Adoption of a system essentially based on two main cycles*

Ministers noted with satisfaction that the objective of a degree structure based on two main cycles, articulating higher education in undergraduate and graduate studies, has been tackled and discussed. Some countries have already adopted this structure and several others are considering it with great interest. It is important to note that in many countries bachelor's and master's degrees, or comparable two cycle degrees, can be obtained at universities as well as at other higher education institutions. Programmes leading to a degree may, and indeed should, have different orientations and various profiles in order to accommodate a diversity of individual, academic and labour market needs as concluded at the Helsinki seminar on bachelor level degrees (February 2001).

*Establishment of a system of credits*

Ministers emphasized that for greater flexibility in learning and qualification processes the adoption of common cornerstones of qualifications, supported by a credit system such as the ECTS or one that is ECTS-compatible, providing both transferability and accumulation functions, is necessary. Together with mutually recognized quality assurance systems such arrangements will facilitate students' access to the European labour market and enhance the compatibility, attractiveness and competitiveness of European higher education. The generalized use of such a credit system and of the Diploma Supplement will foster progress in this direction.

*Promotion of mobility*

Ministers reaffirmed that the objective of improving the mobility of students, teachers, researchers and administrative staff as set out in the Bologna Declaration is of the utmost importance. Therefore, they confirmed their commitment to pursue the removal of all obstacles to the free movement of students, teachers, researchers and administrative staff and emphasized the social dimension of mobility. They took note of the possibilities for mobility offered by the European Community programmes and the progress achieved in this field, eg in launching the Mobility Action Plan endorsed by the European Council in Nice in 2000.

*Promotion of European cooperation in quality assurance*

Ministers recognized the vital role that quality assurance systems play in ensuring high quality standards and in facilitating the comparability of qualifications throughout Europe. They also encouraged closer cooperation between recognition and quality assurance networks. They emphasized the necessity of close European cooperation and mutual trust in and acceptance of national quality assurance systems. Further they encouraged universities and other higher education institutions to disseminate examples of best practice and to design scenarios for mutual acceptance of evaluation and accreditation/certification mechanisms. Ministers called upon the universities and other higher educations institutions, national agencies and the European Network of Quality Assurance in Higher Education (ENQA), in cooperation with corresponding bodies from countries which are not members of ENQA, to collaborate in establishing a common framework of reference and to disseminate best practice.

*Promotion of the European dimensions in higher education*

In order to further strengthen the important European dimensions of higher education and graduate employability Ministers called upon the higher education sector to increase the development of modules, courses and curricula at all levels with "European" content, orientation or organization. This concerns particularly modules, courses and degree curricula offered in partnership by institutions from different countries and leading to a recognized joint degree.

**Furthermore Ministers emphasized the following points**

*Lifelong learning*

Lifelong learning is an essential element of the European Higher Education Area. In the future Europe, built upon a knowledge-based society and economy, lifelong learning strategies are necessary to face the challenges of competitiveness and the use of new technologies and to improve social cohesion, equal opportunities and the quality of life.

*Higher education institutions and students*

Ministers stressed that the involvement of universities and other higher education institutions and of students as competent, active and constructive partners in the establishment and shaping of a European Higher Education Area is needed and welcomed. The institutions have demonstrated the importance they attach to the creation of a compatible and efficient, yet diversified and adaptable European Higher Education Area. Ministers also pointed out that quality is the basic underlying condition for trust, relevance, mobility, compatibility and attractiveness in the European Higher Education Area. Ministers expressed their appreciation of the contributions toward developing study programmes combining academic quality with relevance to lasting employability and called for a continued proactive role of higher education institutions.

Ministers affirmed that students should participate in and influence the organization and content of education at universities and other higher education institutions. Ministers also reaffirmed the need, recalled by students, to take account of the social dimension in the Bologna process.

*Promoting the attractiveness of the European Higher Education Area*

Ministers agreed on the importance of enhancing attractiveness of European higher education to students from Europe and other parts of the world. The readability and comparability of European higher education degrees world-wide should be enhanced by the development of a common framework of qualifications, as well as by coherent quality assurance and accreditation/certification mechanisms and by increased information efforts.

Ministers particularly stressed that the quality of higher education and research is and should be an important determinant of Europe's international attractiveness and competitiveness. Ministers agreed that more attention should be paid to the benefit of a European Higher Education Area with institutions and programmes with different profiles. They called for increased collaboration between the European countries concerning the possible implications and perspectives of transnational education.

**Continued follow-up**

Ministers committed themselves to continue their cooperation based on the objectives set out in the Bologna Declaration, building on the similarities and benefiting from the differences between cultures, languages and national systems, and drawing on all possibilities of intergovernmental cooperation and the ongoing dialogue with European universities and other higher education institutions and student organizations as well as the Community programmes.

Ministers welcomed new members to join the Bologna process after applications from Ministers representing countries for which the European Community programmes Socrates and Leonardo da Vinci or Tempus-Cards are open. They accepted applications from Croatia, Cyprus and Turkey.

Ministers decided that a new follow-up meeting will take place in the second half of 2003 in Berlin to review progress and set directions and priorities for the next stages of the process towards the European Higher Education Area. They confirmed the need for a structure for the follow-up work, consisting of a follow-up group and a preparatory group. The follow-up group should be composed of representatives of all signatories, new participants and the European Commission, and should be chaired by the EU Presidency at the time. The preparatory group should be composed of representatives of the countries hosting the previous ministerial meetings and the next ministerial meeting, two EU member states and two non-EU member states; these latter four representatives will be elected by the follow-up group. The EU Presidency at the time and the European Commission will also be part of the preparatory group. The preparatory group will be chaired by the representative of the country hosting the next ministerial meeting.

The European University Association, the European Association of Institutions in Higher Education (Eurashe), the National Unions of Students in Europe and the Council of Europe should be consulted in the follow-up work.

In order to take the process further, Ministers encouraged the follow-up group to arrange seminars to explore the following areas: cooperation concerning accreditation and quality assurance, recognition issues and the use of credits in the Bologna process, the development of joint degrees, the social dimension, with specific attention to obstacles to mobility, and the enlargement of the Bologna process, lifelong learning and student involvement.

# Appendix V

## 5th European Conference of Ministers responsible for the Cultural Heritage
### Portorož (Slovenia), 5-7 April 2001

## Resolutions and declaration

### Preamble common to the resolutions

Meeting in Portorož (Slovenia) on 6 and 7 April 2001 for the 5th European Conference of Ministers responsible for the Cultural Heritage, the Ministers of the States Parties to the European Cultural Convention, with the support of the observers from the other countries invited,

– stressing that the existence of the Council of Europe is founded on a "common heritage" of ideals and principles enshrined in its Statute;

– referring to the final declarations of the Summits of Heads of State and Government held in Vienna (1993) and Strasbourg (1997) and the 104th Session of the Committee of Ministers in Budapest (1999);

– proclaiming their commitment to the co-operation framework set up by the Convention for the Protection of the Architectural Heritage of Europe (Granada 1985) and the European Convention for the Protection of the Archaeological Heritage (Valletta 1992) and welcoming the opening for signature in the year 2000 of the European Landscape Convention;

– subscribing to the principles of the Declaration on Cultural Diversity adopted by the Committee of Ministers at their 733rd meeting (2000) and stressing the key contribution of the heritage sector to the policies to be implemented in response to that declaration;

– conscious of the possibilities made available by globalisation for the development of intercultural dialogue and universal access to relevant information, but mindful of the need to preserve the diversity and specific values of the heritage of each individual community,

adopt the following resolutions and declaration.

### Resolution No. 1
### on the role of cultural heritage
### and the challenge of globalisation

We, the European Ministers responsible for the cultural heritage,

I. Welcome the considerable progress made since the first conference organised in Brussels in 1969, and the interest now being taken in cultural heritage;

II. Express our satisfaction concerning the adoption of adequate measures on the national and trans-national levels to protect our common European cultural heritage, and to promote and pursue a common European policy in this field within the framework of the Council of Europe;

III. Are committed to taking co-ordinated action, in response to the economic and political challenges of the new century;

IV. Draw the attention of all public authorities and economic decision-makers to the central role of conserving and promoting cultural heritage in:

– implementing the Council of Europe's objectives of strengthening democracy, maintaining peace, bringing about social progress and sustaining cultural diversity;

– drawing up a pan-European development model to address the challenge of globalisation.

V. In this regard, we stress the following principles:

1. *Cultural heritage and globalisation*

We recognise that, in the context of globalisation, the cultural heritage has special value that requires the development of policies to maintain the common interest in this sector:

We underline, therefore, the necessity to:

*a.* ensure that in the information society, everyone has reasonable access to knowledge, culture and cultural heritage;

*b.* ensure that free access to cultural heritage is governed by an ethical approach towards its market strategy, including reinforcing international co-operation to monitor and combat illicit trafficking;

*c.* raise awareness among communities of the value of cultural heritage as an asset for their sustainable development and quality of life;

*d.* ensure that diversity of cultural heritage at the local, regional and national levels:

– gives people a primary sense of identity;

– provides people with an asset in global economic competition;

– contributes to their prosperity and strengthens the stability and social cohesion that encourage investment.

We call upon public authorities to adopt measures to:

– enable local communities to discover their identity and sense of belonging, through improved understanding of the material, linguistic and spiritual values of cultural heritage;

– protect and enhance the authenticity and integrity of cultural heritage;

– preserve the craft trades and small and medium-sized enterprises which specialise in the maintenance and restoration of the regional character of the heritage;

– ensure a balance between training in new technologies and the development and transmission of traditional skills, thus facilitating the availability and use of traditional materials and techniques;

– work alongside respective professional sectors in the growing use of heritage in cultural industries and tourism, and assure quality of training and the adoption of a code of ethics to prevent manipulation;

– foster the international exchange of experience and practitioners, based on an inter-disciplinary approach, which is essential to spread heritage conservation skills evenly throughout Europe;

– devise a sustainable development model that is both democratic and internationally just, to balance the irreplaceable contribution of the market and private investment, linked to the policies being developed within UNESCO and the Council of Europe.

2. *Promotion of mutual understanding and cohesion*

Recognising that:

– the diverse European landscape has a cultural dimension, perceived by people, which forms their cultural environment, and that

– the preservation and fostering of cultural diversity are constituent elements of the identity of communities and individuals,

We are convinced that:

*a*. individuals and communities have a fundamental right to self-defined identities, to know their history and to shape their future through their heritage. They have a right to enjoy their heritage; they equally have an obligation to respect the heritage of others and to consider the common interest in all heritage;

*b*. the values attached to the cultural environment in Europe:

– should be the basis of mutual understanding and contribute to conflict prevention;

– counterbalance the risks of homogenisation inherent in globalisation;

– set quality standards for improving that environment, and

– are a catalyst for creativity;

*c.* We call upon national, regional and local authorities to:

– promote the integrated conservation of cultural heritage, that respects the diverse contribution of past and present communities, their cultures and patterns of use;

– develop heritage policies which intrinsically benefit, preserve and enhance the identity of individuals and communities and cultural diversity;

– ensure the right of communities, their members and non-governmental organisations to participate adequately in consultation and decision-making processes affecting the heritage;

– encourage freedom of access to the heritage consistent with respect for privacy and cultural values;

– take practical steps to raise awareness of the importance of cultural diversity based on mutual understanding;

and upon national authorities in particular to:

– develop international and trans-frontier co-operation and agreements between states, based on reciprocal responsibility for preserving and enhancing the distinctive heritage of relevant communities;

– encourage trans-frontier contacts and shared projects between related communities and individuals;

– facilitate the involvement of non-governmental organisations and experts, from communities in these links.

Accordingly,

– We agree that cultural heritage policies should aim to preserve cultural diversity and encourage inter-cultural dialogue, and should be focussed on initiatives in the field of education, awareness-raising and life-long training, and;

– We reaffirm that understanding and explaining heritage should be the basis of teaching history, and is of major value for training future citizens in Europe. History teaching should not be limited to commenting on national or local heritages, but also put forward its transnational character.

3. *The contribution of heritage to citizenship and democracy*

Recognising that the cultural environment, like the natural environment, is an ideal area for citizen participation, we call upon public authorities to:

*a.* involve the public and communities, alongside professionals, in identifying and protecting cultural heritage;

*b.* establish the legal, financial and professional framework necessary for concerted action by experts, owners, investors, undertakings and civil society;

*c.* develop the concept of shared responsibilities by incorporating the heritage dimension into economic, social and educational strategies, to facilitate sustainable management of the environment;

*d.* since public funds are necessarily limited, encourage, by appropriate measures and incentives:

– the market to sponsor heritage and invest in its less profitable aspects;

– civil society to play an increasing role in the enlarged field of heritage now perceived by people.

We emphasize that citizen participation is not only of value from the cultural and heritage point of view, but also reflects the development of practical citizenship, vital to achieving the Council of Europe's objective of fostering democratic practices.

4. *Enhancing the cultural environment and the ethical role of the Council of Europe*

Recognising that all elements of the European cultural environment embody both market and cultural values, we strongly recommend our governments and the Council of Europe to elaborate and promote:

*a.* ethical development strategies in the global market that aim to promote prosperity, whilst recognising the essential public dimension to sustaining cultural heritage, its authenticity and integrity;

*b.* policies to achieve quality in contemporary architecture, appropriate to its context, which is essential to create the heritage of tomorrow;

*c.* steps to discourage reproductions of vanished buildings and structures, unless they are proven to be compatible with the aim of preserving the integrity of cultural heritage;

*d.* steps to encourage regular maintenance of heritage;

*e.* spatial development policies that recognise the values of the cultural environment, including the contributions of all historical periods, and the full range of cultural communities;

*f.* cultural co-operation under the aegis of the Council of Europe, recognising its indispensable role in identifying changes in society, formulating ethical approaches and constructing inter-sectoral policies, to give practical effect to the democratic principles that are the European common heritage.

Wish to reinforce co-operation between the Council of Europe and the European Union, Unesco and Iccrom, and associate our member states in the taking of decisions about co-operation;

Request the Council of Europe to develop the tools necessary to implement the foregoing principles;

Invite the Secretary-General to transmit the resolutions adopted on the occasion of the 5th ministerial conference to the competent bodies within the Council of Europe and other international organisations, and inform them about actions to be taken in consequence.

**Resolution No. 2
on the Council of Europe's future activities
in the cultural heritage field, 2002 -2005**

We, the European Ministers responsible for the cultural heritage:

I. Congratulate the Council of Europe for its considerable contribution to an improvement in heritage protection and promotion in member states;

II. Underline the importance of the Council's assistance in framing heritage policies and revising legislation, and in building European networks for technical and professional co-operation and development;

III. in the context of activities under the European Cultural Convention, the Granada (1985) and Valetta (1992) Conventions, looking ahead to the application of the

– European Landscape Convention (2000) within this, the European Year of Languages, and bearing in mind all initiatives in the cultural heritage sector, most recently the Europe, a Common Heritage Campaign:

– Applaud the establishment of the European Heritage Network, and the continuing role of technical assistance activities, which are of central importance to promoting the common cultural heritage as one of the pillars of the European cultural co-operation in the information age;

– Agree that the Council of Europe has a specific role to play in identifying, highlighting and promoting social benefits of the cultural heritage, in the fields of community relations, democratisation and social cohesion;

– Point out that the preservation and use of the cultural heritage, as an asset for development and a factor for social cohesion, should contribute to the aims of the Stability Pact for South Eastern Europe concerning democratisation, sustainable development, co-operation and security;

– Request the Committee of Ministers to ensure that a programme for the period 2002-2005 is prepared and implemented encompassing the following activities:

1. *Reference texts*

Adjusting methods of governance by developing reference texts in the field of cultural heritage, including:

*a.* extending the concept of heritage to encompass the cultural environment, and addressing the need to sustain its cultural values (including material, non-material and spiritual), as perceived by people;

*b.* establishing a responsibility to identify, sustain and allow appropriate access to cultural heritage regardless of its current political context, in the context of reciprocal rights and responsibilities towards all cultural heritage in Europe, encouraging trans-national action and co-operation in its conservation;

*c.* promoting ethical, non-discriminatory policies for public access to information about the cultural heritage, encouraging the use of electronic media, and contributing to the development of adequate policies to combat the illicit traffic in cultural assets that may be encouraged by this increased accessibility of information;

*d.* devising a strategy and implementing a programme for the progressive updating and strengthening of the earlier Conventions and Recommendations and other standard texts, and for ensuring their effective dissemination;

*e.* establishing principles for the reconstruction of damaged or destroyed cultural monuments and for fostering regular maintenance of cultural heritage;

*f.* in the framework of the European Landscape Convention, developing core data standards for documenting cultural landscapes.

2. *The European Heritage Network (HEREIN)*

Permanently establishing the European Heritage Network in the Council of Europe, through a structure to be defined in consultation with member states, and with continued support from a range of partners including the European Foundation for Heritage Skills (FEMP), which could be formally placed under the auspices of the Council of Europe. Specifically, the Network should:

*a.* provide a source of authentic core data and experience in the management of the cultural heritage in Europe, available to administrations and the public alike;

*b.* act as an "observatory" to analyse and forecast the benefits of the cultural heritage to a rapidly changing society;

*c.* facilitate the monitoring of the development of heritage policies, and of compliance with the Conventions;

*d.* maintain and develop heritage co-operation networks, and facilitate trans-national co-operation, particularly in the field of archaeology and that of the combating of illicit trafficking in cultural heritage;

*e.* provide a cultural heritage portal, to effectively disseminate information in the electronic age, facilitate the development of interactive professional forums and data networks, and encourage people, especially the young, to engage with the authentic heritage;

*f.* monitor technological developments in order to facilitate the evolution of an information society respectful of cultural and linguistic diversity in Europe, through

– promoting joint consideration of the legal questions connected with the use of digital images of the heritage,

– the definition of methodological tools making possible the interoperability of scientific databases and the creation of specific multimedia products.

3. *Technical co-operation and fieldwork*

On the basis of the experience acquired through the Council of Europe's Technical Co-operation and Consultancy Programme, and from a trans-sectoral perspective including the built environment, the landscape, and the archaeological heritage underlying both, future activities should:

*a.* meet states' specific requests for co-operation and assistance;

*b.* promote the use of common criteria for the preparation and updating of documentation;

*c.* wherever necessary, assist in reforming management and planning techniques and the administrative and legal framework;

*d.* through practical action on the ground, promote the Council of Europe's principles and ethical values laid down in the reference texts, thereby encouraging feedback and an input to discussions at Council of Europe level.

4. *Teaching, training and awareness-raising*

Drawing on its accumulated experience and established tools, future activities by the Council of Europe should:

*a.* highlight the diversity of Europe's common material and non-material heritage, encouraging a transnational understanding of history and of Europe's current situation and future trends, and encouraging education for democratic citizenship;

*b.* use European Heritage Days to these ends, particularly by developing transfrontier activities and the specific involvement of young people;

*c.* lead to an initiative on ethics and techniques of communication, aimed at various types of heritage professionals working with the public;

*d.* promote, particularly to young people, the continuing relevance of traditional skills and common standards and recognition of heritage-related qualifications at the European level, facilitating the free movement, exchange and transfer of traditional and professional skills.

We, the European Ministers,

– request that an implementation programme be drawn up and circulated promptly,

– resolve to consider the support that we can offer to these activities and to secure the broadest participation possible.

**Declaration on the role of voluntary organizations
in the field of cultural heritage**

Meeting in Portorož (Slovenia) on 6-7 April 2001 for their 5th European Conference, the Ministers responsible for the Cultural Heritage of the States party to the European Cultural Convention,

– referring to Article 11 of the European Convention on Human Rights, granting everybody the right to freedom of peaceful assembly and to freedom of association with others;

– taking into account also Article 10 of the same Convention concerning everyone's right to freedom of expression;

– referring to Article 14 of the Convention for the protection of the Architectural Heritage of Europe;

– reiterating the statement made by the Ministers responsible for the cultural heritage at their 4th European Conference in Helsinki in 1996 that "the role of voluntary organisations should be more effectively promoted, used and encouraged by taking into account the major contributions made by voluntary initiatives in building a democratic society";

– pointing to the fact that the year 2001 has been proclaimed the International Year of Volunteers by the United Nations;

– referring to the UNECE Convention on access to information, public participation in decision-making and access to justice in environmental matters;

– referring to Recommendation 1496 (2001) adopted by the Parliamentary Assembly of the Council of Europe on 24 January 2001 on Improving the status and role of volunteers;

– underlining the important conclusions made by the First European Conference on voluntary organisations in the field of cultural heritage held in Oslo on 21-24 September 2000;

– at the same time acknowledging that the main responsibility for the protection of the cultural heritage remains with governmental authorities;

adopt the following declaration on the role of voluntary organisations in the field of cultural heritage.

We, the European Ministers responsible for the Cultural Heritage,

Agree that the general principles valid for all voluntary organisations are also valid for those working in the cultural heritage field;

Request public authorities in our member states to base their action regarding voluntary work upon the following principles;

1. The existence of voluntary organisations is important to building and consolidating societies based on pluralistic political democracy.

2. Voluntary organisations run according to democratic principles are essential in educating people in true democracy.

3. The right to establish voluntary organisations is an integral part of human rights and should be encouraged by all governments.

4. Voluntary organisations should be granted full freedom of speech, whilst respecting the normal limitations necessary in a democratic society.

5. Voluntary organisations should have access to the information necessary to facilitate their role of monitoring and constructive criticism of the heritage protection policies of public authorities.

6. Voluntary organisations should be given an appropriate opportunity to participate in decision-making processes, for instance in spatial planning and the selection of monuments and sites for protection.

7. Voluntary organisations should be encouraged to supplement governmental and other public work, taking on responsibilities that do not normally or naturally fall within the responsibilities of such agencies.

8. Governments should encourage voluntary organisations to take an active part in preventing conflicts by respecting cultural diversity and encouraging the protection of the culture of others.

9. The establishment and work of voluntary organisations should not in any way be hindered by bureaucratic mismanagement.

10. So far as possible, public authorities should implement financial measures to encourage and assist the development of voluntary organisations.

11. Financial measures should be available without limiting the ability of voluntary organisations to fulfil their role as constructive critics of government policies.
12. Financial measures should be transparent and easily accessible in order to achieve democratic accountability in the distribution of available resources.

13. Voluntary organisations are essential for disseminating knowledge to the public at large in the framework of their mission.

14. Co-operation between cultural heritage and other organisations should be encouraged, in order to secure a trans-sectoral and coherent policy for the conservation of the environment as a whole.

15. Voluntary organisations should establish their credibility through their achievements, standards and ability to take responsibility.

16. Voluntary organisations should respect legislation in their field, but should be encouraged to propose improvements if need be.

17. Voluntary organisations should have access to training in order to enhance their competence as active participants in society's protection of the cultural heritage.

We, the Ministers responsible for the cultural heritage urge the Council of Europe to:

– set up a twinning system where associations are made between new voluntary cultural heritage organisations and well established ones;

– secure a regular contact forum in the form of European conferences for voluntary organisations in the cultural heritage field by utilising existing structures, when possible;

– develop the European heritage network (HEREIN) as a portal to an electronic forum where voluntary organisations can communicate and liaise.

*Final declaration*

The European Ministers responsible for the cultural heritage, on the occasion of their 5th Conference, held in Portorož on 6-7 April 2001, express their warm gratitude to the Slovenian government for all its efforts, which ensured the success of the Conference, and their congratulations on the perfect organisation of the event.

# Appendix VI

## Recommendation No. R (98) 5
## of the Committee of Ministers to member states
## concerning heritage education

*(Adopted by the Committee of Ministers on 17 March 1998, at the 623rd meeting of the Ministers' Deputies)*

The Committee of Ministers, pursuant to Article 15.*b* of the Statute of the Council of Europe,

Considering that the aim of the Council of Europe is to achieve a greater unity between its members;

Having regard to the European Cultural Convention signed in Paris on 19 December 1954;

Having regard to the Convention for the Protection of the Architectural Heritage of Europe signed in Granada on 3 October 1985;

Having regard to the European Convention on the Protection of the Archaeological Heritage (revised) signed in Malta on 16 January 1992;

Having regard to the declaration of the heads of state and government of the Council of Europe member states signed in Vienna on 9 October 1993;

Having regard to its previous recommendations:

– on the specialised training of architects, town planners, civil engineers and landscape designers (Recommendation No. R (80) 16);

– on modern languages (Recommendation No. R (82) 18);

– concerning the promotion of an awareness of Europe in secondary schools (Recommendation No. R (83) 4);

– on the role of the secondary school in preparing young people for life (Recommendation No. R (83) 13);

– on the training of teachers in education for intercultural understanding, notably in a context of migration (Recommendation No. R (84) 18);

– on aid for artistic creation (Recommendation No. R (85) 6);

– on teaching and learning about human rights in schools (Recommendation No. R (85) 7);

– on the role of museums in environmental education, information and training (Recommendation No. R (90) 18);

Having regard to Resolution No. 2 of the 2nd European Conference of Ministers responsible for Architectural Heritage on the promotion of architectural heritage in socio-cultural life as a factor in the quality of life (Granada, 3-4 October 1985);

Having regard to the Helsinki Declaration of the 4th European Conference of Ministers responsible for the Cultural Heritage on the political dimension of cultural heritage conservation in Europe (30-31 May 1996);

Having regard to the resolution of the 18th Session of the Standing Conference of European Ministers of Education on the promotion of school links and exchanges in Europe (Madrid, 23-24 March 1994);

Having regard to Recommendation 1111 (1989) of the Parliamentary Assembly of the Council of Europe on the European dimension of education;

Considering that one of the aims of education is to train young people to have respect for diverse cultures, citizenship and democracy;

Bearing in mind that cultural heritage is comprised of cultural contributions and interactions from many sources and periods;

In the light of heritage-based activities already carried out, *inter alia* European heritage classes;

Being convinced that the development of European heritage-based activities requires investment, mobility and appropriate training for teachers and cultural officers;

Taking into account the conclusions of the Brussels seminar (28-30 August 1995) on "Cultural heritage and its educational implications: a factor for tolerance, good citizenship and social integration";

Asserting that educational activities in the heritage field are an ideal way of giving meaning to the future by providing a better understanding of the past,

Recommends member states to adopt appropriate legislative, regulatory, administrative, financial and other measures to initiate and develop heritage education activities and to promote heritage awareness among the young in accordance with the principles set out in the appendix to this recommendation;

Instructs the Secretary General to transmit the text of this recommendation to the non-member states which are parties to the European Cultural Convention.

**Appendix to Recommendation No. R (98) 5**

I. *Scope and definitions*

For the purpose of this recommendation:

i. "cultural heritage" includes any material or non-material vestige of human endeavour and any trace of human activities in the natural environment;

ii. "heritage education" means a teaching approach based on cultural heritage, incorporating active educational methods, cross-curricular approaches, a partnership between the fields of education and culture and employing the widest variety of modes of communication and expression;

iii. "cultural" professionals, associations or organisations are recognised professionals, associations or organisations working in the cultural and environmental field, from the heritage to contemporary creation;

iv. "European heritage classes" consist of an approach to heritage education, including international school exchanges based on a common project and themes related to cultural heritage; they form part of the curriculum but involve fieldwork outside the school; they allow young people at all levels and types of education to discover the richness of heritage in its context and to grasp its European dimension.

II. *Implementing heritage education*

Heritage education, which is cross-curricular by its very nature, should be promoted through the medium of different school subjects at all levels and in all types of teaching.

*a.* Organisation

Initiatives taken by schools, universities, cultural heritage professionals and associations and their governing bodies should be encouraged and facilitated, in so far as they fit into the definitions outlined in Section I.

Efforts of associations and cultural organisations should be supported, *inter alia* in the establishment of centres which host heritage classes, and the participation of cultural professionals should be encouraged.

Evaluation of the results of each action should be undertaken by the partners and/or the relevant ministries, especially that taken at educational, cultural, organisational and financial levels.

*b.* Training

Heritage education presupposes a link with school programmes and appropriate training for teachers.

Theoretical and practical training courses should, wherever possible, be organised for both teachers and cultural professionals.

Heritage staff, at all levels, should be made aware of questions relating to heritage education and, if possible be given training in catering for young visitors.

*c.* Administrative measures

Steps should be taken at the appropriate administrative level to allow and facilitate pupil and teacher travel.

Favourable administrative measures should be adopted for teachers and cultural personnel to enable them to prepare, implement and follow up, in the best possible conditions, educational projects relating to heritage, and in particular heritage classes.

Encouragement should be given to the setting up of educational departments in cultural organisations.

*d.* Finance

All young people, irrespective of their family or financial background, should be able to take part in heritage education activities.

A partnership, which also may cover financial aspects, should be set up on an official basis between the relevant ministries, if possible within existing structures.

The costs incurred in organising European heritage classes (travel, accommodation, preparation) should be borne, wherever possible, at least in part by the relevant authorities.

The organisers of heritage education activities should, if necessary, be assisted in the preparation of a financial plan, as this is not an area for which they are specifically qualified.

III. *Documentation*

The relevant authorities and ministries in each country should be encouraged to produce or commission teaching material relating to cultural heritage.

Heritage education activities should be able to employ the most up-to-date information and communication technologies.

Exchange of material and experience and a better multilateral dissemination of information concerning heritage sites and associated teaching approaches should be ensured. The setting up and a co-ordination of networks in this field would be desirable.

## Appendix VII

## European Convention on the Protection of the Archaelogical Heritage (revised)
## Valetta, 16 January 1992

### Preamble

The member States of the Council of Europe and the other States party to the European Cultural Convention signatory hereto,

Considering that the aim of the Council of Europe is to achieve a greater unity between its members for the purpose, in particular, of safeguarding and realising the ideals and principles which are their common heritage;

Having regard to the European Cultural Convention signed in Paris on 19 December 1954, in particular Articles 1 and 5 thereof;

Having regard to the Convention for the Protection of the Architectural Heritage of Europe signed in Granada on 3 October 1985;

Having regard to the European Convention on Offences relating to Cultural Property signed in Delphi on 23 June 1985;

Having regard to the recommendations of the Parliamentary Assembly relating to archaeology and in particular Recommendations 848 (1978), 921 (1981) and 1072 (1988);

Having regard to Recommendation No. R (89) 5 concerning the protection and enhancement of the archaeological heritage in the context of town and country planning operations;

Recalling that the archaeological heritage is essential to a knowledge of the history of mankind;

Acknowledging that the European archaeological heritage, which provides evidence of ancient history, is seriously threatened with deterioration because of the increasing number of major planning schemes, natural risks, clandestine or unscientific excavations and insufficient public awareness;

Affirming that it is important to institute, where they do not yet exist, appropriate administrative and scientific supervision procedures, and that the need to protect the archaeological heritage should be reflected in town and country planning and cultural development policies;

Stressing that responsibility for the protection of the archaeological heritage should rest not only with the State directly concerned but with all European countries, the aim being to reduce the risk of deterioration and promote conservation by encouraging exchanges of experts and the comparison of experiences;

Noting the necessity to complete the principles set forth in the European Convention for the Protection of the Archaeological Heritage signed in London on 6 May 1969, as a result of evolution of planning policies in European countries,

Have agreed as follows.

## Definition of the archaeological heritage

*Article 1*

1. The aim of this (revised) Convention is to protect the archaeological heritage as a source of the European collective memory and as an instrument for historical and scientific study.

2. To this end shall be considered to be elements of the archaeological heritage all remains and objects and any other traces of mankind from past epochs:

i. the preservation and study of which help to retrace the history of mankind and its relation with the natural environment;

ii. for which excavations or discoveries and other methods of research into mankind and the related environment are the main sources of information; and

iii. which are located in any area within the jurisdiction of the Parties.

3. The archaeological heritage shall include structures, constructions, groups of buildings, developed sites, moveable objects, monuments of other kinds as well as their context, whether situated on land or under water.

## Identification of the heritage and measures for protection

*Article 2*

Each Party undertakes to institute, by means appropriate to the State in question, a legal system for the protection of the archaeological heritage, making provision for:

i. the maintenance of an inventory of its archaeological heritage and the designation of protected monuments and areas;

ii. the creation of archaeological reserves, even where there are no visible remains on the ground or under water, for the preservation of material evidence to be studied by later generations;

iii. the mandatory reporting to the competent authorities by a finder of the chance discovery of elements of the archaeological heritage and making them available for examination.

*Article 3*

To preserve the archaeological heritage and guarantee the scientific significance of archaeological research work, each Party undertakes:

i. to apply procedures for the authorisation and supervision of excavation and other archaeological activities in such a way as:

*a.* to prevent any illicit excavation or removal of elements of the archaeological heritage;

*b.* to ensure that archaeological excavations and prospecting are undertaken in a scientific manner and provided that:

– non-destructive methods of investigation are applied wherever possible;

– the elements of the archaeological heritage are not uncovered or left exposed during or after excavation without provision being made for their proper preservation, conservation and management;

ii. to ensure that excavations and other potentially destructive techniques are carried out only by qualified, specially authorised persons;

iii. to subject to specific prior authorisation, whenever foreseen by the domestic law of the State, the use of metal detectors and any other detection equipment or process for archaeological investigation.

*Article 4*

Each Party undertakes to implement measures for the physical protection of the archaeological heritage, making provision, as circumstances demand:

i. for the acquisition or protection by other appropriate means by the authorities of areas intended to constitute archaeological reserves;

ii. for the conservation and maintenance of the archaeological heritage, preferably *in situ*;

iii. for appropriate storage places for archaeological remains which have been removed from their original location.

**Integrated conservation of the archaeological heritage**

*Article 5*

Each Party undertakes:

i. to seek to reconcile and combine the respective requirements of archaeology and development plans by ensuring that archaeologists participate:

*a.* in planning policies designed to ensure well-balanced strategies for the protection, conservation and enhancement of sites of archaeological interest;

*b.* in the various stages of development schemes;

ii. to ensure that archaeologists, town and regional planners systematically consult one another in order to permit:

*a.* the modification of development plans likely to have adverse effects on the archaeological heritage;

*b.* the allocation of sufficient time and resources for an appropriate scientific study to be made of the site and for its findings to be published;

iii. to ensure that environmental impact assessments and the resulting decisions involve full consideration of archaeological sites and their settings;

iv. to make provision, when elements of the archaeological heritage have been found during development work, for their conservation *in situ* when feasible;

v. to ensure that the opening of archaeological sites to the public, especially any structural arrangements necessary for the reception of large numbers of visitors, does not adversely affect the archaeological and scientific character of such sites and their surroundings.

**Financing of archaeological research and conservation**

*Article 6*

Each Party undertakes:

i. to arrange for public financial support for archaeological research from national, regional and local authorities in accordance with their respective competence;

ii. to increase the material resources for rescue archaeology:

*a.* by taking suitable measures to ensure that provision is made in major public or private development schemes for covering, from public sector or private sector resources, as appropriate, the total costs of any necessary related archaeological operations;

218

*b.* by making provision in the budget relating to these schemes in the same way as for the impact studies necessitated by environmental and regional planning precautions, for preliminary archaeological study and prospection, for a scientific summary record as well as for the full publication and recording of the findings.

**Collection and dissemination of scientific information**

*Article 7*

For the purpose of facilitating the study of, and dissemination of knowledge about, archaeological discoveries, each Party undertakes:

i. to make or bring up to date surveys, inventories and maps of archaeological sites in the areas within its jurisdiction;

ii. to take all practical measures to ensure the drafting, following archaeological operations, of a publishable scientific summary record before the necessary comprehensive publication of specialised studies.

*Article 8*

Each Party undertakes:

i. to facilitate the national and international exchange of elements of the archaeological heritage for professional scientific purposes while taking appropriate steps to ensure that such circulation in no way prejudices the cultural and scientific value of those elements;

ii. to promote the pooling of information on archaeological research and excavations in progress and to contribute to the organisation of international research programmes.

**Promotion of public awareness**

*Article 9*

Each Party undertakes:

i. to conduct educational actions with a view to rousing and developing an awareness in public opinion of the value of the archaeological heritage for understanding the past and of the threats to this heritage;

ii. to promote public access to important elements of its archaeological heritage, especially sites, and encourage the display to the public of suitable selections of archaeological objects.

**Prevention of the illicit circulation of elements of the archaeological heritage**

*Article 10*

Each Party undertakes:

i. to arrange for the relevant public authorities and for scientific institutions to pool information on any illicit excavations identified;

ii. to inform the competent authorities in the State of origin which is a Party to this Convention of any offer suspected of coming either from illicit excavations or unlawfully from official excavations, and to provide the necessary details thereof;

iii. to take such steps as are necessary to ensure that museums and similar institutions whose acquisition policy is under State control do not acquire elements of the archaeological heritage suspected of coming from uncontrolled finds or illicit excavations or unlawfully from official excavations;

iv. as regards museums and similar institutions located in the territory of a Party but the acquisition policy of which is not under State control:

*a.* to convey to them the text of this (revised) Convention;

*b.* to spare no effort to ensure respect by the said museums and institutions for the principles set out in paragraph 3 above;

v. to restrict, as far as possible, by education, information, vigilance and co-operation, the transfer of elements of the archaeological heritage obtained from uncontrolled finds or illicit excavations or unlawfully from official excavations.

*Article 11*

Nothing in this (revised) Convention shall affect existing or future bilateral or multilateral treaties between Parties, concerning the illicit circulation of elements of the archaeological heritage or their restitution to the rightful owner.

**Mutual technical and scientific assistance**

*Article 12*

The Parties undertake:

i. to afford mutual technical and scientific assistance through the pooling of experience and exchanges of experts in matters concerning the archaeological heritage;

ii. to encourage, under the relevant national legislation or international agreements binding them, exchanges of specialists in the preservation of the archaeological heritage, including those responsible for further training.

**Control of the application of the (revised) Convention**

*Article 13*

For the purposes of this (revised) Convention, a committee of experts, set up by the Committee of Ministers of the Council of Europe pursuant to Article 17 of the Statute of the Council of Europe, shall monitor the application of the (revised) Convention and in particular:

i. report periodically to the Committee of Ministers of the Council of Europe on the situation of archaeological heritage protection policies in the States Parties to the (revised) Convention and on the implementation of the principles embodied in the (revised) Convention;

ii. propose measures to the Committee of Ministers of the Council of Europe for the implementation of the (revised) Convention's provisions, including multilateral activities, revision or amendment of the (revised) Convention and informing public opinion about the purpose of the (revised) Convention;

iii. make recommendations to the Committee of Ministers of the Council of Europe regarding invitations to States which are not members of the Council of Europe to accede to this (revised) Convention.

**Final clauses**

*Article 14*

1. This (revised) Convention shall be open for signature by the member States of the Council of Europe and the other States party to the European Cultural Convention.

It is subject to ratification, acceptance or approval. Instruments of ratification, acceptance or approval shall be deposited with the Secretary General of the Council of Europe.

2. No State party to the European Convention on the Protection of the Archaeological Heritage, signed in London on 6 May 1969, may deposit its instrument of ratification, acceptance or approval unless it has already denounced the said Convention or denounces it simultaneously.

3. This (revised) Convention shall enter into force six months after the date on which four States, including at least three member States of the Council of Europe, have expressed their consent to be bound by the (revised) Convention in accordance with the provisions of the preceding paragraphs.

4. Whenever, in application of the preceding two paragraphs, the denunciation of the Convention of 6 May 1969 would not become effective simultaneously with the entry into force of this (revised) Convention, a Contracting State may, when depositing its instrument of ratification, acceptance or approval, declare that it will continue to apply the Convention of 6 May 1969 until the entry into force of this (revised) Convention.

5. In respect of any signatory State which subsequently expresses its consent to be bound by it, the (revised) Convention shall enter into force six months after the date of the deposit of the instrument of ratification, acceptance or approval.

*Article 15*

1. After the entry into force of this (revised) Convention, the Committee of Ministers of the Council of Europe may invite any other State not a member of the Council and the European Economic Community, to accede to this (revised) Convention by a decision taken by the majority provided for in Article 20.d of the Statute of the Council of Europe and by the unanimous vote of the representatives of the Contracting States entitled to sit on the Committee.

2. In respect of any acceding State or, should it accede, the European Economic Community, the (revised) Convention shall enter into force six months after the date of deposit of the instrument of accession with the Secretary General of the Council of Europe.

*Article 16*

1. Any State may, at the time of signature or when depositing its instrument of ratification, acceptance, approval or accession, specify the territory or territories to which this (revised) Convention shall apply.

2. Any State may at any later date, by a declaration addressed to the Secretary General of the Council of Europe, extend the application of this (revised) Convention to any other territory specified in the declaration. In respect of such territory the (revised) Convention shall enter into force six months after the date of receipt of such declaration by the Secretary General.

3. Any declaration made under the two preceding paragraphs may, in respect of any territory specified in such declaration, be withdrawn by a notification addressed to the Secretary General. The withdrawal shall become effective six months after the date of receipt of such notification by the Secretary General.

*Article 17*

1. Any Party may at any time denounce this (revised) Convention by means of a notification addressed to the Secretary General of the Council of Europe.

2. Such denunciation shall become effective six months following the date of receipt of such notification by the Secretary General.

*Article 18*

The Secretary General of the Council of Europe shall notify the member States of the Council of Europe, the other States party to the European Cultural Convention and any State or the European Economic Community which has acceded or has been invited to accede to this (revised) Convention of:

i. any signature;

ii. the deposit of any instrument of ratification, acceptance, approval or accession;

iii. any date of entry into force of this (revised) Convention in accordance with Articles 14, 15 and 16.

iv. any other act, notification or communication relating to this (revised) Convention.

In witness whereof the undersigned, being duly authorised thereto, have signed this revised Convention.

Done at Valletta, this 16th day of January 1992, in English and French, both texts being equally authentic, in a single copy which shall be deposited in the archives of the Council of Europe. The Secretary General of the Council of Europe shall transmit certified copies to each member State of the Council of Europe, to the other States party to the European Cultural Convention, and to any non-member State or the European Economic Community invited to accede to this (revised) Convention.

# Appendix VIII

## Convention for the Protection
## of the Architectural Heritage of Europe
## Granada, 3 October 1985

The member States of the Council of Europe, signatory hereto,

Considering that the aim of the Council of Europe is to achieve a greater unity between its members for the purpose, *inter alia*, of safeguarding and realising the ideals and principles which are their common heritage;

Recognising that the architectural heritage constitutes an irreplaceable expression of the richness and diversity of Europe's cultural heritage, bears inestimable witness to our past and is a common heritage of all Europeans;

Having regard to the European Cultural Convention signed in Paris on 19 December 1954 and in particular to Article 1 thereof;

Having regard to the European Charter of the Architectural Heritage adopted by the Committee of Ministers of the Council of Europe on 26 September 1975 and to Resolution (76) 28, adopted on 14 April 1976, concerning the adaptation of laws and regulations to the requirements of integrated conservation of the architectural heritage;

Having regard to Recommendation 880 (1979) of the Parliamentary Assembly of the Council of Europe on the conservation of the European architectural heritage;

Having regard to Recommendation No. R (80) 16 of the Committee of Ministers to member States on the specialised training of architects, town planners, civil engineers and landscape designers, and to Recommendation No. R (81) 13 of the Committee of Ministers, adopted on 1 July 1981, on action in aid of certain declining craft trades in the context of the craft activity;

Recalling the importance of handing down to future generations a system of cultural references, improving the urban and rural environment and thereby fostering the economic, social and cultural development of States and regions;

Acknowledging the importance of reaching agreement on the main thrust of a common policy for the conservation and enhancement of the architectural heritage,

Have agreed as follows:

### Definition of the architectural heritage

*Article 1*

For the purposes of this Convention, the expression "architectural heritage" shall be considered to comprise the following permanent properties:

1. monuments: all buildings and structures of conspicuous historical, archaeological, artistic, scientific, social or technical interest, including their fixtures and fittings;

2. groups of buildings: homogeneous groups of urban or rural buildings conspicuous for their historical, archaeological, artistic, scientific, social or technical interest which are sufficiently coherent to form topographically definable units;

3. sites: the combined works of man and nature, being areas which are partially built upon and sufficiently distinctive and homogeneous to be topographically definable and are of conspicuous historical, archaeological, artistic, scientific, social or technical interest.

## Identification of properties to be protected

*Article 2*

For the purpose of precise identification of the monuments, groups of buildings and sites to be protected, each Party undertakes to maintain inventories and in the event of threats to the properties concerned, to prepare appropriate documentation at the earliest opportunity.

## Statutory protection procedures

*Article 3*

Each Party undertakes:

1. to take statutory measures to protect the architectural heritage;

2. within the framework of such measures and by means specific to each State or region, to make provision for the protection of monuments, groups of buildings and sites.

*Article 4*

Each Party undertakes:

1. to implement appropriate supervision and authorisation procedures as required by the legal protection of the properties in question;

2. to prevent the disfigurement, dilapidation or demolition of protected properties. To this end, each Party undertakes to introduce, if it has not already done so, legislation which:

a. requires the submission to a competent authority of any scheme for the demolition or alteration of monuments which are already protected, or in respect of which protection proceedings have been instituted, as well as any scheme affecting their surroundings;

*b.* requires the submission to a competent authority of any scheme affecting a group of buildings or a part thereof or a site which involves demolition of buildings

– the erection of new buildings
– substantial alterations which impair the character of the buildings or the site;

*c.* permits public authorities to require the owner of a protected property to carry out work or to carry out such work itself if the owner fails to do so;

*d.* allows compulsory purchase of a protected property.

*Article 5*

Each Party undertakes to prohibit the removal, in whole or in part, of any protected monument, except where the material safeguarding of such monuments makes removal imperative. In these circumstances the competent authority shall take the necessary precautions for its dismantling, transfer and reinstatement at a suitable location.

**Ancillary measures**

*Article 6*

Each Party undertakes:

1. to provide financial support by the public authorities for maintaining and restoring the architectural heritage on its territory, in accordance with the national, regional and local competence and within the limitations of the budgets available;

2. to resort, if necessary, to fiscal measures to facilitate the conservation of this heritage;

3. to encourage private initiatives for maintaining and restoring the architectural heritage.

*Article 7*

In the surroundings of monuments, within groups of buildings and within sites, each Party undertakes to promote measures for the general enhancement of the environment.

*Article 8*

With a view to limiting the risks of the physical deterioration of the architectural heritage, each Party undertakes:

1. to support scientific research for identifying and analysing the harmful effects of pollution and for defining ways and means to reduce or eradicate these effects;

2. to take into consideration the special problems of conservation of the architectural heritage in anti-pollution policies.

## Sanctions

*Article 9*

Each Party undertakes to ensure within the power available to it that infringements of the law protecting the architectural heritage are met with a relevant and adequate response by the competent authority. This response may in appropriate circumstances entail an obligation on the offender to demolish a newly erected building which fails to comply with the requirements or to restore a protected property to its former condition.

## Conservation policies

*Article 10*

Each Party undertakes to adopt integrated conservation policies which:

1. include the protection of the architectural heritage as an essential town and country planning objective and ensure that this requirement is taken into account at all stages both in the drawing up of development plans and in the procedures for authorising work;

2. promote programmes for the restoration and maintenance of the architectural heritage;

3. make the conservation, promotion and enhancement of the architectural heritage a major feature of cultural, environmental and planning policies;

4. facilitate whenever possible in the town and country planning process the conservation and use of certain buildings whose intrinsic importance would not warrant protection within the meaning of Article 3, paragraph 1, of this Convention but which are of interest from the point of view of their setting in the urban or rural environment and of the quality of life;

5. foster, as being essential to the future of the architectural heritage, the application and development of traditional skills and materials.

*Article 11*

Due regard being had to the architectural and historical character of the heritage, each Party undertakes to foster:

– the use of protected properties in the light of the needs of contemporary life;
– the adaptation when appropriate of old buildings for new uses.

*Article 12*

While recognising the value of permitting public access to protected properties, each Party undertakes to take such action as may be necessary to ensure that the consequences of permitting this access, especially any structural development, do not adversely affect the architectural and historical character of such properties and their surroundings.

*Article 13*

In order to facilitate the implementation of these policies, each Party undertakes to foster, within its own political and administrative structure, effective co-operation at all levels between conservation, cultural, environmental and planning activities.

**Participation and associations**

*Article 14*

With a view to widening the impact of public authority measures for the identification, protection, restoration, maintenance, management and promotion of the architectural heritage, each Party undertakes:

1. to establish in the various stages of the decision-making process, appropriate machinery for the supply of information, consultation and co-operation between the State, the regional and local authorities, cultural institutions and associations, and the public;

2. to foster the development of sponsorship and of non-profit-making associations working in this field.

**Information and training**

*Article 15*

Each Party undertakes:

1. to develop public awareness of the value of conserving the architectural heritage, both as an element of cultural identity and as a source of inspiration and creativity for present and future generations;

2. to this end, to promote policies for disseminating information and fostering increased awareness, especially by the use of modern communication and promotion techniques, aimed in particular:

*a.* at awakening or increasing public interest, as from school-age, in the protection of the heritage, the quality of the built environment and architecture;

*b.* at demonstrating the unity of the cultural heritage and the links that exist between architecture, the arts, popular traditions and ways of life at European, national and regional levels alike.

*Article 16*

Each Party undertakes to promote training in the various occupations and craft trades involved in the conservation of the architectural heritage.

**European co-ordination of conservation policies**

*Article 17*

The Parties undertake to exchange information on their conservation policies concerning such matters as:

1. the methods to be adopted for the survey, protection and conservation of properties having regard to historic developments and to any increase in the number of properties concerned;

2. the ways in which the need to protect the architectural heritage can best be reconciled with the needs of contemporary economic, social and cultural activities;

3. the possibilities afforded by new technologies for identifying and recording the architectural heritage and combating the deterioration of materials as well as in the fields of scientific research, restoration work and methods of managing and promoting the heritage;

4. ways of promoting architectural creation as our age's contribution to the European heritage.

*Article 18*

The Parties undertake to afford, whenever necessary, mutual technical assistance in the form of exchanges of experience and of experts in the conservation of the architectural heritage.

*Article 19*

The Parties undertake, within the framework of the relevant national legislation, or the international agreements, to encourage European exchanges of specialists in the conservation of the architectural heritage, including those responsible for further training.

*Article 20*

For the purposes of this Convention, a Committee of Experts set up by the Committee of Ministers of the Council of Europe pursuant to Article 17 of the Statute of the Council of Europe shall monitor the application of the Convention and in particular:

1. report periodically to the Committee of Ministers of the Council of Europe on the situation of architectural heritage conservation policies in the States Parties to the Convention, on the implementation of the principles embodied in the Convention and on its own activities;

2. propose to the Committee of Ministers of the Council of Europe measures for the implementation of the Convention's provisions, such measures being deemed to include multilateral activities, revision or amendment of the Convention and public information about the purpose of the Convention;

3. make recommendations to the Committee of Ministers of the Council of Europe regarding invitations to States which are not members of the Council of Europe to accede to this Convention.

*Article 21*

The provisions of this Convention shall not prejudice the application of such specific more favourable provisions concerning the protection of the properties described in Article 1 as are embodied in:

– the Convention for the Protection of World Cultural and Natural Heritage of 16 November 1972;

– the European Convention on the Protection of the Archaeological Heritage of 6 May 1969.

**Final clauses**

*Article 22*

1. This Convention shall be open for signature by the member States of the Council of Europe. It is subject to ratification, acceptance or approval. Instruments of ratification, acceptance or approval shall be deposited with the Secretary General of the Council of Europe.

2. This Convention shall enter into force on the first day of the month following the expiration of a period of three months after the date on which three member States of the Council of Europe have expressed their consent to be bound by the Convention in accordance with the provisions of the preceding paragraph.

3. In respect of any member State which subsequently expresses it consent to be bound by it, the Convention shall enter into force on the first day of the month following the expiration of a period of three months after the date of the deposit of the instrument of ratification, acceptance or approval.

*Article 23*

1. After the entry into force of this Convention, the Committee of Ministers of the Council of Europe may invite any State not a member of the Council and the European Economic Community to accede to this Convention by a decision taken by the majority provided for in Article 20.d of the Statute of the Council of Europe and by the unanimous vote of the representatives of the Contracting States entitled to sit on the Committee.

2. In respect of any acceding State or, should it accede, the European Economic Community, the Convention shall enter into force on the first day of the month following the expiration of a period of three months after the date of deposit of the instrument of accession with the Secretary General of the Council of Europe.

*Article 24*

1. Any State may, at the time of signature or when depositing its instrument of ratification, acceptance, approval or accession, specify the territory or territories to which this Convention shall apply.

2. Any State may at any later date, by a declaration addressed to the Secretary General of the Council of Europe, extend the application of this Convention to any other territory specified in the declaration. In respect of such territory the Convention shall enter into force on the first day of the month following the expiration of a period of three months after the date of receipt of such declaration by the Secretary General.

3. Any declaration made under the two preceding paragraphs may, in respect of any territory specified in such declaration, be withdrawn by a notification addressed to the Secretary General. The withdrawal shall become effective on the first day of the month following the expiration of a period of six months after the date of receipt of such notification by the Secretary General.

*Article 25*

1. Any State may, at the time of signature or when depositing its instrument of ratification, acceptance, approval or accession, declare that it reserves the right not to comply, in whole or in part, with the provisions of Article 4, paragraphs c and d. No other reservations may be made.

2. Any Contracting State which has made a reservation under the preceding paragraph may wholly or partly withdraw it by means of a notification addressed to the Secretary General of the Council of Europe. The withdrawal shall take effect on the date of receipt of such notification by the Secretary General.

3. A Party which has made a reservation in respect of the provisions mentioned in paragraph 1 above may not claim the application of that provision by any other Party; it may, however, if its reservation is partial or conditional, claim the application of that provision in so far as it has itself accepted it.

*Article 26*

1. Any Party may at any time denounce this Convention by means of a notification addressed to the Secretary General of the Council of Europe.

2. Such denunciation shall become effective on the first day of the month following the expiration of a period of six months after the date of receipt of such notification by the Secretary General.

*Article 27*

The Secretary General of the Council of Europe shall notify the member States of the Council of Europe, any State which has acceded to this Convention and the European Economic Community if it has acceded, of:

*a.* any signature;

*b.* the deposit of any instrument of ratification, acceptance, approval or accession;

*c.* any date of entry into force of this Convention in accordance with Articles 22, 23 and 24;

*d.* any other act, notification or communication relating to this Convention.

In witness whereof the undersigned, being duly authorised thereto, have signed this Convention.

Done at Granada, this 3rd day of October 1985, in English and French, both texts being equally authentic, in a single copy which shall be deposited in the archives of the Council of Europe. The Secretary General of the Council of Europe shall transmit certified copies to each member State of the Council of Europe and to any State or to the European Economic Community invited to accede to this Convention.

# Appendix IX

## Recommendation Rec(2005)13
## of the Committee of Ministers to member states
## on the governance and management of university heritage

*(Adopted by the Committee of Ministers on 7 December 2005*
*at the 950th meeting of the Ministers' Deputies)*

### Preamble

The Committee of Ministers of the Council of Europe, under the terms of Article 15.*b* of the Statute of the Council of Europe,

Considering that the aim of the Council of Europe is to achieve greater unity among its members and that this aim can be pursued notably by common action in educational and cultural matters;

Having regard to the European Cultural Convention of 1954 (ETS No. 18);

Having regard to the Convention for the Protection of the Architectural Heritage of Europe (Granada Convention) (ETS No. 121) and to the European Convention on the Protection of the Archaeological Heritage (Revised) (Valletta Convention) (ETS No. 143);

Having regard to the Final Declaration and the Action Plan adopted by the Second Summit of Heads of State and Government of the Council of Europe (October 1997);

Having regard to the "Europe, a Common Heritage" campaign, undertaken between 1999 and 2000 on the decision of the Second Summit, and in particular to the project on the heritage of European universities within this campaign;

Having regard to the Joint Declaration of the European Ministers of Education signed in Bologna on 19 June 1999 launching the Bologna Process of higher education reform aiming to establish a European Higher Education Area by 2010;

Considering that the heritage of European universities encompasses elements of key importance to higher education today, such as academic and institutional autonomy, the ability to adapt and renew while preserving core values of independent scholarship, and freedom of teaching and learning, and that these are fully compatible with the values of the Council of Europe;

Considering that university autonomy is an integral part of the heritage of European universities and one of the key principles of higher education in Europe;

Considering that this very university autonomy has confirmed the uniqueness of university heritage;

Considering that cultural heritage is the subject of international legal instruments, such as the Granada and Valletta Conventions, that address general issues of cultural heritage without specific reference to the heritage of universities;

Considering that the responsibility for the governance and management of the university heritage is shared between governments, other public authorities at national, regional and local levels and higher education institutions;

Considering the role played in the governance and management of university heritage by non-governmental organisations at international, national and regional levels;

Considering that the newer standard-setting texts on cultural heritage within the context of the Council of Europe provide a wider definition of the concept of cultural heritage with more emphasis on beliefs, perceptions, traditions and concepts that make reference to intellectual heritage;

Having regard to the Hague Convention for the Protection of Cultural Property in the Event of Armed Conflict of 14 May 1954 and its Second Protocol of 26 March 1999, the UNESCO Convention for the Safeguarding of the Intangible Cultural Heritage of 17 October 2003 and the World Intellectual Property Organisation's normative texts directly related to intellectual heritage, such as the Berne Convention for the Protection of Literary and Artistic Works;

Considering that cultural heritage is subject to national legislation, most of which deals with heritage in broader terms rather than specific aspects of heritage, such as university heritage and that, in some countries, higher education legislation may contain provisions that are also relevant to university heritage, but that there is little or no synergy between these two categories of laws;

Considering that no international standards exist specifically for university heritage and that policies and strategies for the protection of this heritage are highly diverse and range from fully developed structures to an absence of definition of management responsibilities other than informal precedent;

Considering that higher education institutions have a double mission as concerns training in heritage: on the one hand, they have a mission to train high level specialists in all heritage-related fields, while on the other hand, they also have a mission to provide training in the specific heritage of universities for both heritage specialists and members of the academic community specialising in other areas;

Considering that the European dimension is an integral part of university heritage, and vice versa, that universities are, by their history, their heritage and their current activities, European and international institutions par excellence, and that the European dimension should guide all activities related to university heritage,

Recommends that the governments of member states:

*a.*     take steps to implement in their policy, law and practice the principles set out in the appendix to this recommendation;

*b.*     promote the implementation of the principles and measures contained in the appendix where this is not the direct responsibility of governments;

*c.*     promote the implementation of these measures by relevant public authorities at all levels as well as higher education institutions;

*d.*     ensure that this recommendation is distributed as widely as possible among all persons and bodies concerned.

*Appendix to Recommendation Rec(2005)13*

**Scope**

1.     The present recommendation aims to set out guidelines for and good practice in the governance and management of the heritage of European universities.

2.     The provisions of this recommendation are applicable to higher education institutions and bodies seeking to adhere to the traditions and values that this heritage represents as defined in the present recommendation, and that assume responsibility for the protection and enhancement of these traditions and values as a common European heritage, regardless of the age of these institutions.

3.     This recommendation is addressed to governments. However, in view of the shared responsibility for the governance and management of university heritage, its provisions may be implemented not only by governments, but also by other public authorities at national, regional and local levels, higher education institutions and public bodies responsible for the management and protection of cultural heritage, as the case may be.

**Definitions**

*University/higher education institution*

4.     For the purposes of the present recommendation, the terms "university" and "higher education institution" shall designate an establishment providing higher education and being recognised by the competent authority as belonging to its system of higher education. For the purposes of the present text, the terms shall be used indiscriminately, even if it is realised that in some higher education systems, a formal and/or legal distinction is made between various kinds of higher education institutions, and that the right to the use of the term "university" may be protected by law.

5.        For the purposes of this recommendation, the "heritage of universities" shall be understood to encompass all tangible and intangible heritage related to higher education institutions, bodies and systems as well as to the academic community of scholars and students, and the social and cultural environment of which this heritage is a part. The "heritage of universities" is understood as being all tangible and intangible traces of human activity relating to higher education. It is an accumulated source of wealth with direct reference to the academic community of scholars and students, their beliefs, values, achievements and their social and cultural function as well as modes of transmission of knowledge and capacity for innovation.

## Institutional heritage policies

6.        The heritage of European universities concerns individual higher education institutions as well as the academic community of scholars and students collectively, and European society at large. Higher education institutions should be encouraged to establish transparent institutional policies for protecting and raising awareness of their heritage both within the institutions and in the larger society. In so doing, institutions could make explicit their understanding, preservation and enhancement of their heritage and the goals for its conservation and for raising awareness of it, as well as specify the structure, instruments and means with which the institution intends to implement these policies, including its decision-making structures and a clear planning process.

## Legislative framework

7.        Competent public authorities and higher education institutions should be encouraged to make full use of existing laws and of external and internal regulations for the protection and preservation of the heritage of universities.

8.        Competent public authorities and higher education institutions should, however, be encouraged to review their laws and/or internal regulations with a view to adopting adequate provisions to protect their heritage where such do not already exist. In their internal regulations, universities should be encouraged to take account of possible measures for protecting and raising awareness of the heritage of universities as outlined in the present recommendation through legislation as well as guidelines established by professional organisations.

9.        The status of the university heritage and parts thereof should be clarified through law or internal university regulations, as the case may be.

## Heritage governance and management at higher education institutions

10.        University leaders should be encouraged to consider all parts of the heritage of a higher education institution as falling under their ultimate legal, administrative and moral responsibility.

11.     Universities should be encouraged to define, as appropriate in the context of the particular institution, the political and administrative responsibility for the university heritage as well as appropriate reporting mechanisms.

12.     Higher education institutions should be encouraged to make their goals and policies for the university heritage explicit, for example through the adoption of a heritage charter for the institution or a specific heritage plan.

13.     Institutions and units managing parts of the university heritage, such as museums, collections, libraries, archives, building services or university departments, should be encouraged to make explicit their goals and policies for the parts of the university heritage that fall under their responsibility, taking due account of the overall heritage policies of the higher education institution of which they are a part.

14.     The management of the university heritage and parts thereof should conform to the best national and international standards established by competent heritage bodies or authorities within or outside of the university.

15.     In considering major overall decisions and developments, including strategic plans for the institution, plans for the use of its buildings and their surroundings and other development plans, elected bodies as well as the administration of higher education institutions should be encouraged to give explicit consideration to the impact of such plans and decisions on the university heritage.

16.     Universities should be encouraged to make acquisitions, bequests, loans, deposits and disposals an integral part of institutional policy and allow them to benefit from adequate conservation measures and administrative and financial safeguards, including insurance policies.

**Finance**

17.     The financing of the policies for university heritage falls under the shared responsibility of government and of higher education institutions. In systems with public financing of higher education – whether entirely or partially – the competent public authorities should include provisions for the financing of the policies for the university heritage in the budgets allocated to higher education institutions. The institutions should in their turn be encouraged to make provision for the financing of their heritage policies within their own budget, whether publicly or privately funded, and seek to obtain additional funding from external sources.

18.     Higher education institutions and bodies should be encouraged to provide and maintain suitable physical accommodation for their heritage and to provide balanced and reasonable funding for its protection and enhancement.

19.     To the extent that the upkeep and protection of university heritage is financed through the general university budget, rather than through earmarked provisions from public or other sources, higher education institutions should be

encouraged to set up the budget in such a way as to make it possible to identify the appropriations for heritage purposes.

20.      Where required, institutions should be encouraged to seek supplementary external funds to enhance their heritage and implement their heritage policies. Such funds may be sought from local, regional, national or international sources.

**Access**

21.      As far as compatible with the main missions of the university and with international and national standards of ethical practice, universities should be encouraged to make their heritage accessible to members of the academic community and/or the general public, as appropriate.

22.      In some cases, access may need to be restricted in order to protect and conserve specific parts of this heritage or for reasons that have to do with the research and teaching of the institution. In such cases, institutions should be encouraged to make every effort to achieve a reasonable balance between heritage conservation needs, the needs of research and teaching and the desirability of providing wide access for the general public. However, at no time should the conservation of university heritage be endangered by institutional policies concerning access to this heritage.

23.      Institutions should be encouraged to give access to their university heritage for members of the general public at affordable prices and within reasonable opening hours.

24.      Higher education institutions and bodies should be encouraged to take appropriate measures to safeguard and protect their heritage.

25.      As far as possible and in accordance with their general heritage policies, universities should be encouraged to take appropriate measures and develop methods for the promotion of the value, nature and interest of this heritage today.

**Professionalisation**

26.      Higher education institutions, in co-operation with ministries or agencies responsible for higher education and cultural heritage and/or relevant professional organisations, as appropriate, should be encouraged to consider qualifications requirements, career structures and professional development plans for different categories of staff working on university heritage. In particular, they should be encouraged to credit academic staff with appropriate academic merit for their work with museums, collections, archives, libraries and other academic work related to university heritage.

27.      Higher education institutions should be encouraged to consider elaborating specific instructions for heritage-related posts, emphasising the specific professional requirements.

28.     They should be encouraged to advertise internationally at least those heritage-related posts that require a high level of heritage expertise, with a view to making it possible to fill some posts with foreign experts. Governments should take steps to abolish any remaining legislation stipulating that certain posts at higher education institutions or heritage institutions may only be filled by nationals.

29.     Higher education institutions and bodies as well as ministries responsible for higher education and/or cultural heritage should seek to set up fora and networks, both nationally and internationally, for professional exchange and development among heritage professionals working on university heritage.

## Training

30.     Higher education institutions should be encouraged to establish training programmes in heritage-related fields. They should aim to provide balanced competences and skills combining an overview and a common-heritage approach with training in the specific knowledge and skills required of the various heritage-related professions as well as "instrumental" skills and, as far as possible, should be integrated with and draw on existing heritage units at the institution.

31.     Students in heritage-related fields should be strongly encouraged to train for at least one semester at a foreign university, and universities should be encouraged to make every effort to recognise the period spent at a foreign institution as part of the degree to be earned from the student's home institution. Higher education institutions should also be encouraged to seek co-operation with other institutions with a view to offering joint, advanced-level heritage courses involving staff and students from several universities.

## Research

32.     With due regard for the principle of institutional autonomy and for the freedom of academic staff to select the topics of their own research, higher education institutions should encourage research on heritage by their own staff as well as by other qualified researchers, taking an interdisciplinary and comparative approach and, as appropriate, seeking to co-ordinate such research.

33.     Research councils, international research programmes, foundations and other bodies funding research should be encouraged to support programmes and projects to further research both on heritage in general and more specifically on the heritage of universities, in particular programmes and projects involving specialists from a variety of disciplines (conservation, restoration, inventories, core data systems and applied high technology) and/or from a variety of higher education institutions from various countries.

34.     Higher education institutions and bodies should be encouraged to make all parts of their heritage available for research purposes in so far as this does not entail a risk for the conservation of this heritage. In the latter case, they should be encouraged to seek alternative solutions for the proper use of this heritage for research purposes.

**Awareness raising**

35.     Higher education institutions should be encouraged to make focused efforts to raise awareness of their heritage in the academic community of scholars and students, in their local communities, among political decision makers and in civil society at large.

36.     Higher education institutions should be encouraged to include in their awareness-raising efforts activities which aim to improve knowledge and understanding of their heritage among pupils and teachers at schools, in particular local schools, in order to help them identify with this heritage and see it as a part of the heritage of their community and region as well as a part of the common heritage of Europe.

37.     Higher education institutions should be encouraged to develop policies and strategies for co-operating with media on a regular basis to raise awareness of their university heritage. They should also be encouraged to prepare publications on their history and heritage and to aim at least some of them at general readers and be available at an affordable price.

38.     Higher education institutions should be encouraged to provide staff members responsible for communication, external relations and awareness-raising activities with a background in the heritage of the institution as well as in the heritage of European universities.

**Relations with the local community**

39.     True to their mission of teaching, research and awareness raising, higher education institutions should, in general terms, be encouraged to seek to develop and maintain close connections with the local communities of which they are a part and offer their services and expertise to these communities as appropriate.

40.     Higher education institutions should be encouraged to seek to develop close relations with local authorities as well as with civil society in the communities in which they are located. Local and regional authorities should, for their part, also be encouraged to seek to develop and maintain close relations with higher education institutions in their area.

**International co-operation**

41.     Governments should encourage universities as well as relevant public authorities to explore and make use of all possibilities to establish European and international co-operation activities in heritage-related fields, including, as appropriate, programmes of international organisations and institutions, such as the Council of Europe, UNESCO, the European Union, the European Science Foundation, University Museums and Collections (UMAC), International Council of Museums (ICOM/ICOMOS) or the International Council on Archives (ICA),

regional co-operation programmes, university networks and bilateral university co-operation.

42.　　In the same way, universities should be encouraged to promote heritage research projects, including a comparative and/or European dimension, in particular where such projects include co-operation between staff at various European universities.

43.　　Governments should encourage higher education institutions as well as relevant public authorities to make full use of the opportunities offered for increased international co-operation within the framework of a European higher education area and of Council of Europe conventions and other legal instruments.

# Appendix X

## Explanatory report to Recommendation Rec(2005)13 of the Committee of Ministers to member states on the governance and management of university heritage

### Introduction and context

In 1999-2000, the Council of Europe conducted a campaign entitled "Europe, a common heritage". The decision to launch this campaign was made at the highest level – at the 2nd Summit of Heads of State and Government of the Council of Europe (Strasbourg, October 1997) – and it came to encompass a high number of national and transnational projects and events.

Within the campaign, five transnational projects were carried out under a covenant between the Council of Europe and the European Commission and co-financed by the two institutions. One of these was also a joint project between two different parts of the Council of Europe, namely those responsible for cultural heritage – the secretariat of the campaign – and for higher education and research, as well as between the two committees responsible for these areas.

This project focused on the heritage of European universities, it involved some 12 universities[96] and was carried out through four thematic meetings, each of which involved a number of invited experts in addition to the representatives of the participating universities as well as, for the final meeting, the CRE:[97]

i.      Alcalá de Henares (launching of the project, 9-10 December 1999);

ii.     Montpellier (the intellectual heritage of European universities, 13-14 March 2000);

iii.    Bologna (the material traces of the heritage of European universities, 28-29 July 2000);

iv.     Kraków (the European dimension of the university heritage, 23-24 October 2000).

The purpose of the project was to raise awareness of the key role of universities in the cultural heritage of Europe as well as to encourage universities to co-operate at European level to define a common approach to their common problems and deficiencies with regard to their heritage. It thus had a double aim: the heritage of European universities and the European university as heritage. The transmission,

---

96. The universities of Alcalá, Bologna, Cluj-Napoca, Coimbra, İstanbul, Kraków, Louvain/Leuven, Montpellier, Santiago de Compostela, Tartu, Vilnius and Zagreb.
97. On 31 March 2001, the CRE (Conférence des recteurs européens – the European Rectors' Conference) merged with the Confederation of Rectors' Conference of the European Union to form the EUA – European University Association.

generation and implementation of human knowledge, academic attitudes and social values were key factors in the project, which aimed to make the university conscious of its role as a multicultural space of learning and teaching, conceived as a project of and for society.

As a transversal effort, the project sought to strike a balance between the concerns of institutional policy makers, such as rectors and deans, and heritage specialists working in these universities. While the experts involved included two of the foremost specialists on the history of European universities, the project was careful to distinguish between history and heritage and to emphasise the function of transmission, which is a key aspect of the heritage concept.

The first phase of the project gave rise to a publication,[98] it provided a platform for discussion and exchange of experience, and it identified four areas in which traditional and newer universities could co-operate to raise awareness of their heritage both within the academic community of students and teachers and in society at large:

–	by bringing together the **information on university heritage** which is already available and by making new information available through a common format, using the new information technologies and by setting up a common Web portal;

–	by developing **European standards and norms** on preserving and raising awareness of the cultural heritage of European universities;

–	through **European courses** which encourage the mobility of students and teachers and by introducing heritage programmes at all levels of study, and teacher training courses for heritage methodology in its European dimension, bearing in mind the reforms outlined in the Bologna Declaration;

–	through **a network** of European universities concerned with their heritage. The purpose of a network would be to bring together universities with a specific commitment to their heritage as well as to raise awareness of this heritage among a wider public, in particular schoolchildren.

This was, of course, a quite ambitious agenda, and it was decided to focus the second phase of the project on considering possible European standards and norms.

Moreover, it was decided to focus this work on standards for governance and management of the university heritage, as the first phase of the project had revealed considerable deficiencies with regard to institutional policies in this area. In fact, few universities seem to have institutional policies for their heritage, as opposed to policies for specific parts of that heritage, such as individual museums or collections. The standards would have to take account of the fact that university

98. Nuria Sanz and Sjur Bergan (eds.): *The Heritage of European Universities* (Strasbourg 2002: Council of Europe Publishing, ISBN 92-871-4960-7 (English version)); Nuria Sanz et Sjur Bergan (sous la direction de): *Le patrimoine des universités européennes* (Strasbourg 2002: Editions du Conseil de l'Europe, 92-871-4959-3 (French version)).

autonomy is an integral part of the heritage of European universities and one of the key principles of higher education in Europe.

## Dimensions of the university heritage

The work on standards for the governance of the university heritage has relied on a clear view of what constitutes this heritage, of which the first part of the project demonstrated some of the main elements.

Firstly, historical universities provide a **holistic approach** for heritage purposes not easily found elsewhere. In this sense, they constitute relevant and global heritage laboratories. Throughout their history, universities have faced many difficulties that they have been able to surmount by being highly flexible institutions. Consciousness of the university heritage will help universities face the challenges they are currently facing in their mission as centres of teaching, learning and development of new knowledge in rapidly changing societies.

Secondly, the university functions as a **laboratory** of ideas, policies and practice with regard to all aspects of the cultural heritage: archives, libraries, buildings, historical gardens and mobile collections. It thus provides a more complete compendium of heritage than any other individual institution. This global context needs to be addressed specifically.

Thirdly, policies for the **intangible heritage** of universities were an important aspect of the project. In this sense, the university constitutes an important point of reference in beginning to define and valorise the intellectual heritage of Europe as a part of our intangible heritage. The uniqueness of the intellectual heritage is shown through the integrative power and freedom of learning and scientific research with regard to language, aesthetic, mythical, religious and historical endeavour. Intangible/immaterial heritage implies ethical practice, a way of thought and understanding that shape the fundaments of communal academic life, transmitted through the tradition, including rites, customs, values and principles.

Yet, while we have so far found the distinction between tangible and intangible heritage[99] useful for operational purposes, it should be underlined that it is not clear cut and that to some extent it is even artificial and many – possibly most – heritage elements embody both aspects. We have so far maintained the distinction between tangible and intangible to draw attention to the intellectual heritage.

Fourthly, the university is a quintessentially European institution. The **European dimension** of the intellectual heritage of universities draws its power from the heterogeneity of a multiple national experience. Yet, it is a salient feature of the heritage of European universities that this diversity is played out on the background of a common heritage. Conceptualisation and visions of a common European tradition should include flexibility, respect, preservation, responsibility, acceptance of diversity and conscience of transmission. Universities should not, however, limit their horizons to Europe: in accordance with their mission, they should also be open

---

99. Sometimes also referred to, less precisely, as "material" and "immaterial" heritage.

to the wider world. In the first part of the project, this was in particular underlined by the universities of Coimbra and Istanbul,[100] each on the background of its particular experience with Latin America and Africa in the first case and with the Middle East and as a "bridge between East and West" in the second.

Last, but not least, it should be underlined that while the initial project had to be based on a small group of universities with relatively long traditions, it is important to underline that the **university heritage is a common value for all universities**, both the traditional universities and new ones that may want to adhere to a sustainable tradition in a prospective way. To take just one example among many: in the case of the Serbian universities, the years of the Milošević regime, and in particular the 1998 Law on Universities, implied a break with and departure from the heritage of European universities, at least in institutional terms, in that the regime appointed university leadership played a political rather than educational or cultural role. Yet, the European university heritage was upheld both by individual staff and students and by the Alternative Academic Education Network (AAEN). The AAEN as well as individual staff and students thus laid the ground for the return of Serbian universities to the European university heritage following the political changes of October 2000.

The point should also be made explicitly that the European university heritage is not the exclusive domain of older universities. Rather, many of the universities that have been established over the past generation have participated in the European university heritage in an essential way, above all by trying to organise training programmes to meet a demand from heritage professionals. Therefore, the considerations of standards for the management of the university heritage includes not only all aspects of this heritage, but also all academic institutions that are a part of it, regardless of the year in which they were established.

**Preamble**

The Preamble outlines the context of the recommendation and refers to relevant texts adopted by the Council of Europe and in other contexts. Attention is in particular drawn to the fact that the present recommendation constitutes the first intergovernmental international standards conceived specifically for the university heritage.

**Scope (paragraphs 1-3)**

This part of the text outlines the scope, purpose and ambition of the recommendation. It should in particular be noted that in view of the wide variety of current models for the governance of university heritage and the likelihood that these varieties will persist in view of different traditions as to central authority, faculty organisation and autonomy, budget systems, the organisation of museums and collections, the position of university libraries and archives and other factors, the aim of the present recommendation is to outline key elements of which account

---

100. In their answers to the questionnaires for the fourth meeting of the project (Kraków, 23-24 October 2000).

should be taken in the governance and management of the university heritage rather than recommend one specific model for all circumstances.

The concept of university heritage is understood in a wide sense of the term (see also Definitions, below) and applies to all higher education institutions and bodies that, on the one hand, seek to adhere to the traditions and values embodied in this heritage and, on the other hand, assume responsibility for the protection and enhancement of this heritage.

In view of the fact that responsibility for the governance and management of the university heritage is shared between governments, other public authorities at national, regional and local level, higher education institutions and public bodies responsible for the management and protection of cultural heritage and that the precise competence in this area varies among the states to which this recommendation is addressed, the provisions of the recommendation are addressed to all of these bodies, as appropriate in each individual case.

**Definitions (paragraphs 4 and 5)**

The definition of "university/higher education institution" is standard and reflects the fact that precise definitions differ among the countries to which the recommendation is directed. It is adapted from the Council of Europe/UNESCO Convention on the Recognition of Qualifications concerning Higher Education in the European Region (ETS No. 165). In this context, reference is made to the scope of the concept of university heritage as outlined above.

The definition of the "heritage of universities" is comprehensive and emphasises the academic community of scholars and students and their beliefs, values, achievements and their social and cultural function as well as modes of transmission and knowledge innovation. For practical reasons, reference is often made to intangible and tangible heritage, while keeping in mind that the two interact and are elements of an indissociable whole in which one element cannot exist without the other. The heritage of European universities includes:

i.    the transmission of human experience, aspirations and achievements as well as the development of knowledge within or related to higher education institutions and bodies;

ii.    the concept of the identity of scholars and students as an academic community;

iii.    the traditions, methods and output of teaching, learning and research within higher education institutions and bodies;

iv.    the freedom of academic teaching and research;

v.    the autonomy of universities;

vi.    the freedom of thought, belief and expression;

vii.    the values and ethics of higher education institutions and bodies and of the academic community, including openness, tolerance, respect and acceptance and a critical attitude;

viii.    the search for new knowledge, intellectual discoveries and intellectual development as a duty incumbent on the members of the academic community;

ix.    the traditions and customs, rules and regulations of higher education institutions and bodies and of the academic community emanating from these values;

x.    the academic tradition of open, public dialogue and critical discourse;

xi.    the production of social value and the social responsibility of higher education institutions and body and the academic community;

xii.    protected buildings used by higher education institutions or bodies for purposes pertaining to the functions of such institutions;

xiii.    the cultural environment of which the higher education institution or body is a part, such as a university town, urban traces or a *quartier universitaire*;

xiv.    museums, collections and movable heritage of private or public origin, in current academic use or otherwise, of an artistic, archaeological, historic, educational, scientific, natural or technical character;

xv.    historic libraries and library collections;

xvi.    historic documentary, administrative and academic archives;

xvii.    historic and botanical gardens, research stations and nature reserves;

xviii.    historical and ceremonial items, such as gowns and insignia;

xix.    other traces of human activity relating to higher education.

**Institutional heritage policies (paragraph 6)**

This paragraph underlines the triple focus of the recommendation: higher education institutions, the academic community of scholars and students and society at large. It further underlines the need for institutions to establish heritage policies, which emerged as one of the major deficiencies in the surveys conducted in the first phase of the project on the heritage of European universities.

As with the other parts of the recommendation that are addressed to higher education institutions and their leadership, the recommendations are phrased in the form of encouragement and seeks to avoid unnecessary detail. In general terms, it could be argued that institutional policies should seek to make explicit the institution's understanding, preservation and enhancement of its heritage and the goals for its conservation and for raising awareness of it as well as specify the structure, instruments and means with which the institution intends to implement these policies, including its decision making structures and a clear planning process.

**Legislative framework (paragraphs 7-9)**

The recommendation underlines the need to provide legal protection for the university heritage, by using existing laws as far as possible, and encourages competent public authorities as well as higher education institutions to review existing laws and internal regulations to this effect.

Paragraph 10 underlines the desirability of clarifying the relationship between the university and the different units constituting this heritage, such as museums, collections, libraries, archives and built heritage. This is particularly urgent in systems where faculties and other units have a high degree of autonomy from the central decision making bodies of the university, and where the scope for institutional heritage policies is correspondingly reduced. This would be the case in, but not limited to, most countries of the former Yugoslavia, where faculties are independent legal persons.

**Heritage governance and management at higher education institutions (paragraphs 10-16)**

The ultimate responsibility for the university heritage should lie with the leadership of the higher education institution. This responsibility should extend to making explicit goals for the university heritage as well as to defining policies to achieve these goals and to consider the impact of institutional policies in other areas on the university heritage. In this context, institutions should also be encouraged to make explicit the means by which they plan to implement their goals.

It is further important that those with specific responsibility for the university heritage, whether these be elected or administrative officers or collective bodies, such as advisory committees, have direct access to the institutional leadership to the extent possible.

While this responsibility may be vested in one central body or administration or be distributed according to the type of heritage (e.g. built heritage, museums, collections, libraries, archives, intellectual heritage) or its physical location (faculty level, or between various parts of the university if these are physically separated), the higher education institution should be encouraged to ensure a measure of co-ordination at central level to ensure coherent policies and transparent and easily accessible information. This could be achieved through an administrative unit with responsibility for the heritage policies of the institution, an elected official with similar responsibilities, through an advisory committee of both heritage specialists and other representatives of the academic community, possibly also of experts from outside the institution and/or representatives of the wider community.

The recommendation further underlines the need for university heritage management to conform to and be guided by the best national and international standards established by competent heritage bodies or authorities.

## Finance (paragraphs 17-20)

The budget is a key instrument for implementing institutional higher education policies, which will remain ineffective unless they are backed by financial commitments. Budget policies should therefore be an important part of policies for the university heritage. Institutions should be encouraged to set up their financial systems so as to make it possible to identify the budget resource allocated to heritage, and to seek funding for heritage related purposes in accordance with their institutional heritage policies. The structure of budget and information systems also gives an indication of which activities are considered important, in that these are the ones for which the system is often able to provide detailed information, whereas less important activities may easily be grouped in an "other items" category. As far as possible, institutions and public authorities should be able to identify funds spent on the university heritage.

## Access (paragraphs 21-25)

The issue of access to the university heritage for the general public is an important one. The recommendation seeks to weigh the interests of heritage conservation, teaching and research and access for the general public. On the one hand, access for the general public is important with a view to creating awareness of the university heritage, while on the other hand, conservation concerns may make it necessary to restrict access permanently or temporarily. The recommendation suggests that access be as wide as possible, but not at the cost of endangering the university heritage. The measures taken to safeguard the university heritage should be differentiated in accordance with the value of and the threat to the different elements that make up this heritage. The recommendation also underlines the need that access be made effective, once the level of access has been decided, based on the considerations outlined in the recommendation, i.e. that opening hours and prices be reasonable as judged by local standards and conditions, for example in terms of the cost of living.

## Professionalisation (paragraphs 26-29)

These paragraphs underline the need to valorise the specific professional competence of heritage specialists within higher education institutions. Whereas research results, and to some extent teaching ability, are the determining factors in academic careers, in filling heritage related posts, due account should be given to specific professional requirements for such posts, which may include management experience, experience in organising and running exhibitions, experience in conservation and restoration, or other specific heritage related professional experience. Conversely, high-level heritage related experience should also be considered of academic merit in related fields. In particular, it would seem important to include knowledge and experience of heritage and heritage management among the required qualifications for posts as heads of museums, collections, libraries, archives or other heritage related units, and that such responsibilities not be automatically linked to chairs in specific departments.

The provisions of paragraph 29 correspond fairly closely to international best practice for the advertising of academic posts. It should be noted that language proficiency requirements may be stipulated. The recommendation to abolish any nationality requirements has previously been made in general terms for all academic positions in Recommendation No. R (85) 21 of the Committee of Ministers on mobility of academic staff.

**Training (paragraphs 30 and 31)**

Higher education institutions have an important mission in training future heritage specialists and heritage methodologists, both for the general heritage area and for the heritage that specifically concerns higher education. Heritage related training programmes could therefore aim at giving students balanced competences and skills in heritage and not be limited to certain aspects or disciplines of heritage, such as archaeology or history of art and at offering students the opportunity to develop a comparative perspective.

Heritage related training programmes should be designed so as to take full advantage of the reform of degree structures towards a two tier ("Bachelor/Master") structure as well as other reforms of the Bologna Process aiming to establish a European Higher Education Area by 2010, including the further development and use of the European Credit Transfer System (ECTS).

Higher education institutions should also be encouraged to include an international experience in their heritage training and methodology programmes, either by making use of established exchange programmes such as ERASMUS, ERASMUS Mundus, CEEPUS[101] or NORDPLUS, or by co-operating with other institutions with a view to offering joint programmes. Interesting examples of such initiatives in other fields include the Community of Mediterranean Universities (CMU), which offers a number of such courses in various areas, known as CMU schools, where the minimum requirement is the participation of at least three institutions from different countries. Courses will be given at one of the participating institutions, either in the language of the institution or in a language that is widely used internationally. The Nordic Agricultural University is another relevant model, in that it is an institutionalised co-operation (and not an independent institution) drawing on the courses and resources of the agricultural universities of the five Nordic countries offering specific courses on behalf of all five institutions and open to all their qualified students.

**Research (paragraphs 32-34)**

These paragraphs have a double objective: on the one hand, they underline the need to stimulate research and research co-operation in heritage related areas, both in terms of co-operation between researchers in various academic disciplines and

---

101. Central European Exchange Program for University Studies.

across institutional and national borders. On the other hand, it also underlines the need for institutions to put their own heritage at the disposal of research or, where this for good reason is not possible, to seek alternative solutions.

**Awareness raising (paragraphs 35-38)**

Heritage is heritage only to the extent it is transmitted, and awareness raising is therefore an important aspect of any heritage policy. In the case of university heritage, there is certainly need for awareness raising within the academic community of staff and students, but also in society at large.

To be effective, institutions need to elaborate policies for awareness raising and differentiate their efforts according to specific target groups and objectives, and the recommendation lists a number of possible measures. Where these include popularisation of the history and heritage of the university, it is important that these conform to the standards of scholarship. Of the large number of institutional histories published on the occasion of institutional anniversaries and therefore referred to as "jubilee publications", relatively few would currently seem to meet these requirements. As a part of their awareness raising efforts, higher education institutions should be encouraged to develop policies and strategies for co-operating with media on a regular basis and to provide staff members responsible for communication, external relations and awareness raising activities with an adequate background in the heritage of European universities as well as of the specific institution at which they are employed.

**Relations with the local community (paragraphs 39 and 40)**

The term "university town" indicates that a university is a part of a local community, and in the case of some universities, a very important part. This is the case of Alcalá, Bologna, Coimbra, Kraków, Santiago de Compostela and Tartu, to take just a few examples from the institutions participating in the project. Nevertheless, the relationship between the university and the local community are not always well developed, and they are certainly not always easy. The recommendation underlines the need for higher education institutions to engage with the local community of which they are a part also as concerns their heritage, at both institutional level and with the civic community. In the heritage field, universities could for example encourage their specialists in heritage related areas to serve on or offer advice to heritage boards and other bodies concerned with the heritage of the local community and to make their heritage available to the community on a permanent basis and through special arrangements such as "Open days" – such as the European Heritage Days – exhibitions or campaigns. For their part, municipal leaders and bodies should seek to develop relations with the higher education institutions located in their community and seek the opinion of higher education institutions on municipal plans and projects that may affect the university heritage.

**International co-operation (paragraphs 41-43)**

The university is a European and international institution par excellence, and this is also reflected in its heritage and values. The recommendation underlines the need to develop this dimension through institutional policies for the university heritage, whether through international organisations and programmes, university or professional networks, bilateral co-operation and other means. Institutions should give due consideration to including heritage related programmes in their existing international co-operation as well as to developing new co-operation where required. One example could be co-operation in applied technologies for conservation. The recommendation makes specific reference to new development of considerable relevance to international co-operation on the university heritage: the emerging European Higher Education Area, and it underlines the importance of the Council of Europe's legal standards.

The NGOs to which reference is made in paragraph 43 are UMAC,[102] ICOM/ICOMOS[103] and the ICA.[104]

---

102. International Committee for University Museums and Collections.
103. The International Council of Museums.
104. The International Council on Archives.

# Sales agents for publications of the Council of Europe
# Agents de vente des publications du Conseil de l'Europe

**BELGIUM/BELGIQUE**
La Librairie Européenne -
The European Bookshop
Rue de l'Orme, 1
B-1040 BRUXELLES
Tel.: +32 (0)2 231 04 35
Fax: +32 (0)2 735 08 60
E-mail: order@libeurop.be
http://www.libeurop.be

Jean De Lannoy
Avenue du Roi 202 Koningslaan
B-1190 BRUXELLES
Tel.: +32 (0)2 538 43 08
Fax: +32 (0)2 538 08 41
E-mail: jean.de.lannoy@dl-servi.com
http://www.jean-de-lannoy.be

**CANADA and UNITED STATES/**
**CANADA et ÉTATS-UNIS**
Renouf Publishing Co. Ltd.
1-5369 Canotek Road
OTTAWA, Ontario K1J 9J3, Canada
Tel.: +1 613 745 2665
Fax: +1 613 745 7660
Toll-Free Tel.: (866) 767-6766
E-mail: orders@renoufbooks.com
http://www.renoufbooks.com

**CZECH REPUBLIC/**
**RÉPUBLIQUE TCHÈQUE**
Suweco CZ, s.r.o.
Klecakova 347
CZ-180 21 PRAHA 9
Tel.: +420 2 424 59 204
Fax: +420 2 848 21 646
E-mail: import@suweco.cz
http://www.suweco.cz

**DENMARK/DANEMARK**
GAD
Vimmelskaftet 32
DK-1161 KØBENHAVN K
Tel.: +45 77 66 60 00
Fax: +45 77 66 60 01
E-mail: gad@gad.dk
http://www.gad.dk

**FINLAND/FINLANDE**
Akateeminen Kirjakauppa
PO Box 128
Keskuskatu 1
FIN-00100 HELSINKI
Tel.: +358 (0)9 121 4430
Fax: +358 (0)9 121 4242
E-mail: akatilaus@akateeminen.com
http://www.akateeminen.com

**FRANCE**
La Documentation française
(diffusion/distribution France entière)
124, rue Henri Barbusse
F-93308 AUBERVILLIERS CEDEX
Tél.: +33 (0)1 40 15 70 00
Fax: +33 (0)1 40 15 68 00
E-mail: prof@ladocumentationfrancaise.fr
http://www.ladocumentationfrancaise.fr

Librairie Kléber
1 rue des Francs Bourgeois
F-67000 STRASBOURG
Tel.: +33 (0)3 88 15 78 88
Fax: +33 (0)3 88 15 78 80
E-mail: francois.wolfermann@librairie-kleber.fr
http://www.librairie-kleber.com

**GERMANY/ALLEMAGNE**
**AUSTRIA/AUTRICHE**
UNO Verlag GmbH
August-Bebel-Allee 6
D-53175 BONN
Tel.: +49 (0)228 94 90 20
Fax: +49 (0)228 94 90 222
E-mail: bestellung@uno-verlag.de
http://www.uno-verlag.de

**GREECE/GRÈCE**
Librairie Kauffmann s.a.
Stadiou 28
GR-105 64 ATHINAI
Tel.: +30 210 32 55 321
Fax: +30 210 32 30 320
E-mail: ord@otenet.gr
http://www.kauffmann.gr

**HUNGARY/HONGRIE**
Euro Info Service kft.
1137 Bp. Szent István krt. 12.
H-1137 BUDAPEST
Tel.: +36 (06)1 329 2170
Fax: +36 (06)1 349 2053
E-mail: euroinfo@euroinfo.hu
http://www.euroinfo.hu

**ITALY/ITALIE**
Licosa SpA
Via Duca di Calabria, 1/1
I-50125 FIRENZE
Tel.: +39 0556 483215
Fax: +39 0556 41257
E-mail: licosa@licosa.com
http://www.licosa.com

**MEXICO/MEXIQUE**
Mundi-Prensa México, S.A. De C.V.
Río Pánuco, 141 Delegacion Cuauhtémoc
06500 MÉXICO, D.F.
Tel.: +52 (01)55 55 33 56 58
Fax: +52 (01)55 55 14 67 99
E-mail: mundiprensa@mundiprensa.com.mx
http://www.mundiprensa.com.mx

**NETHERLANDS/PAYS-BAS**
De Lindeboom Internationale Publicaties b.v.
M.A. de Ruyterstraat 20 A
NL-7482 BZ HAAKSBERGEN
Tel.: +31 (0)53 5740004
Fax: +31 (0)53 5729296
E-mail: books@delindeboom.com
http://www.delindeboom.com

**NORWAY/NORVÈGE**
Akademika
Postboks 84 Blindern
N-0314 OSLO
Tel.: +47 2 218 8100
Fax: +47 2 218 8103
E-mail: support@akademika.no
http://akademika.no

**POLAND/POLOGNE**
Ars Polona JSC
25 Obroncow Street
PL-03-933 WARSZAWA
Tel.: +48 (0)22 509 86 00
Fax: +48 (0)22 509 86 10
E-mail: arspolona@arspolona.com.pl
http://www.arspolona.com.pl

**PORTUGAL**
Livraria Portugal
(Dias & Andrade, Lda.)
Rua do Carmo, 70
P-1200-094 LISBOA
Tel.: +351 21 347 42 82 / 85
Fax: +351 21 347 02 64
E-mail: info@livrariaportugal.pt
http://www.livrariaportugal.pt

**RUSSIAN FEDERATION/**
**FÉDÉRATION DE RUSSIE**
Ves Mir
9a, Kolpacnhyi per.
RU-101000 MOSCOW
Tel.: +7 (8)495 623 6839
Fax: +7 (8)495 625 4269
E-mail: zimarin@vesmirbooks.ru
http://www.vesmirbooks.ru

**SPAIN/ESPAGNE**
Mundi-Prensa Libros, s.a.
Castelló, 37
E-28001 MADRID
Tel.: +34 914 36 37 00
Fax: +34 915 75 39 98
E-mail: liberia@mundiprensa.es
http://www.mundiprensa.com

**SWITZERLAND/SUISSE**
Van Diermen Editions – ADECO
Chemin du Lacuez 41
CH-1807 BLONAY
Tel.: +41 (0)21 943 26 73
Fax: +41 (0)21 943 36 05
E-mail: info@adeco.org
http://www.adeco.org

**UNITED KINGDOM/ROYAUME-UNI**
The Stationery Office Ltd
PO Box 29
GB-NORWICH NR3 1GN
Tel.: +44 (0)870 600 5522
Fax: +44 (0)870 600 5533
E-mail: book.enquiries@tso.co.uk
http://www.tsoshop.co.uk

**UNITED STATES and CANADA/**
**ÉTATS-UNIS et CANADA**
Manhattan Publishing Company
468 Albany Post Road
CROTTON-ON-HUDSON, NY 10520, USA
Tel.: +1 914 271 5194
Fax: +1 914 271 5856
E-mail: Info@manhattanpublishing.com
http://www.manhattanpublishing.com

**Council of Europe Publishing/Editions du Conseil de l'Europe**
F-67075 Strasbourg Cedex
Tel.: +33 (0)3 88 41 25 81 – Fax: +33 (0)3 88 41 39 10 – E-mail: publishing@coe.int – Website: http://book.coe.int